WARBEARS™

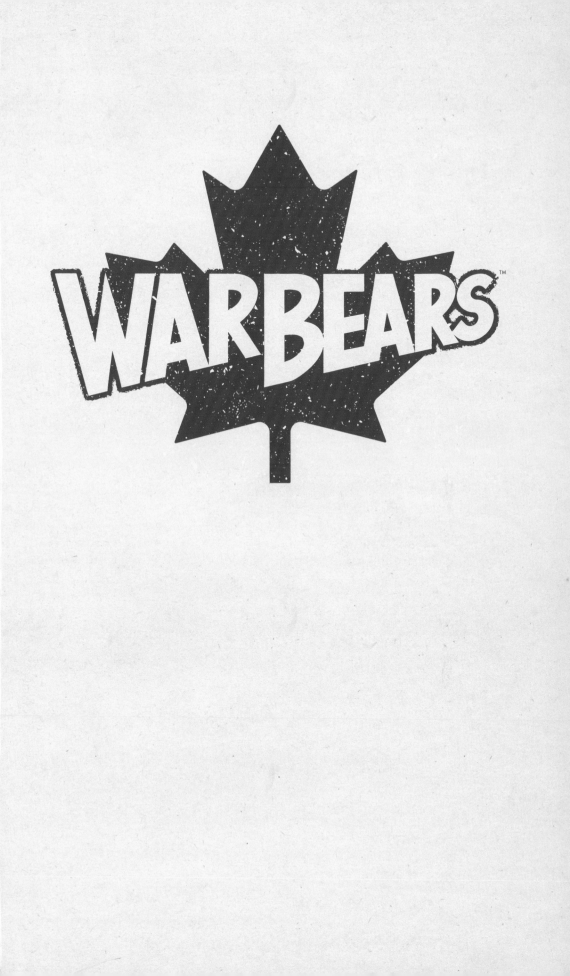

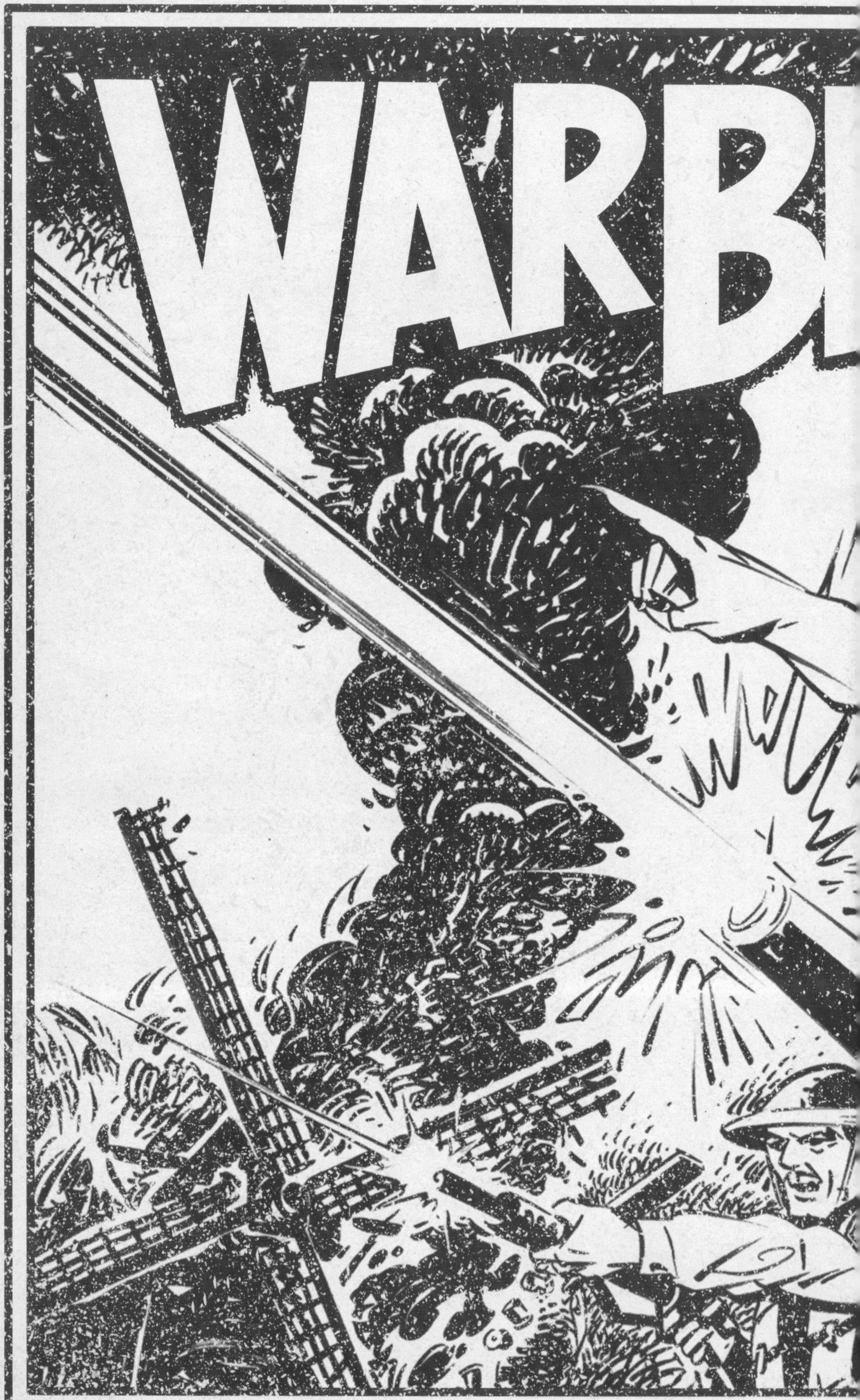
WARB

STORY BY
MARGARET ATWOOD
& KEN STEACY

ARTWORK BY
KEN STEACY

COVER BY
KEN STEACY

DARK HORSE BOOKS

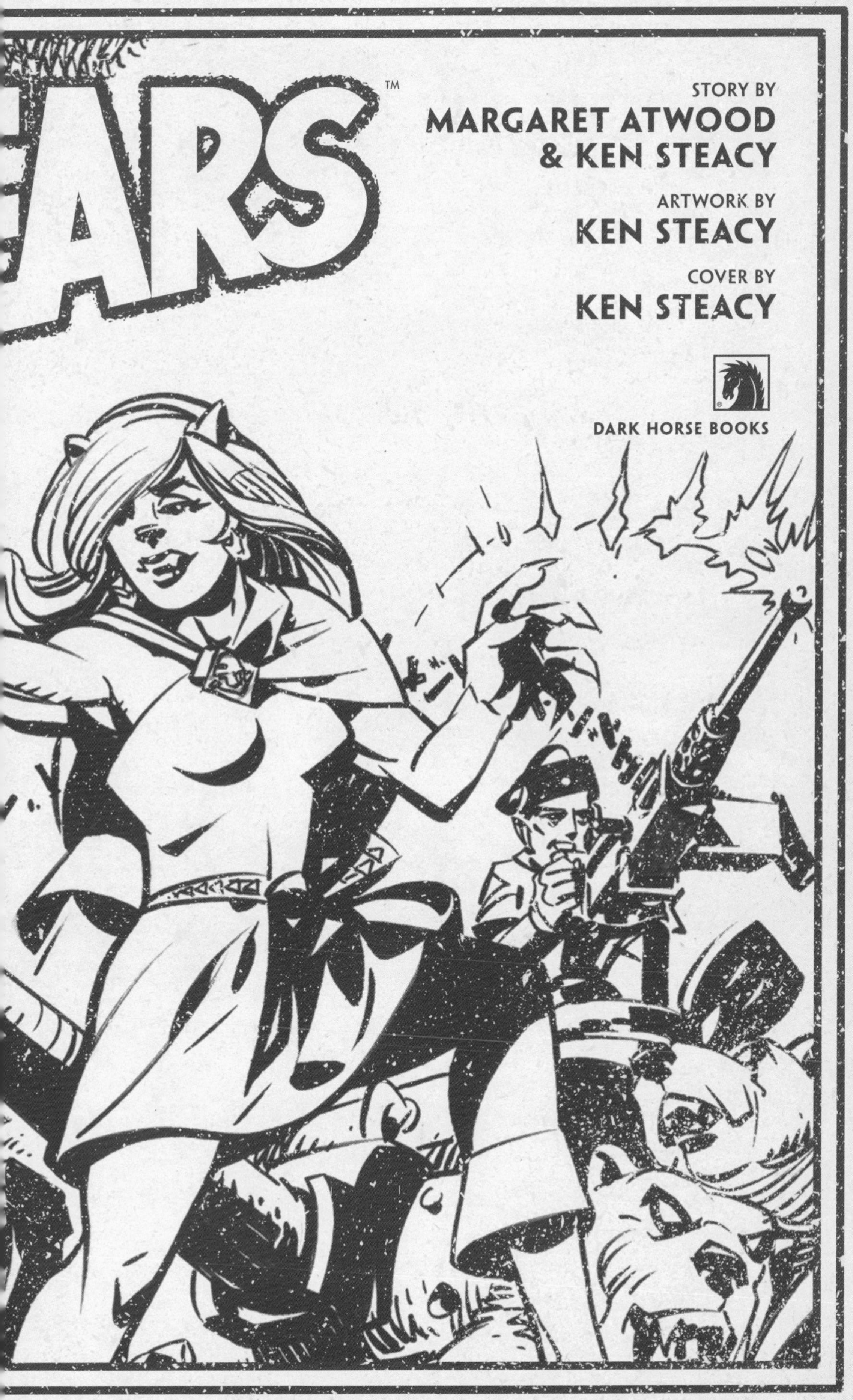

PRESIDENT AND PUBLISHER **MIKE RICHARDSON**
EDITOR **DANIEL CHABON**
ASSISTANT EDITOR **BRETT ISRAEL**
DESIGNER **JASON RALL**
DIGITAL ART TECHNICIAN **JOSIE CHRISTENSEN**

EXECUTIVE VICE PRESIDENT **NEIL HANKERSON**
CHIEF FINANCIAL OFFICER **TOM WEDDLE**
VICE PRESIDENT OF PUBLISHING **RANDY STRADLEY**
CHIEF BUSINESS DEVELOPMENT OFFICER **NICK MCWHORTER**
VICE PRESIDENT OF MARKETING **MATT PARKINSON**
VICE PRESIDENT OF INFORMATION TECHNOLOGY **DALE LAFOUNTAIN**
VICE PRESIDENT OF PRODUCTION AND SCHEDULING **CARA NIECE**
VICE PRESIDENT OF BOOK TRADE AND DIGITAL SALES **MARK BERNARDI**
GENERAL COUNSEL **KEN LIZZI**
EDITOR IN CHIEF **DAVE MARSHALL**
EDITORIAL DIRECTOR **DAVEY ESTRADA**
SENIOR BOOKS EDITOR **CHRIS WARNER**
DIRECTOR OF SPECIALTY PROJECTS **CARY GRAZZINI**
ART DIRECTOR **LIA RIBACCHI**
DIRECTOR OF PRINT PURCHASING **VANESSA TODD-HOLMES**
DIRECTOR OF DIGITAL ART AND PREPRESS **MATT DRYER**
DIRECTOR OF INTERNATIONAL PUBLISHING AND LICENSING **MICHAEL GOMBOS**
DIRECTOR OF CUSTOM PROGRAMS **KARI YADRO**
DIRECTOR OF INTERNATIONAL LICENSING **KARI TORSON**

Published by Dark Horse Books
A division of Dark Horse Comics LLC
10956 SE Main Street
Milwaukie, OR 97222

DarkHorse.com
To find a comics shop in your area, visit comicshoplocator.com

First edition: February 2019
ISBN 978-1-50670-898-0
Digital ISBN 978-1-50670-888-1

10 9 8 7 6 5 4 3 2 1
Printed in China

Collects issues #1–#3 of the Dark Horse Comics series *War Bears*.

Library of Congress Cataloging-in-Publication Data

Names: Atwood, Margaret, 1939- author. | Steacy, Ken, author, artist.
Title: War bears / story by Margaret Atwood & Ken Steacy ; art and chapter
  breaks by Ken Steacy.
Description: First edition. | Milwaukie, OR : Dark Horse Books, February
  2019. | "Collects issues #1-#3 of the Dark Horse Comics series War Bears."
Identifiers: LCCN 2018042959 | ISBN 9781506708980
Subjects: LCSH: Graphic novels.
Classification: LCC PN6727.A886 W37 2019 | DDC 741.5/973–dc23
LC record available at https://lccn.loc.gov/2018042959

FOREWORD

Welcome to *War Bears*, and the world of the Canadian black and white comics of World War II!

The story had several origins. I knew about the "Canadian whites" partly because, having been born in 1939, I was old enough to remember the tail end of them, and also old enough to have read the colored American comics that flooded into Canada after the end of the war. Our generation of late forties kids was comics-oriented, as television had not yet made its 1950s consumer rollout.

Then, in 1971, The *Great Canadian Comic Book* appeared, in which my old college friend Alan Walker was instrumental, and I learned more about these comics. Many years later, I found myself participating in a crowdfunding effort managed by graphics curator, historian, producer, and publisher Hope Nicholson, its goal the republication of a lost comic called *Brok Windsor*. Through this effort I met Hope, who was of crucial assistance in the creation of *Angel Catbird*, my own cat-and-bird graphic novel, illustrated by the wonderful Johnnie Christmas.

Then, in 2017, along came Canada's sesquicentennial, and the *Globe and Mail* commissioned a series of stories from fiction writers. The mandate was to pick a date from Canadian history and build a story around it. I chose VE Day—which was a huge celebration, with dancing in the streets, paper streamers, all of that—but which was also the day that signaled the end of the Canadian comics.

My central figure is the somewhat hapless writer-illustrator of a successful series called *Oursonette*—a shape-changing bear-woman with two bear helpers, who (of course) fights Nazis, just like Wonder Woman or Nelvana, though with a few more clothes on. On this day—so happy for most in Toronto—he knows he must say goodbye to his beloved Oursonette, and that he will soon be drawing soap flakes and women joyful about their whiter-than-white laundry. As one did as a commercial illustrator.

The Great Canadian Comic Book was helpful for research, and if you are interested in that world, there's a new overview of the Bell Features writer-illustrators who drew Nelvana, Johnny Canuck, Thunderfist, Nitro, The Invisible Commando, The Penguin—what a strange disguise!—and many more: *Heroes Of the Home Front*, by Ivan Kocmarek. Surrealism had nothing on these artists!

Ken Steacy was chosen by the *Globe* to illustrate "Oursonette," given his WW2 interests and researches and his high standards of visual accuracy. He fell in love with Oursonette, we collaborated—although the main work on the script is his—and the rest, as we say, is history. Comics history.

Enjoy!

MARGARET ATWOOD

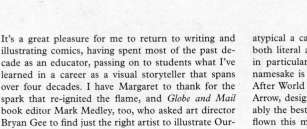

It's a great pleasure for me to return to writing and illustrating comics, having spent most of the past decade as an educator, passing on to students what I've learned in a career as a visual storyteller that spans over four decades. I have Margaret to thank for the spark that re-ignited the flame, and *Globe and Mail* book editor Mark Medley, too, who asked art director Bryan Gee to find just the right artist to illustrate Oursonette's introduction. He in turn asked his partner, illustration historian Dr. Jaleen Grove, who would best be suited to the task, and I'm very grateful for her robust response: "Ken Steacy, of course!"

Margaret and I share a fascination with Canuck history, particularly that which relates to WWII. I knew that extensive research would be required to ensure period fidelity and avoid anachronisms, and spent an enormous amount of time and effort assembling reference material which informed both the artwork and the dialogue.

Being a stickler for accuracy owes much to my being the son of a Royal Canadian Air Force fighter pilot, who thankfully never tried to dissuade me from so

atypical a career path for a military brat. References both literal and ironic abound in this series, but one in particular bears mention: our protagonist Alain's namesake is Battle of Britain ace Janusz Zurakowski. After World War II he was a test pilot for the Avro Arrow, designed and built here in Canada, and arguably the best interceptor of its time. My dad would've flown this magnificent aircraft, but sadly it was cancelled during the heat of the Cold War.

The RCAF's motto is *Per Ardua Ad Astra*, "through adversity to the stars," but anyone who's really good at what they do makes it look effortless, and those efforts invariably make us thirst for more. That was my experience when reading "Oursonette" for the first time; I just had to know more about Al, and Gloria, and Mike—what went before, and what happened next? You hold in your hands the answers to those questions, which I hope you will read with as much enjoyment as Margaret and I had during their creation.

KEN STEACY

INTRODUCTIONS

World War II was a desperate time for all; for our European allies, the battles and bombings were right at their doorstep; most of Europe was under the cruel boot-heels of the Nazi invaders. Canada and the United States were luckier; the War didn't touch our shores, but we knew the desperation. We gave up meat for the cause, gave up sugar, butter, leather for our shoes, gasoline for our cars. Of course it was worth it; we knew the terrible price we would have to pay if we lost. We did without or made do. In the US that meant oleomargarine instead of butter and chicory instead of coffee. It also meant hiring women to do what had previously been men's jobs. We sent our young men off to war with hopes and prayers, and women rushed in to fill their places: in the factories, on the farms, driving the trucks and buses, building the planes and ships—and drawing comics. For the first time, the publishers of the almost all-male comic books hired more women artists than ever before.

And Canadians had to make do without their colorful American comic books, because the War Exchange Conservation Act prohibited imports of non-essential goods from the US to Canada, and what could be more non-essential than comics? (Many of us would disagree!) So Canadians made do. They formed their own comic book companies, printing comics in black and white that featured Canadian heroes like *Nelvana of the Northern Lights* (my own personal favorite) and *Brok Windsor*. And in Margaret Atwood's and Ken Steacy's bittersweet fictional series, *Oursonette*, the French speaking were-bear.

The horrible war ended with victory for our side, for which we are all grateful, and the boys came home. In America and Canada, the returning GIs got their old jobs back, and the women were sent back to the kitchens, not to emerge for at least the next twenty years. And for Canada, it meant the return of American comic books and the end of that magical time known as the Golden Age of Canadian comics.

As for Oursonette, a pretty lass with a big black nose, covered in fluffy white fur, who punches Nazis, what's not to love?

TRINA ROBBINS

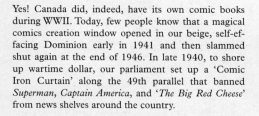

Yes! Canada did, indeed, have its own comic books during WWII. Today, few people know that a magical comics creation window opened in our beige, self-effacing Dominion early in 1941 and then slammed shut again at the end of 1946. In late 1940, to shore up wartime dollar, our parliament set up a 'Comic Iron Curtain' along the 49th parallel that banned *Superman*, *Captain America*, and '*The Big Red Cheese*' from news shelves around the country.

But there were only a dozen or so comic-less weeks at the start of 1941 because that was all the time needed for a pair of enterprising publishers, two thousand miles apart in Toronto and Vancouver, to take advantage of the vacuum and start up a double-barrelled, homegrown, Canadian comic book industry. Kids had folding heroes again, but this time they were our own. These comics also contained information about our war efforts abroad and at home (remember that Pearl Harbor was a good number of months away). They even offered an early form of social networking for kids from coast to coast through contests and club pages.

There has been an unwarranted neglect (bordering on a cultural amnesia) of these first Canadian comics. Their small, but I think effective, role in contributing to the elusive 'Canadian identity' we were so desperately trying to condense by the time of the Centennial in 1967 is disregarded and dismissed. As the culture of comics has come to ascendency among the masses and in academia during the last few decades, it perks up my sense of Canadian pride whenever we pull out and dig into that old trunk of forgotten comics in our nation's dusty attic.

Margaret Atwood did this when, for the subject of a short story published in the Sesquicentennial issue of the *Globe and Mail*, she chose to remember Canada's wartime comics. That playful little story, "Oursonette," is reprinted in this volume.

Ken Steacy has artfully extrapolated this story both backward, as a short prequel, and forward, with a near-to-present-day coda that caps it off neatly. This has resulted in the three-issue comic book run called *War Bears* that has been collected here in a first-rate package.

I can't think of when Ken Steacy's artwork and storytelling has been better. He captures the 'film noir' bleakness of the war years at home and peppers that part of the story with a multitude of Canadian references and allusions that will make you smile—you might even have to look a few up.

I think you will enjoy Gloria and Mike and Al's story as well as Oursonette's black-and-white wartime exploits. The best thing about *War Bears* is that it recognizes that there were human beings behind those black-and-white panels. Today just about all of them are gone, but the need to remember and acknowledge what they did isn't. Margaret Atwood and Ken Steacy have provided us with a stepping stone towards this and towards gathering these wartime creators into our Canadian cultural fold again.

IVAN KOCMAREK

EDUCATIONAL PROJECTS INC. · DOUBLE 'A' COMICS · BELL FEATURES · MAPLE LEAF PUBLISHING CO. COMIC BOOKS

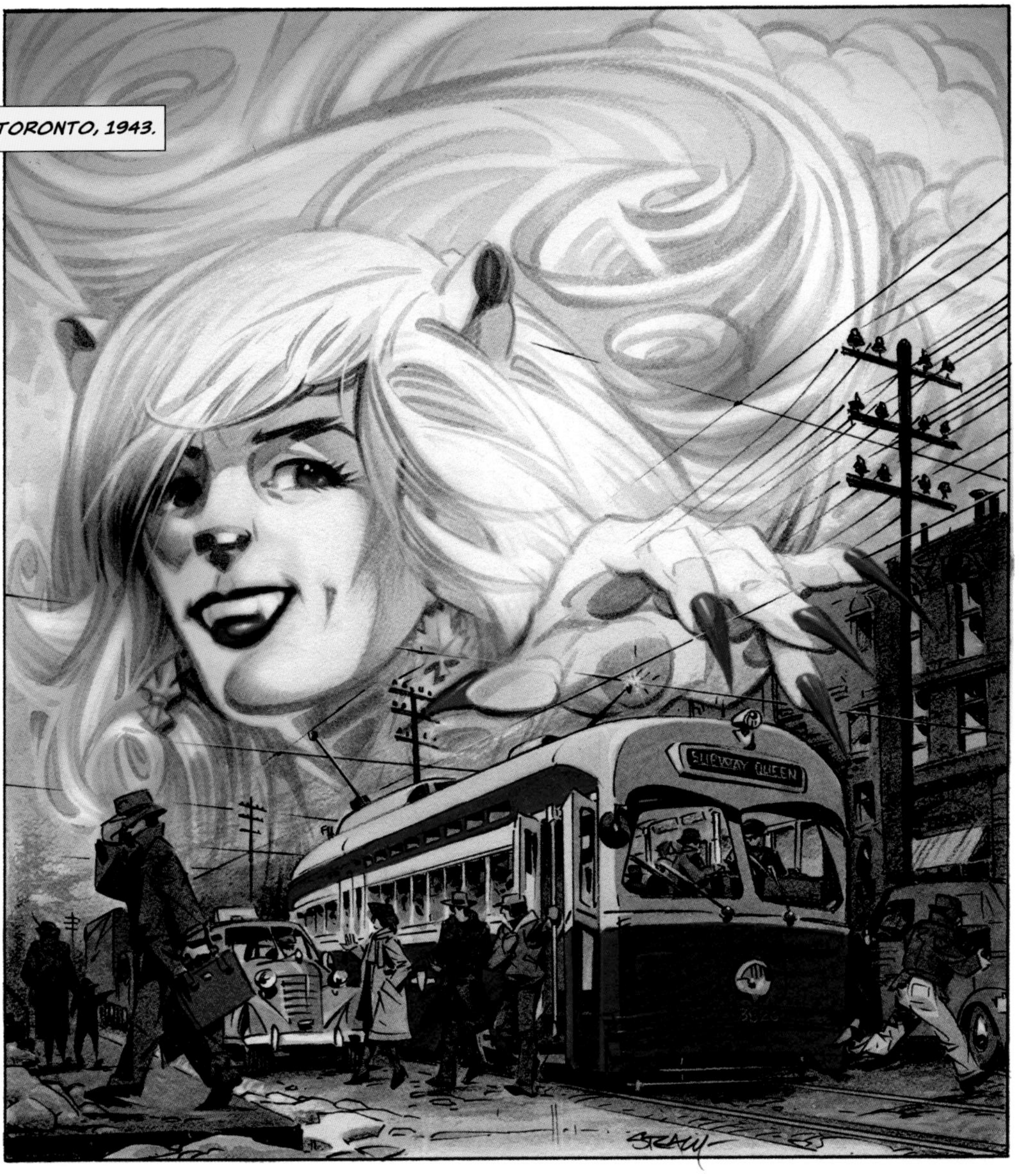
TORONTO, 1943.

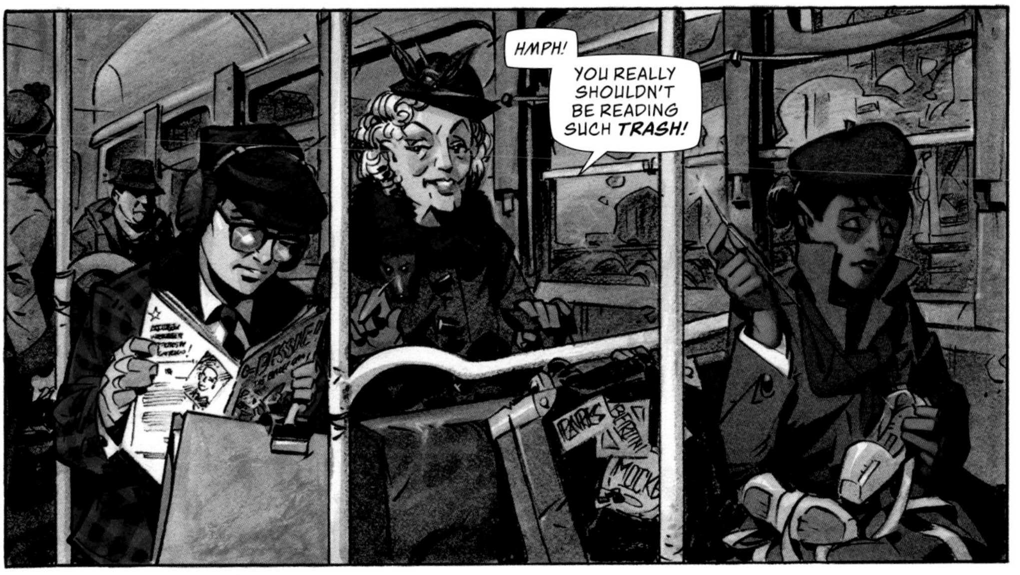
HMPH!
YOU REALLY SHOULDN'T BE READING SUCH TRASH!

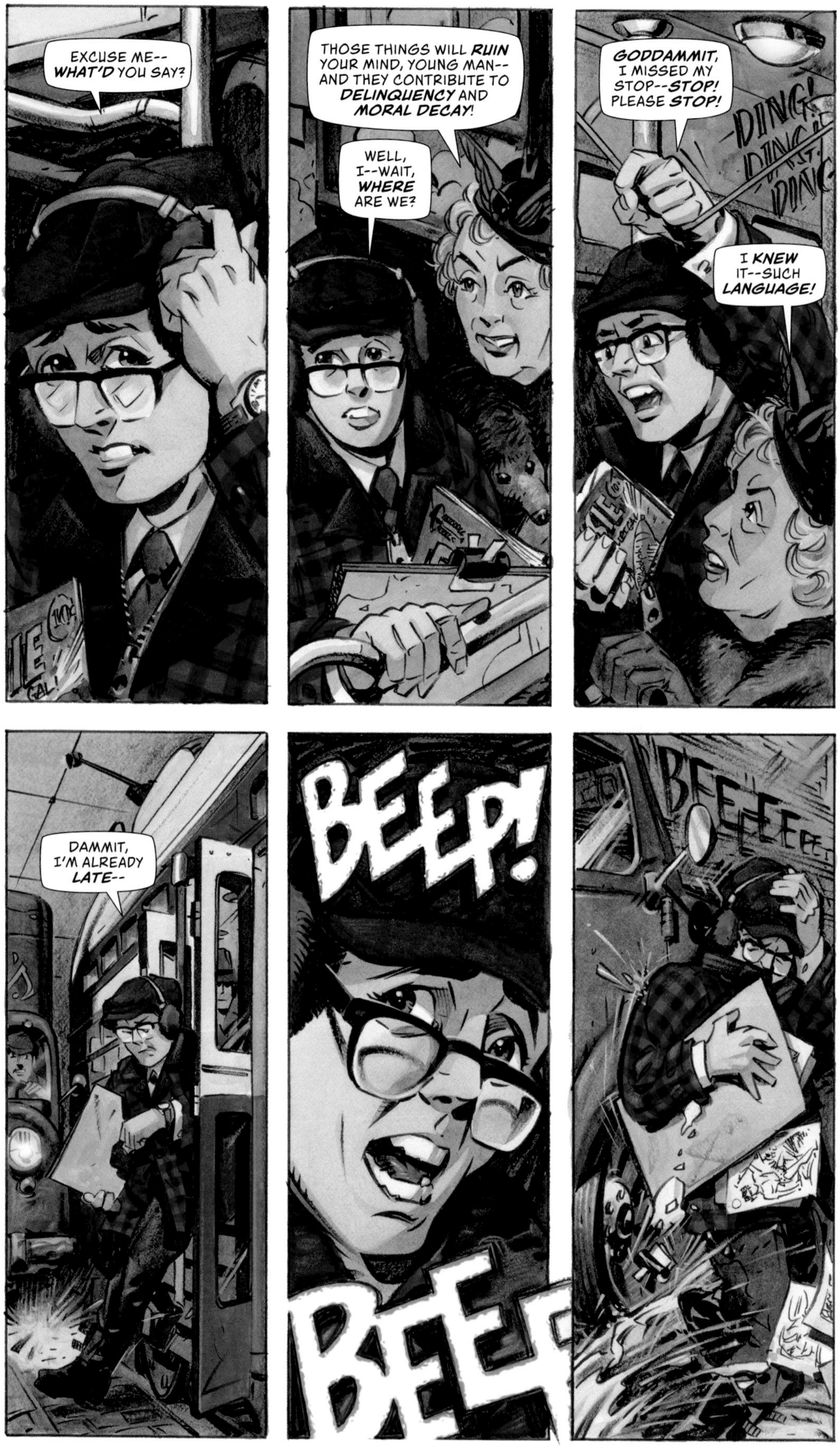

EXCUSE ME-- WHAT'D YOU SAY?
THOSE THINGS WILL RUIN YOUR MIND, YOUNG MAN-- AND THEY CONTRIBUTE TO DELINQUENCY AND MORAL DECAY!
WELL, I--WAIT, WHERE ARE WE?
GODDAMMIT, I MISSED MY STOP--STOP! PLEASE STOP!
DING! DING! DING!
I KNEW IT--SUCH LANGUAGE!
DAMMIT, I'M ALREADY LATE--
BEEP!

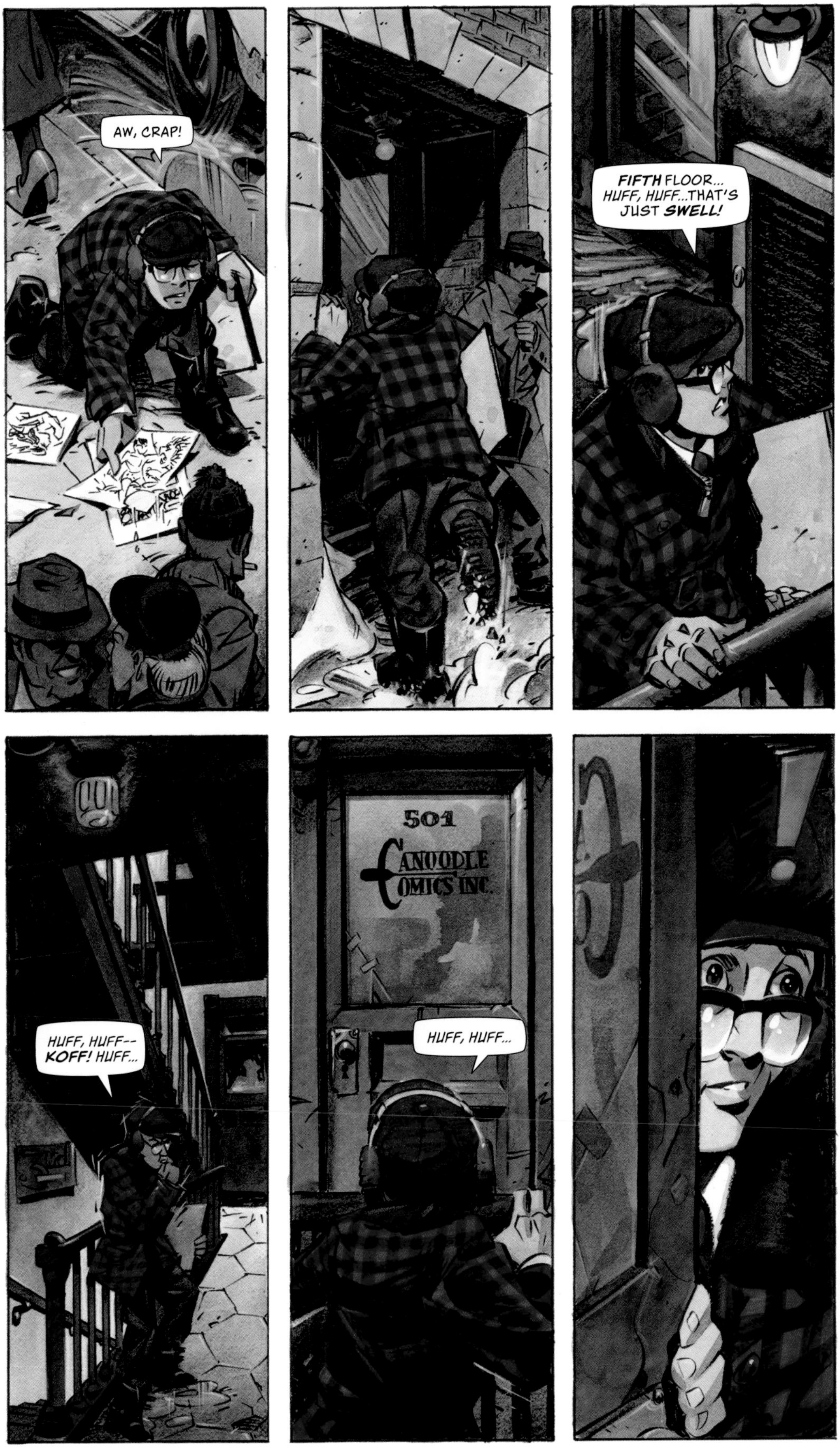
AW, CRAP!
FIFTH FLOOR... HUFF, HUFF...THAT'S JUST SWELL!
HUFF, HUFF-- KOFF! HUFF...
501
CANOODLE COMICS INC.
HUFF, HUFF...

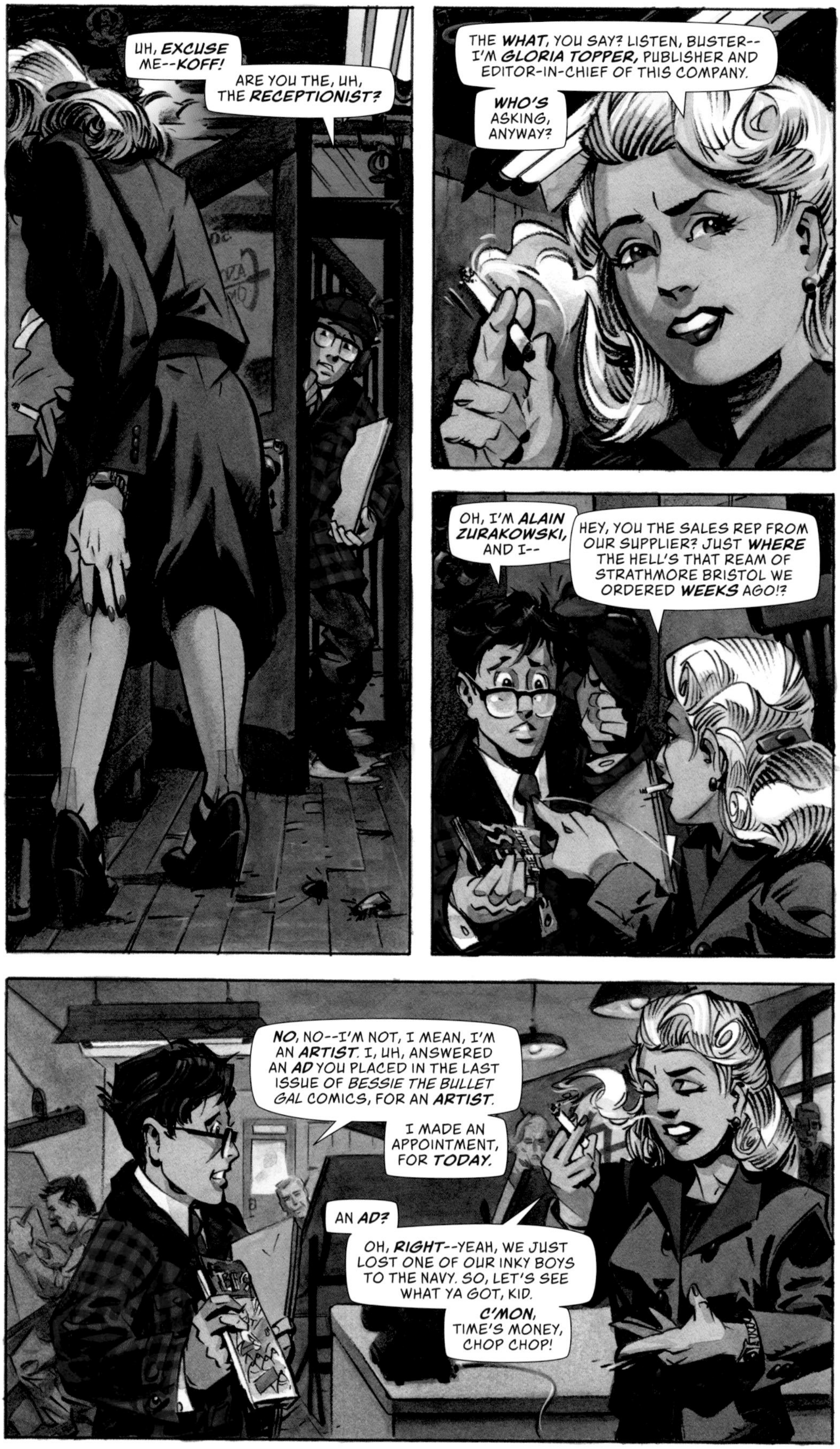
UH, EXCUSE ME--KOFF!
ARE YOU THE, UH, THE RECEPTIONIST?
THE WHAT, YOU SAY? LISTEN, BUSTER--I'M GLORIA TOPPER, PUBLISHER AND EDITOR-IN-CHIEF OF THIS COMPANY.
WHO'S ASKING, ANYWAY?
OH, I'M ALAIN ZURAKOWSKI, AND I--
HEY, YOU THE SALES REP FROM OUR SUPPLIER? JUST WHERE THE HELL'S THAT REAM OF STRATHMORE BRISTOL WE ORDERED WEEKS AGO!?
NO, NO--I'M NOT, I MEAN, I'M AN ARTIST. I, UH, ANSWERED AN AD YOU PLACED IN THE LAST ISSUE OF BESSIE THE BULLET GAL COMICS, FOR AN ARTIST.
I MADE AN APPOINTMENT, FOR TODAY.
AN AD?
OH, RIGHT--YEAH, WE JUST LOST ONE OF OUR INKY BOYS TO THE NAVY. SO, LET'S SEE WHAT YA GOT, KID.
C'MON, TIME'S MONEY, CHOP CHOP!

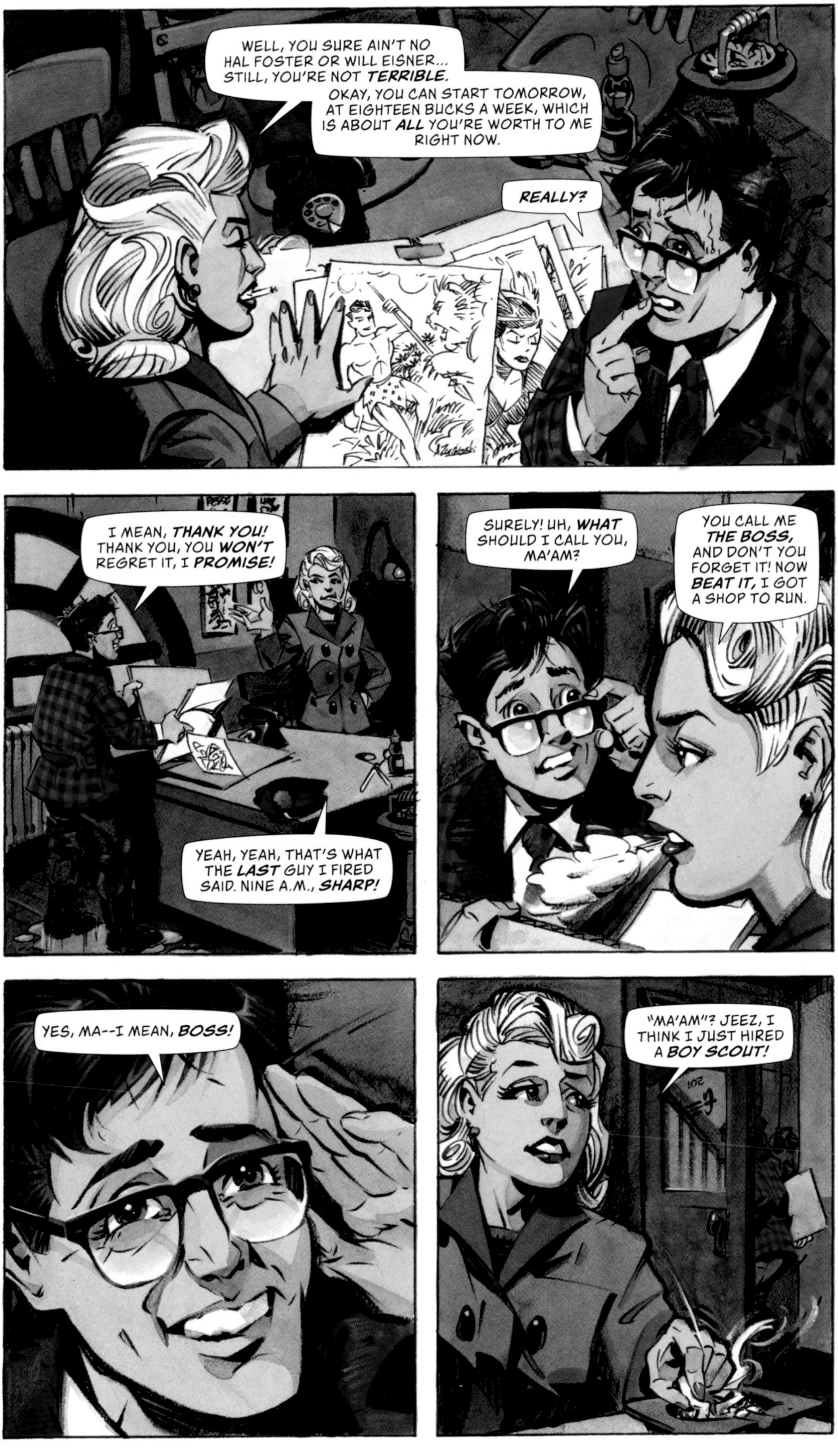
WELL, YOU SURE AIN'T NO HAL FOSTER OR WILL EISNER... STILL, YOU'RE NOT **TERRIBLE.**
OKAY, YOU CAN START TOMORROW, AT EIGHTEEN BUCKS A WEEK, WHICH IS ABOUT **ALL** YOU'RE WORTH TO ME RIGHT NOW.
REALLY?
I MEAN, **THANK YOU!** THANK YOU, YOU **WON'T** REGRET IT, I **PROMISE!**
YEAH, YEAH, THAT'S WHAT THE **LAST** GUY I FIRED SAID. NINE A.M., **SHARP!**
SURELY! UH, **WHAT** SHOULD I CALL YOU, MA'AM?
YOU CALL ME **THE BOSS,** AND DON'T YOU FORGET IT! NOW **BEAT IT,** I GOT A SHOP TO RUN.
YES, MA--I MEAN, **BOSS!**
"MA'AM"? JEEZ, I THINK I JUST HIRED A **BOY SCOUT!**

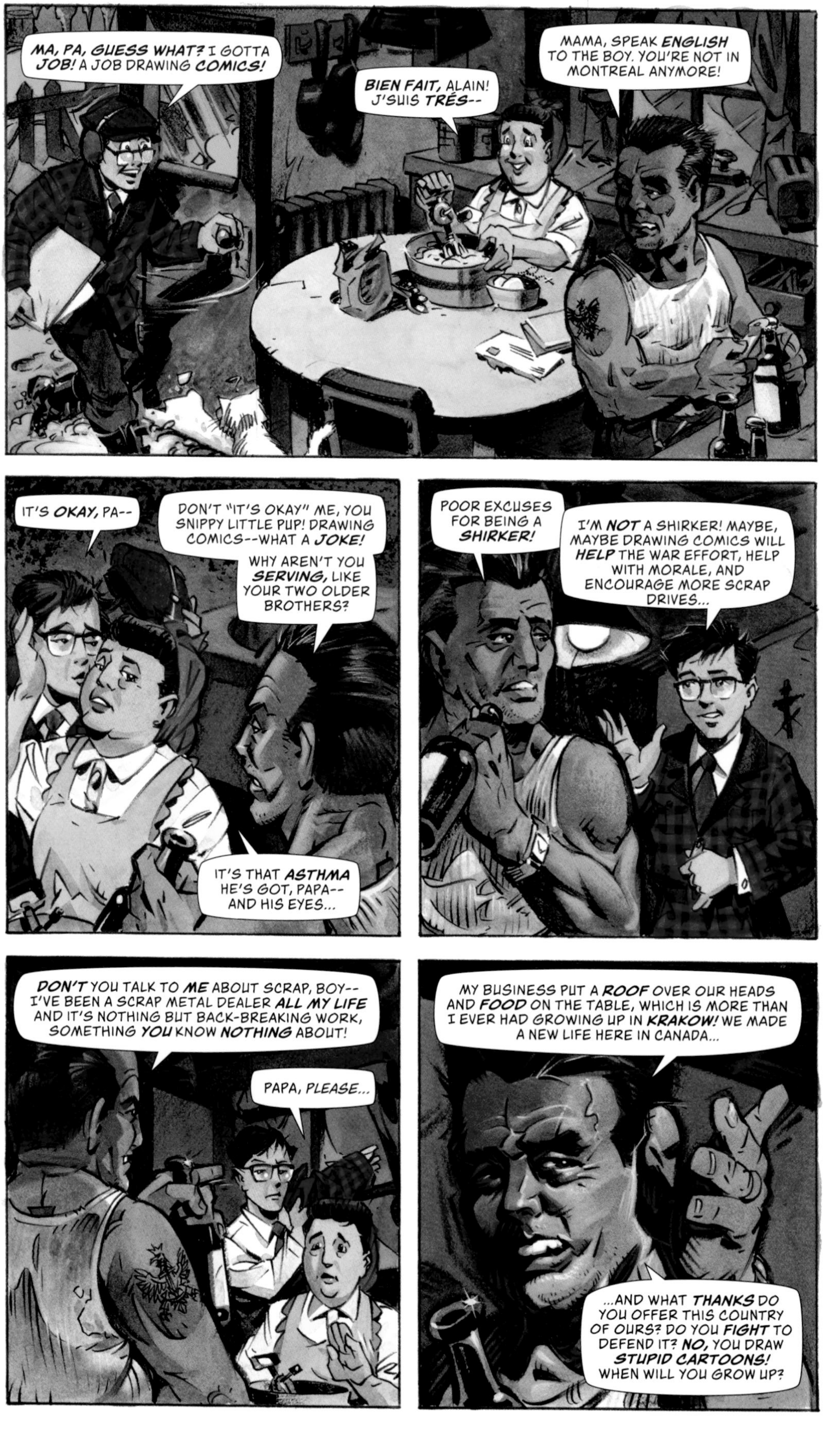
MA, PA, GUESS WHAT? I GOTTA JOB! A JOB DRAWING COMICS!
BIEN FAIT, ALAIN! J'SUIS TRÉS--
MAMA, SPEAK ENGLISH TO THE BOY. YOU'RE NOT IN MONTREAL ANYMORE!
IT'S OKAY, PA--
DON'T "IT'S OKAY" ME, YOU SNIPPY LITTLE PUP! DRAWING COMICS--WHAT A JOKE!
WHY AREN'T YOU SERVING, LIKE YOUR TWO OLDER BROTHERS?
IT'S THAT ASTHMA HE'S GOT, PAPA-- AND HIS EYES...
POOR EXCUSES FOR BEING A SHIRKER!
I'M NOT A SHIRKER! MAYBE, MAYBE DRAWING COMICS WILL HELP THE WAR EFFORT, HELP WITH MORALE, AND ENCOURAGE MORE SCRAP DRIVES...
DON'T YOU TALK TO ME ABOUT SCRAP, BOY-- I'VE BEEN A SCRAP METAL DEALER ALL MY LIFE AND IT'S NOTHING BUT BACK-BREAKING WORK, SOMETHING YOU KNOW NOTHING ABOUT!
PAPA, PLEASE...
MY BUSINESS PUT A ROOF OVER OUR HEADS AND FOOD ON THE TABLE, WHICH IS MORE THAN I EVER HAD GROWING UP IN KRAKOW! WE MADE A NEW LIFE HERE IN CANADA...
...AND WHAT THANKS DO YOU OFFER THIS COUNTRY OF OURS? DO YOU FIGHT TO DEFEND IT? NO, YOU DRAW STUPID CARTOONS! WHEN WILL YOU GROW UP?

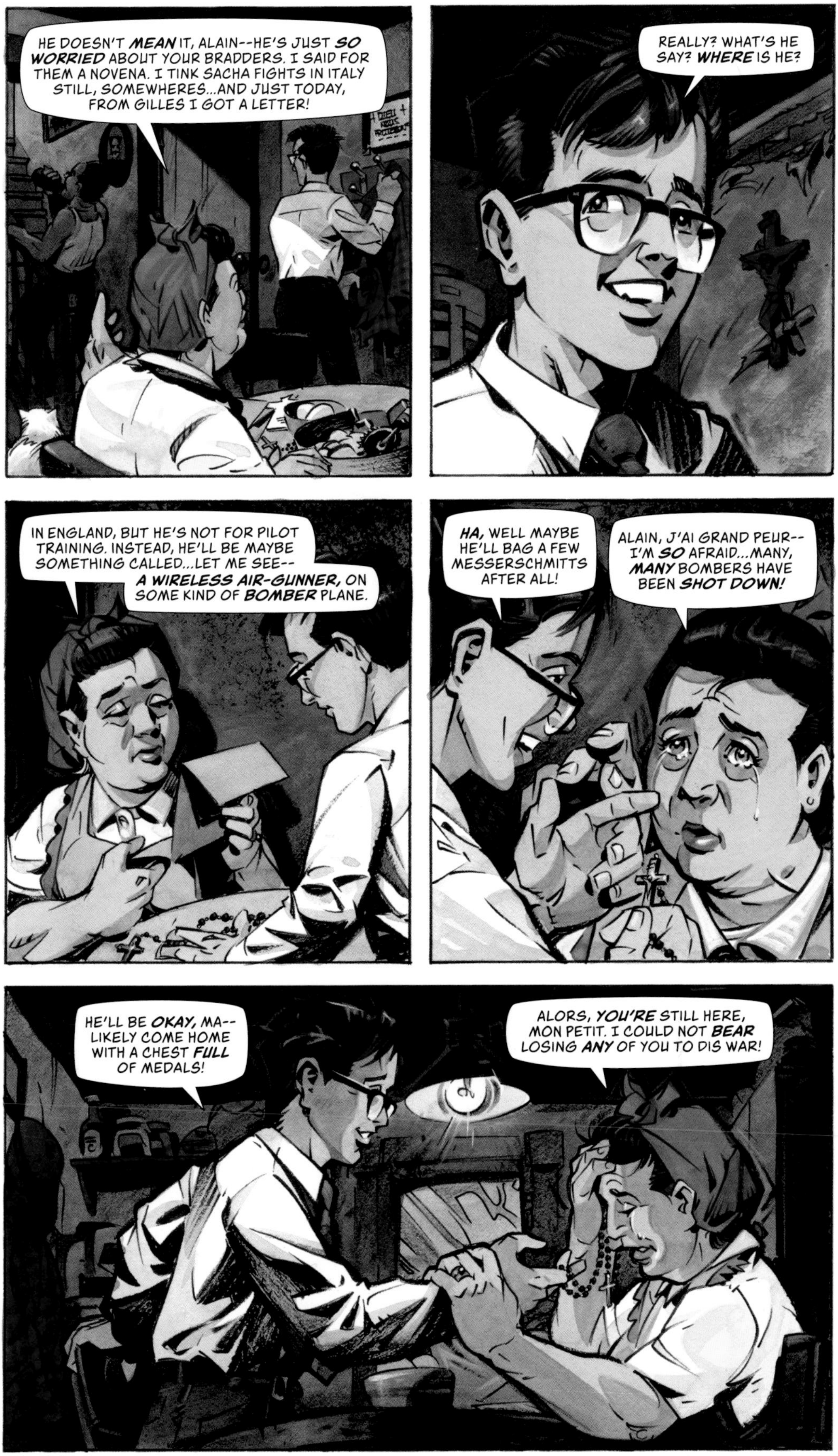
HE DOESN'T MEAN IT, ALAIN--HE'S JUST SO WORRIED ABOUT YOUR BRADDERS. I SAID FOR THEM A NOVENA. I TINK SACHA FIGHTS IN ITALY STILL, SOMEWHERES...AND JUST TODAY, FROM GILLES I GOT A LETTER!
REALLY? WHAT'S HE SAY? WHERE IS HE?
IN ENGLAND, BUT HE'S NOT FOR PILOT TRAINING. INSTEAD, HE'LL BE MAYBE SOMETHING CALLED...LET ME SEE--
A WIRELESS AIR-GUNNER, ON SOME KIND OF BOMBER PLANE.
HA, WELL MAYBE HE'LL BAG A FEW MESSERSCHMITTS AFTER ALL!
ALAIN, J'AI GRAND PEUR--I'M SO AFRAID...MANY, MANY BOMBERS HAVE BEEN SHOT DOWN!
HE'LL BE OKAY, MA--LIKELY COME HOME WITH A CHEST FULL OF MEDALS!
ALORS, YOU'RE STILL HERE, MON PETIT. I COULD NOT BEAR LOSING ANY OF YOU TO DIS WAR!

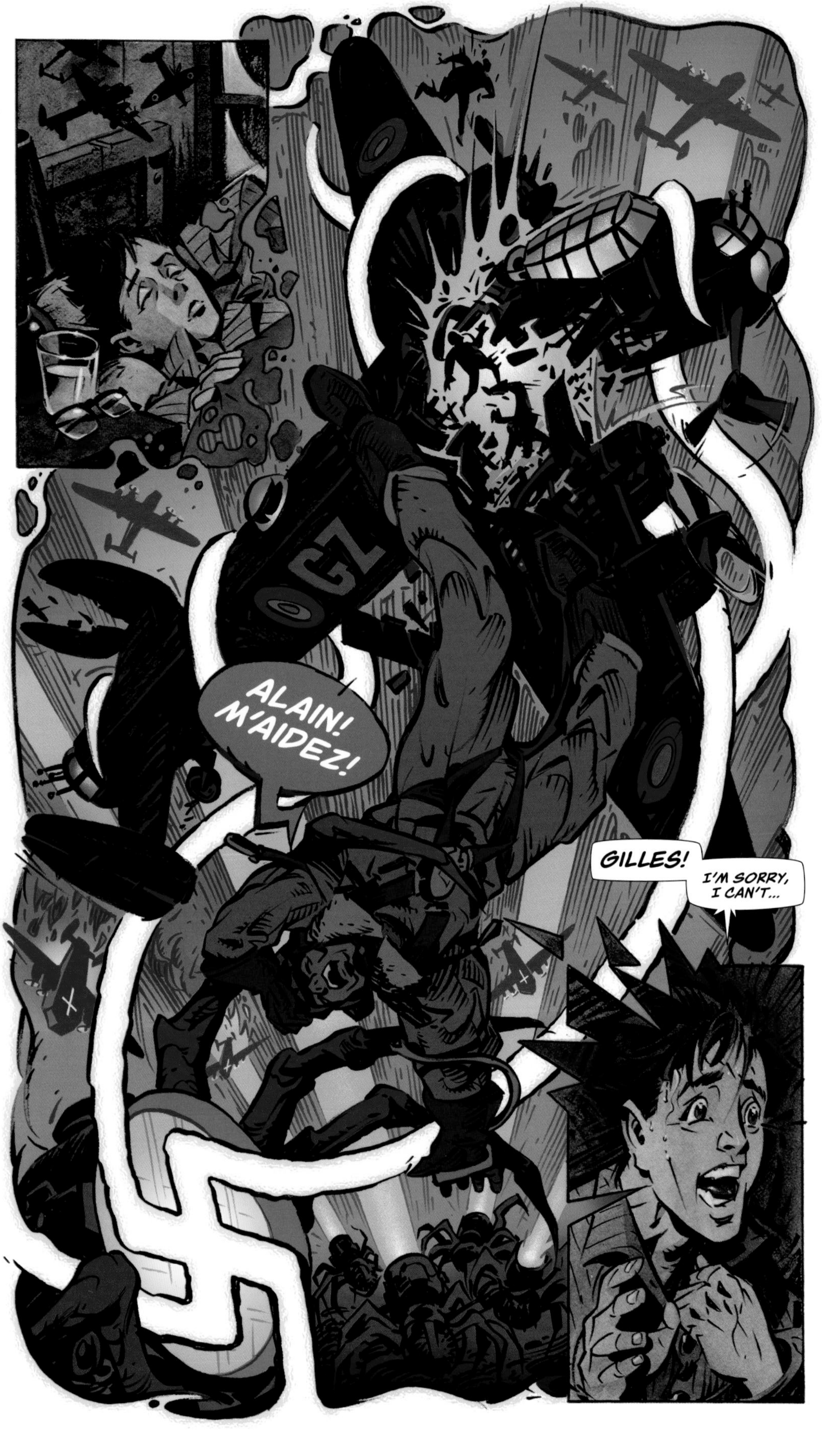
ALAIN! M'AIDEZ!
GILLES!
I'M SORRY, I CAN'T...

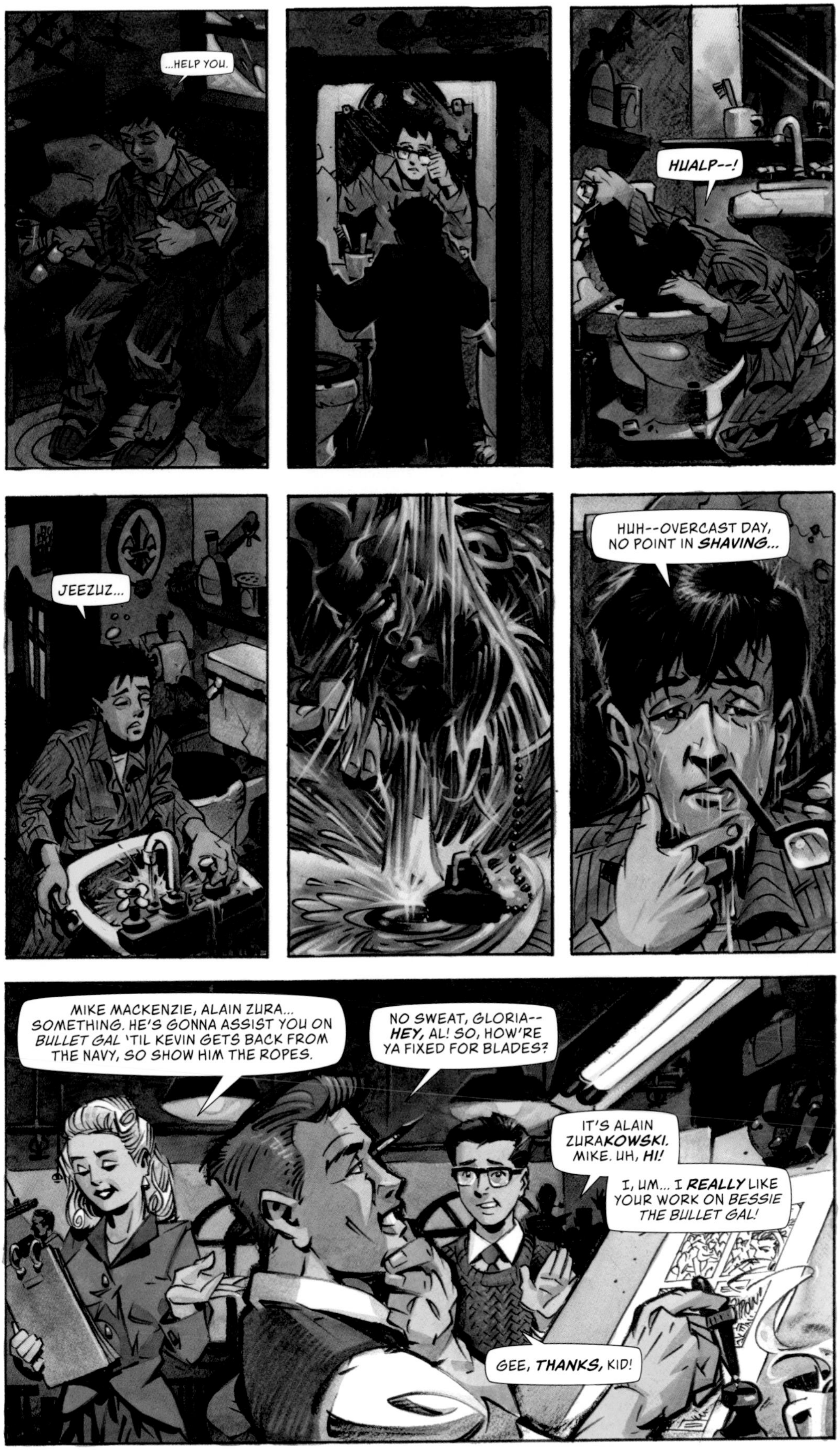
...HELP YOU.
HUALP--!
JEEZUZ...
HUH--OVERCAST DAY, NO POINT IN **SHAVING...**
MIKE MACKENZIE, ALAIN ZURA... SOMETHING. HE'S GONNA ASSIST YOU ON *BULLET GAL* 'TIL KEVIN GETS BACK FROM THE NAVY, SO SHOW HIM THE ROPES.
NO SWEAT, GLORIA-- **HEY,** AL! SO, HOW'RE YA FIXED FOR BLADES?
IT'S ALAIN ZURA**KOWSKI.** MIKE. UH, HI!
I, UM... I **REALLY** LIKE YOUR WORK ON BESSIE THE BULLET GAL!
GEE, **THANKS,** KID!

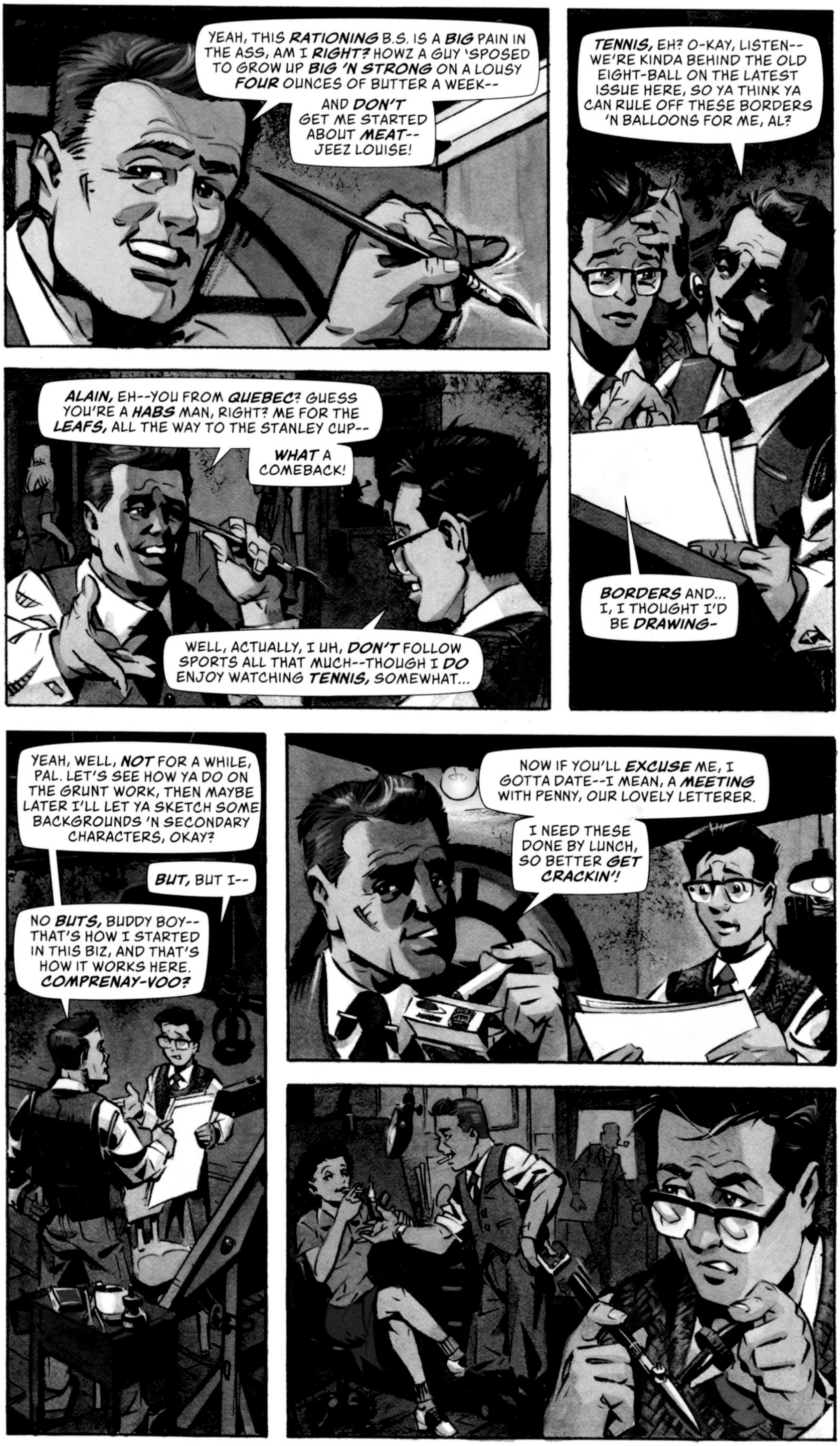
YEAH, THIS RATIONING B.S. IS A BIG PAIN IN THE ASS, AM I RIGHT? HOWZ A GUY 'SPOSED TO GROW UP BIG 'N STRONG ON A LOUSY FOUR OUNCES OF BUTTER A WEEK--
AND DON'T GET ME STARTED ABOUT MEAT-- JEEZ LOUISE!
ALAIN, EH--YOU FROM QUEBEC? GUESS YOU'RE A HABS MAN, RIGHT? ME FOR THE LEAFS, ALL THE WAY TO THE STANLEY CUP--
WHAT A COMEBACK!
WELL, ACTUALLY, I UH, DON'T FOLLOW SPORTS ALL THAT MUCH--THOUGH I DO ENJOY WATCHING TENNIS, SOMEWHAT...
TENNIS, EH? O-KAY, LISTEN-- WE'RE KINDA BEHIND THE OLD EIGHT-BALL ON THE LATEST ISSUE HERE, SO YA THINK YA CAN RULE OFF THESE BORDERS 'N BALLOONS FOR ME, AL?
BORDERS AND... I, I THOUGHT I'D BE DRAWING-
YEAH, WELL, NOT FOR A WHILE, PAL. LET'S SEE HOW YA DO ON THE GRUNT WORK, THEN MAYBE LATER I'LL LET YA SKETCH SOME BACKGROUNDS 'N SECONDARY CHARACTERS, OKAY?
BUT, BUT I--
NO BUTS, BUDDY BOY-- THAT'S HOW I STARTED IN THIS BIZ, AND THAT'S HOW IT WORKS HERE. COMPRENAY-VOO?
NOW IF YOU'LL EXCUSE ME, I GOTTA DATE--I MEAN, A MEETING WITH PENNY, OUR LOVELY LETTERER.
I NEED THESE DONE BY LUNCH, SO BETTER GET CRACKIN'!

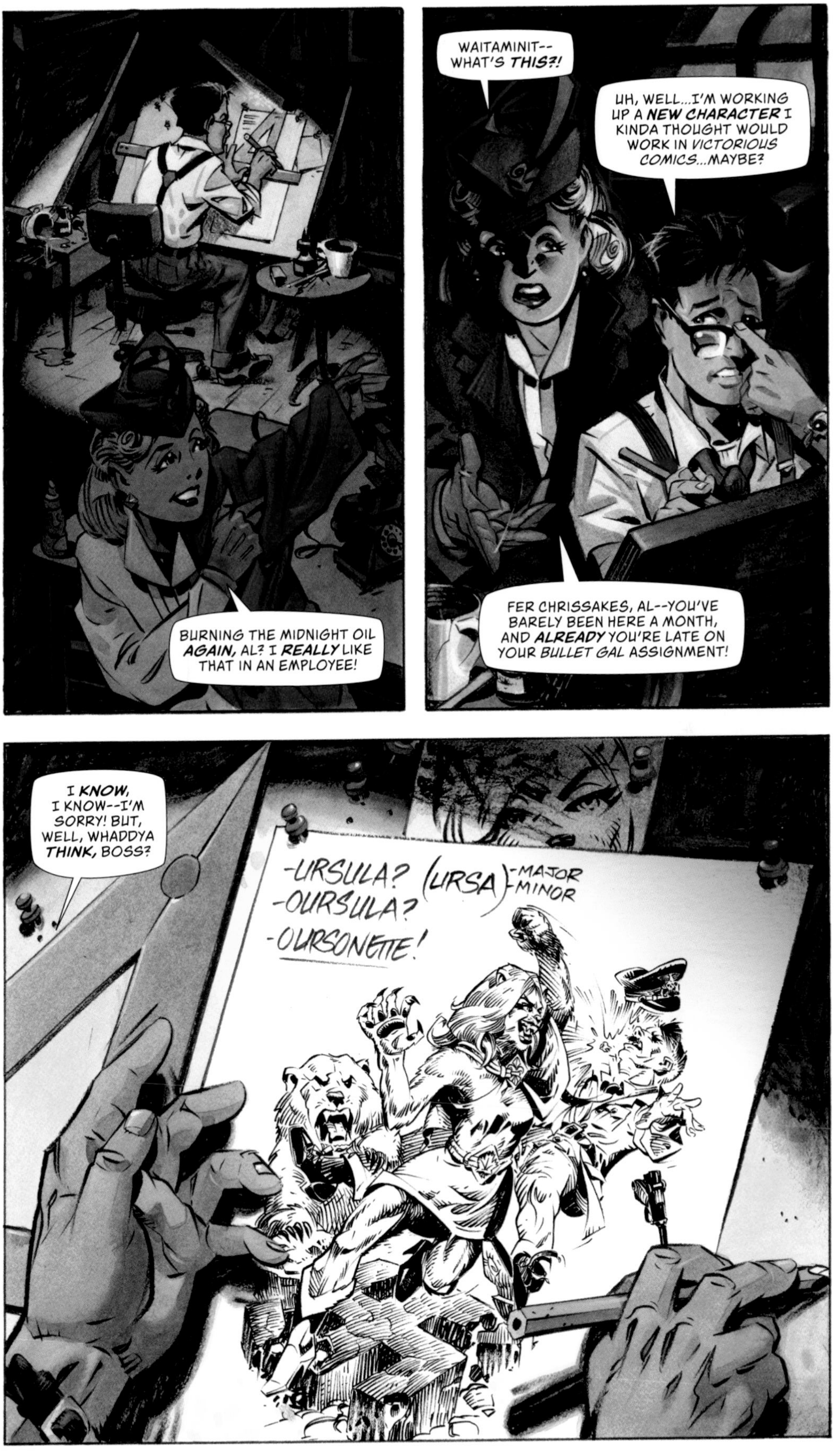
BURNING THE MIDNIGHT OIL AGAIN, AL? I REALLY LIKE THAT IN AN EMPLOYEE!
WAITAMINIT-- WHAT'S THIS?!
UH, WELL...I'M WORKING UP A NEW CHARACTER I KINDA THOUGHT WOULD WORK IN VICTORIOUS COMICS...MAYBE?
FER CHRISSAKES, AL--YOU'VE BARELY BEEN HERE A MONTH, AND ALREADY YOU'RE LATE ON YOUR BULLET GAL ASSIGNMENT!
I KNOW, I KNOW--I'M SORRY! BUT, WELL, WHADDYA THINK, BOSS?
-URSULA? (URSA)-MAJOR -MINOR
-OURSULA?
-OURSONETTE!

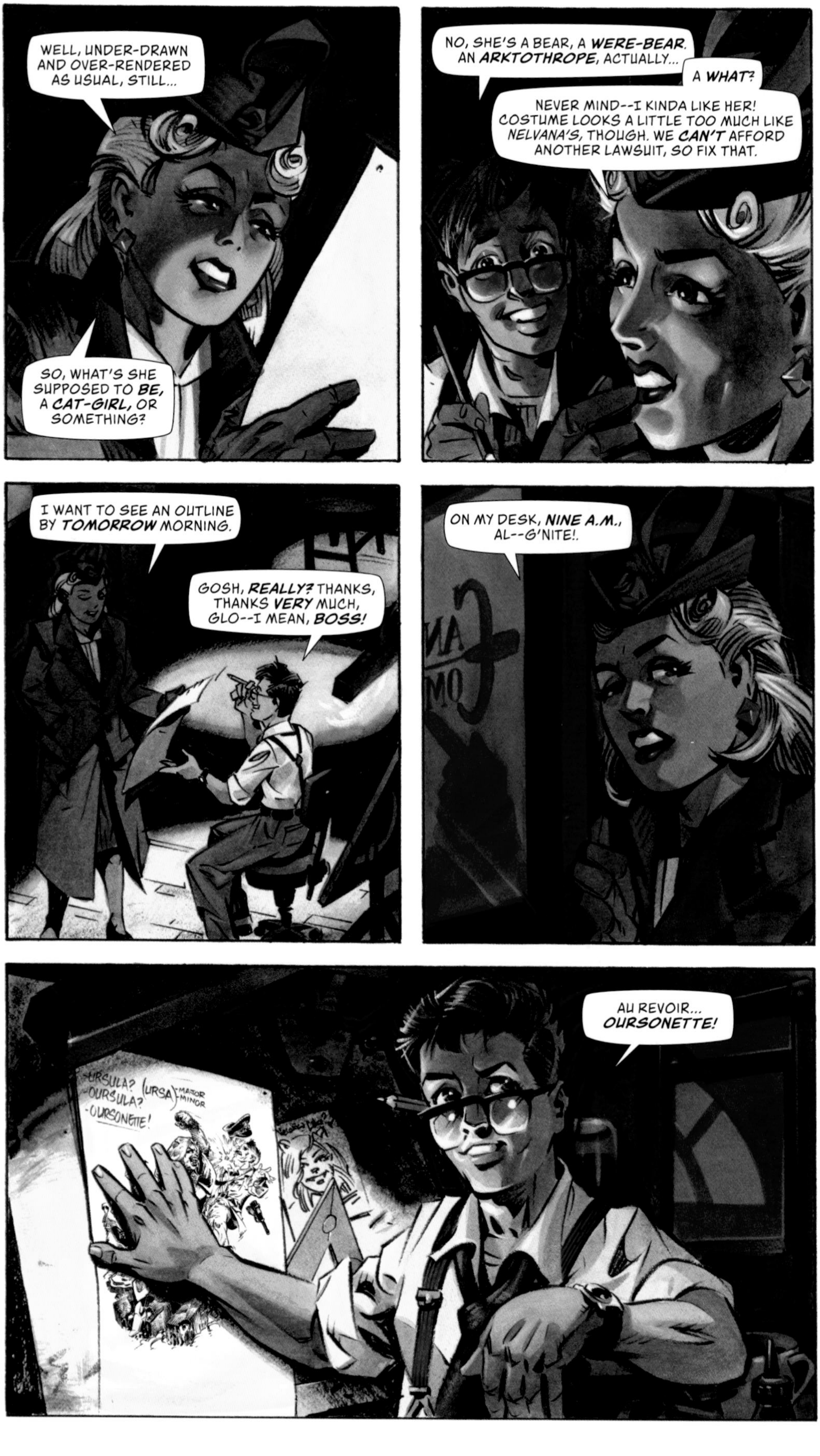
WELL, UNDER-DRAWN AND OVER-RENDERED AS USUAL, STILL...
SO, WHAT'S SHE SUPPOSED TO BE, A CAT-GIRL, OR SOMETHING?
NO, SHE'S A BEAR, A WERE-BEAR. AN ARKTOTHROPE, ACTUALLY...
A WHAT?
NEVER MIND--I KINDA LIKE HER! COSTUME LOOKS A LITTLE TOO MUCH LIKE NELVANA'S, THOUGH. WE CAN'T AFFORD ANOTHER LAWSUIT, SO FIX THAT.
I WANT TO SEE AN OUTLINE BY TOMORROW MORNING.
GOSH, REALLY? THANKS, THANKS VERY MUCH, GLO--I MEAN, BOSS!
ON MY DESK, NINE A.M., AL--G'NITE!.
-URSULA? (URSA) MAJOR MINOR
-OURSULA?
-OURSONETTE!
AU REVOIR... OURSONETTE!

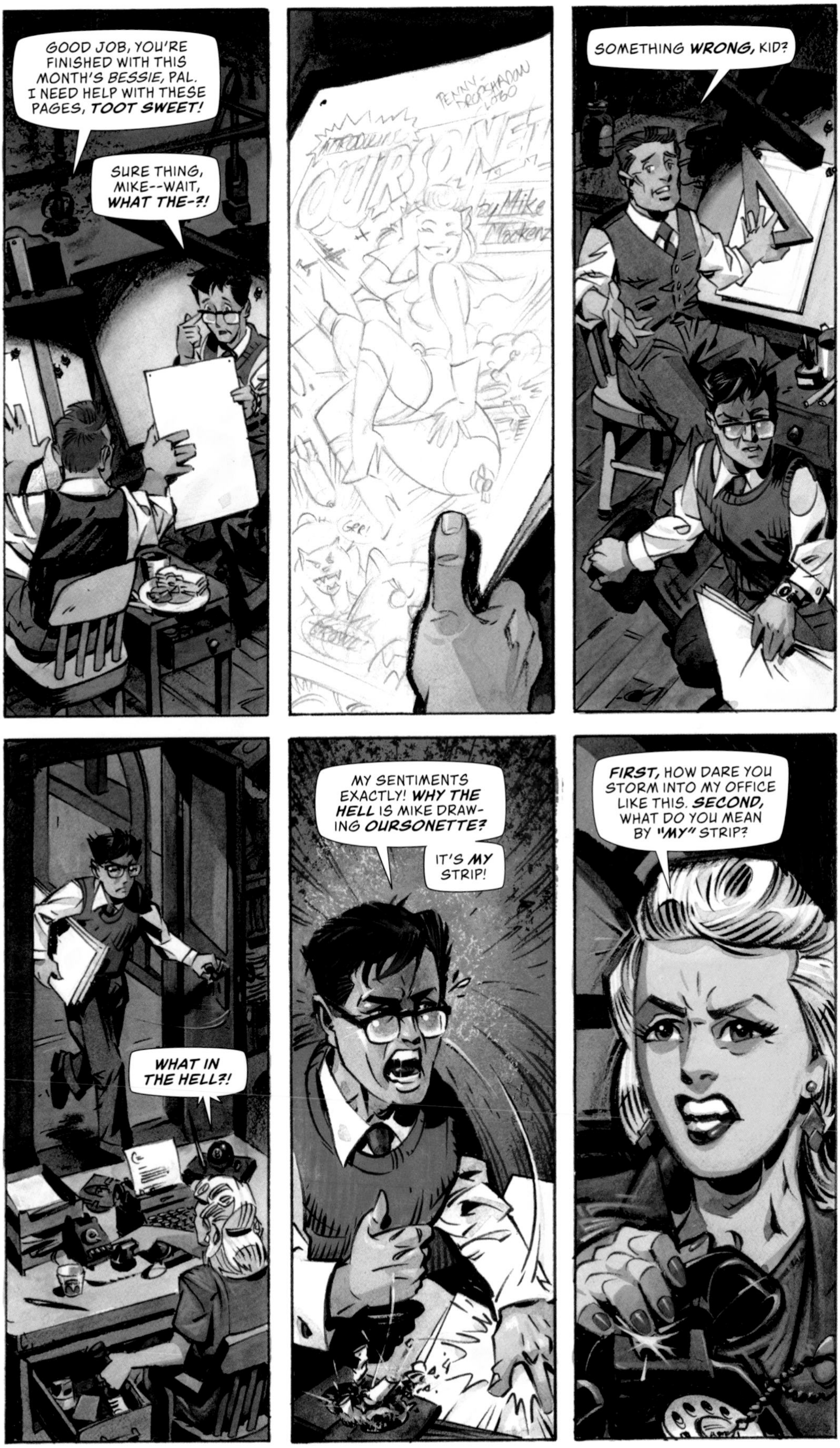
GOOD JOB, YOU'RE FINISHED WITH THIS MONTH'S *BESSIE*, PAL. I NEED HELP WITH THESE PAGES, ***TOOT SWEET!***
SURE THING, MIKE--WAIT, ***WHAT THE-?!***
SOMETHING ***WRONG,*** KID?
WHAT IN THE HELL?!
MY SENTIMENTS EXACTLY! ***WHY THE HELL*** IS MIKE DRAWING ***OURSONETTE?***
IT'S ***MY*** STRIP!
FIRST, HOW DARE YOU STORM INTO MY OFFICE LIKE THIS. ***SECOND,*** WHAT DO YOU MEAN BY ***"MY"*** STRIP?

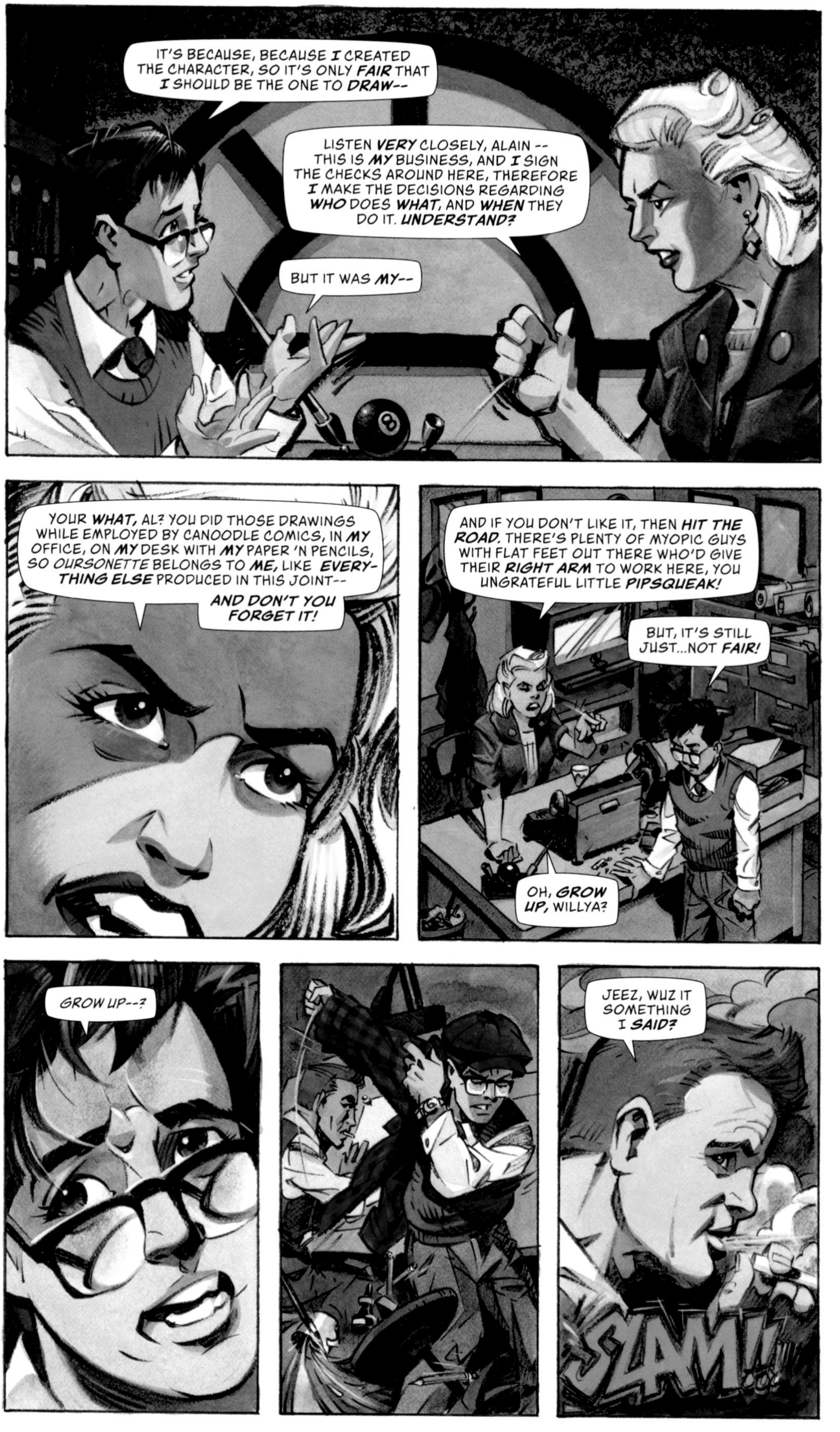
IT'S BECAUSE, BECAUSE I CREATED THE CHARACTER, SO IT'S ONLY FAIR THAT I SHOULD BE THE ONE TO DRAW--
LISTEN VERY CLOSELY, ALAIN -- THIS IS MY BUSINESS, AND I SIGN THE CHECKS AROUND HERE, THEREFORE I MAKE THE DECISIONS REGARDING WHO DOES WHAT, AND WHEN THEY DO IT. UNDERSTAND?
BUT IT WAS MY--
YOUR WHAT, AL? YOU DID THOSE DRAWINGS WHILE EMPLOYED BY CANOODLE COMICS, IN MY OFFICE, ON MY DESK WITH MY PAPER 'N PENCILS, SO OURSONETTE BELONGS TO ME, LIKE EVERY-THING ELSE PRODUCED IN THIS JOINT--
AND DON'T YOU FORGET IT!
AND IF YOU DON'T LIKE IT, THEN HIT THE ROAD. THERE'S PLENTY OF MYOPIC GUYS WITH FLAT FEET OUT THERE WHO'D GIVE THEIR RIGHT ARM TO WORK HERE, YOU UNGRATEFUL LITTLE PIPSQUEAK!
BUT, IT'S STILL JUST...NOT FAIR!
OH, GROW UP, WILLYA?
GROW UP--?
JEEZ, WUZ IT SOMETHING I SAID?
SLAM!!

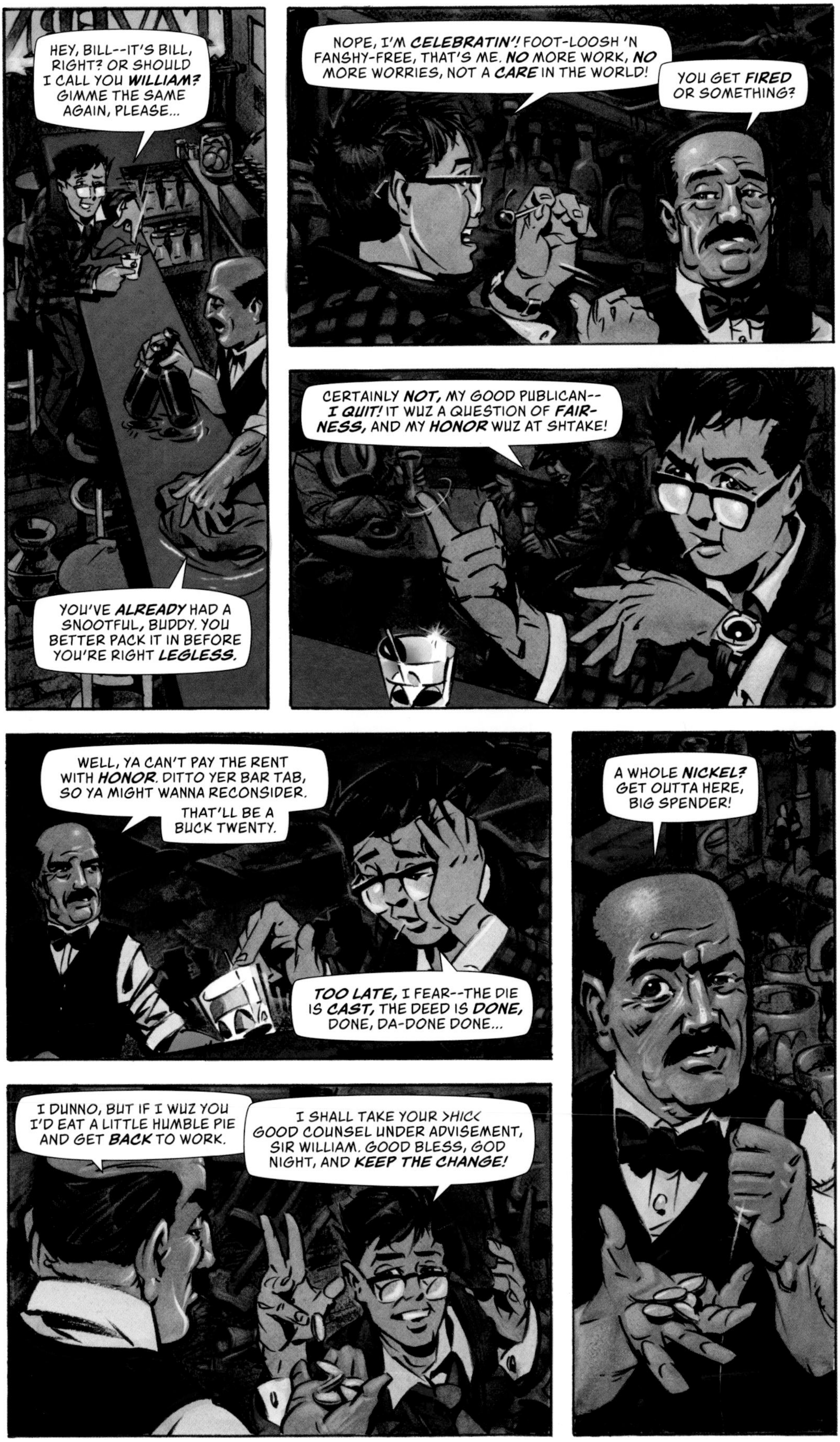
HEY, BILL--IT'S BILL, RIGHT? OR SHOULD I CALL YOU WILLIAM? GIMME THE SAME AGAIN, PLEASE...
YOU'VE ALREADY HAD A SNOOTFUL, BUDDY. YOU BETTER PACK IT IN BEFORE YOU'RE RIGHT LEGLESS.
NOPE, I'M CELEBRATIN'! FOOT-LOOSH 'N FANSHY-FREE, THAT'S ME. NO MORE WORK, NO MORE WORRIES, NOT A CARE IN THE WORLD!
YOU GET FIRED OR SOMETHING?
CERTAINLY NOT, MY GOOD PUBLICAN--I QUIT! IT WUZ A QUESTION OF FAIR-NESS, AND MY HONOR WUZ AT SHTAKE!
WELL, YA CAN'T PAY THE RENT WITH HONOR. DITTO YER BAR TAB, SO YA MIGHT WANNA RECONSIDER.
THAT'LL BE A BUCK TWENTY.
TOO LATE, I FEAR--THE DIE IS CAST, THE DEED IS DONE, DONE, DA-DONE DONE...
I DUNNO, BUT IF I WUZ YOU I'D EAT A LITTLE HUMBLE PIE AND GET BACK TO WORK.
I SHALL TAKE YOUR >HIC< GOOD COUNSEL UNDER ADVISEMENT, SIR WILLIAM. GOOD BLESS, GOD NIGHT, AND KEEP THE CHANGE!
A WHOLE NICKEL? GET OUTTA HERE, BIG SPENDER!

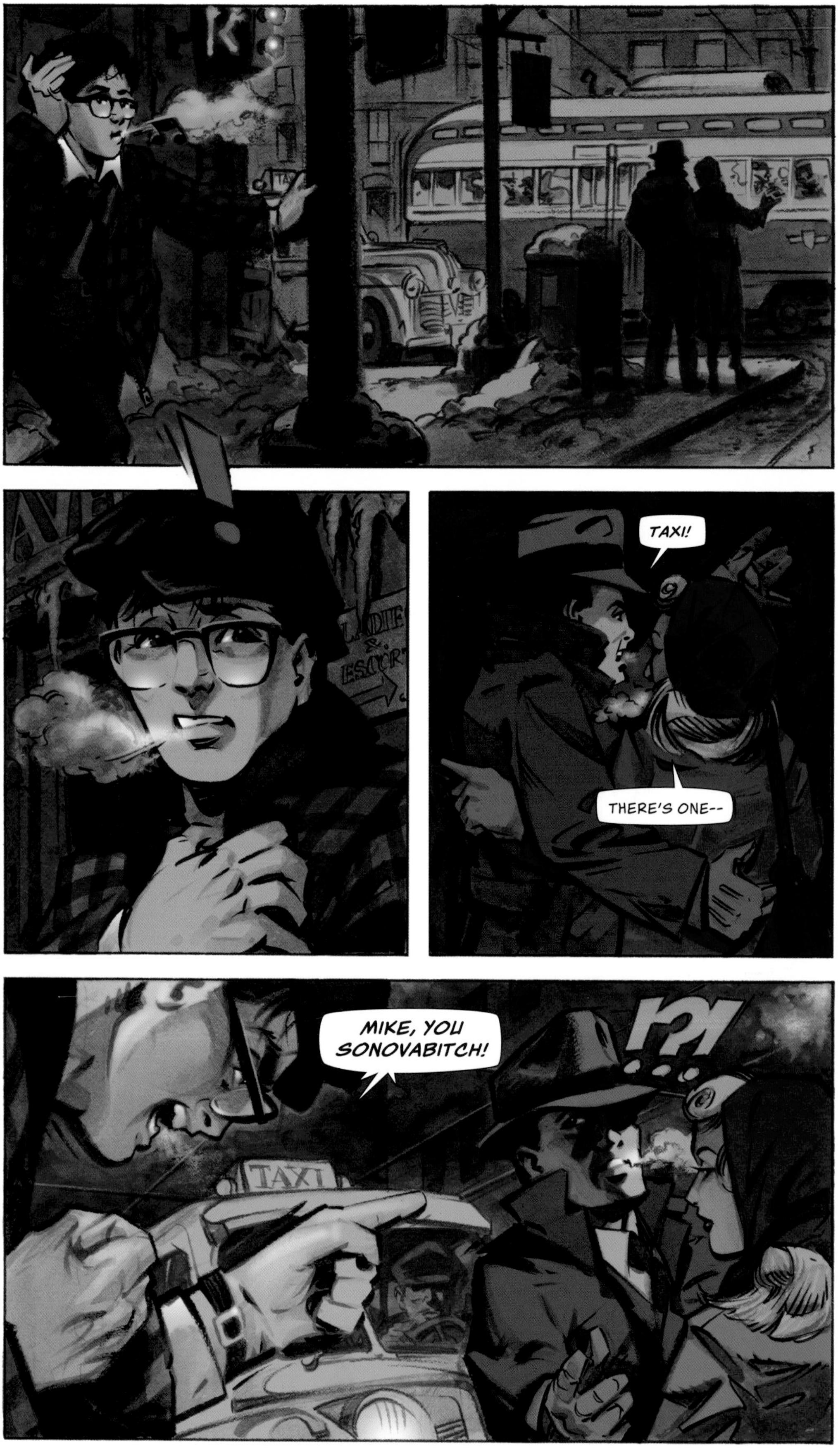
!
TAXI!
THERE'S ONE--
MIKE, YOU SONOVABITCH!
!?!

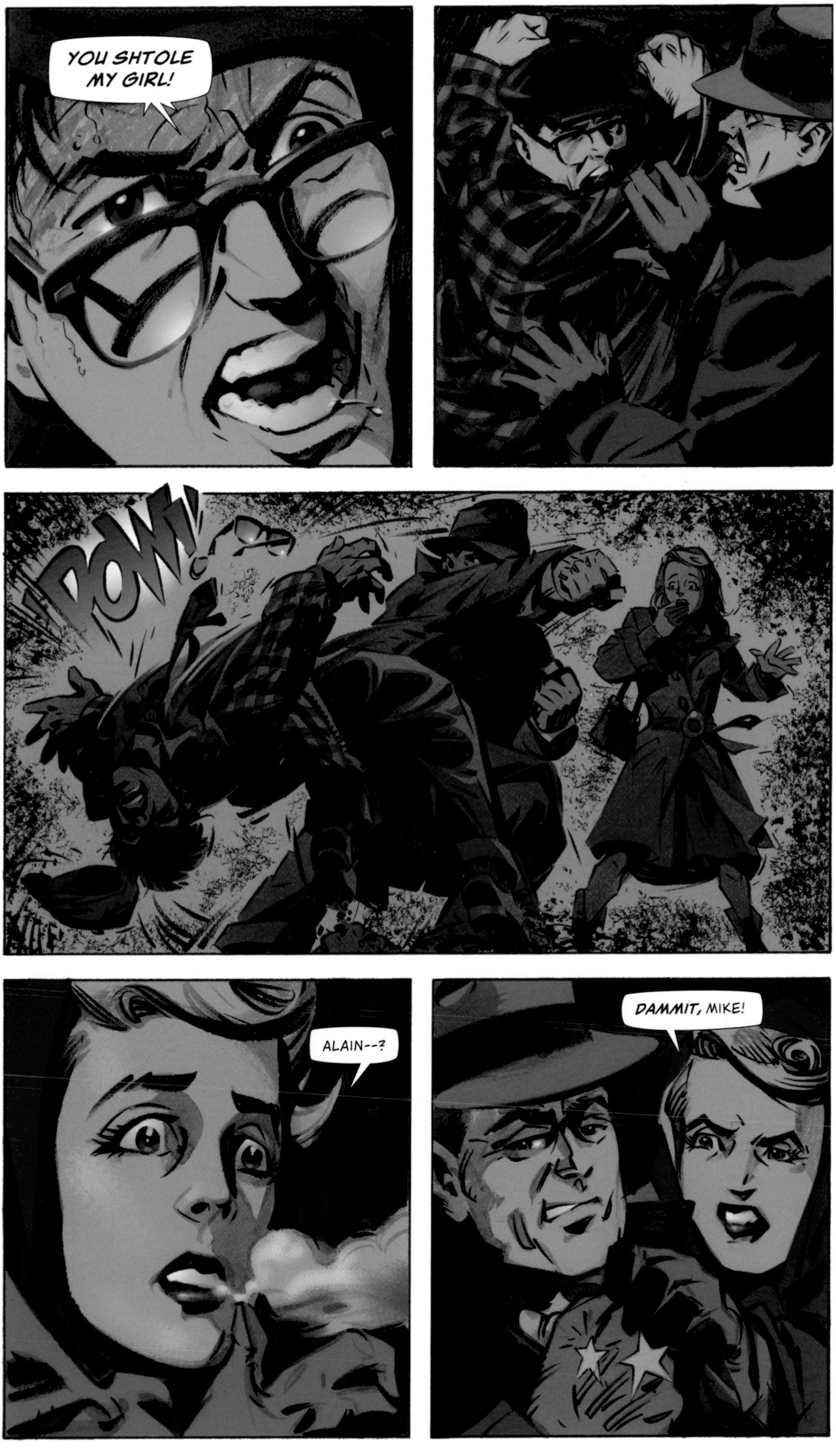
YOU SHTOLE MY GIRL!
POW!
ALAIN--?
DAMMIT, MIKE!

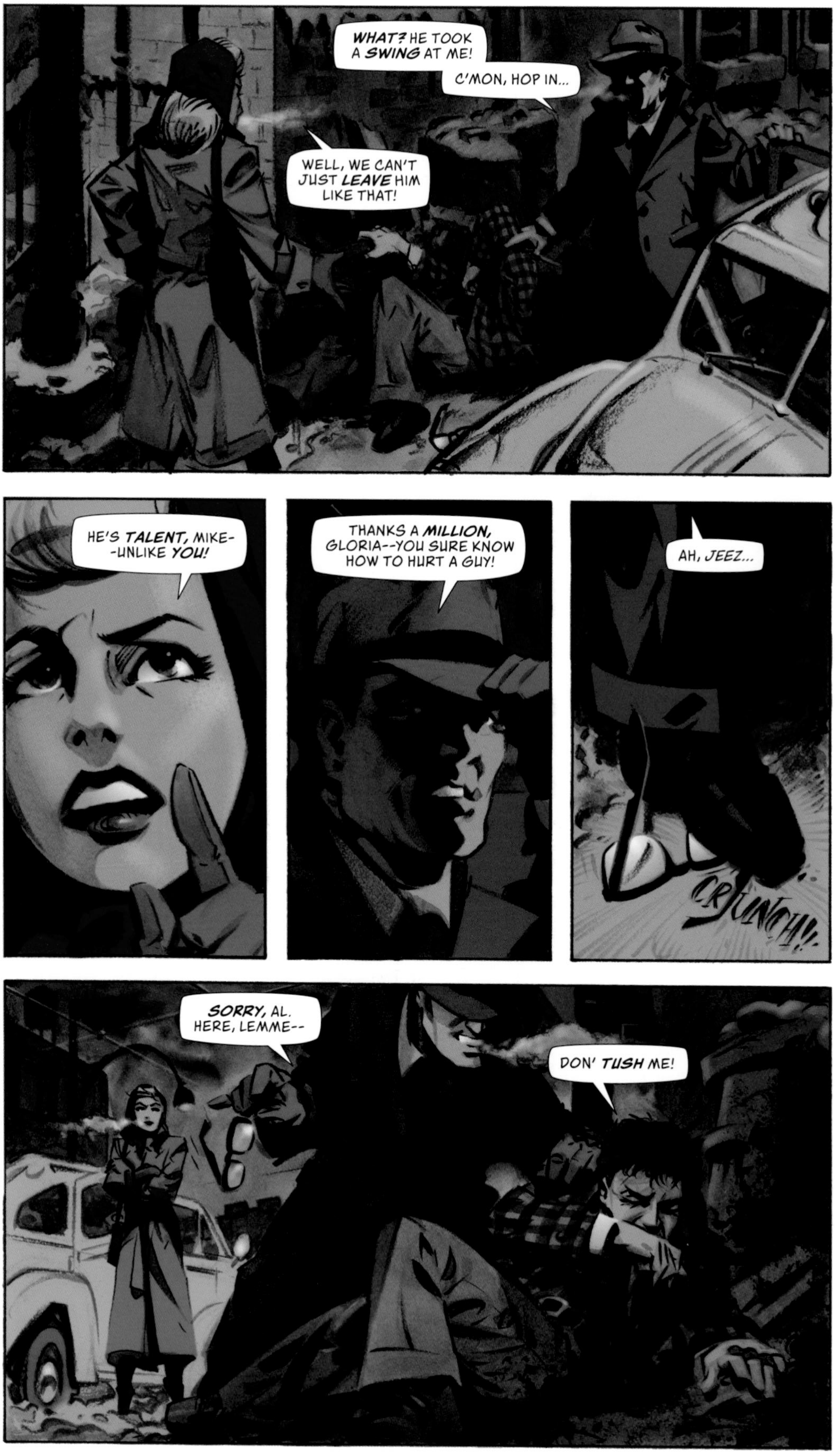
WHAT? HE TOOK A SWING AT ME!
C'MON, HOP IN...
WELL, WE CAN'T JUST LEAVE HIM LIKE THAT!
HE'S TALENT, MIKE--UNLIKE YOU!
THANKS A MILLION, GLORIA--YOU SURE KNOW HOW TO HURT A GUY!
AH, JEEZ...
CRUNCH!!
SORRY, AL. HERE, LEMME--
DON' TUSH ME!

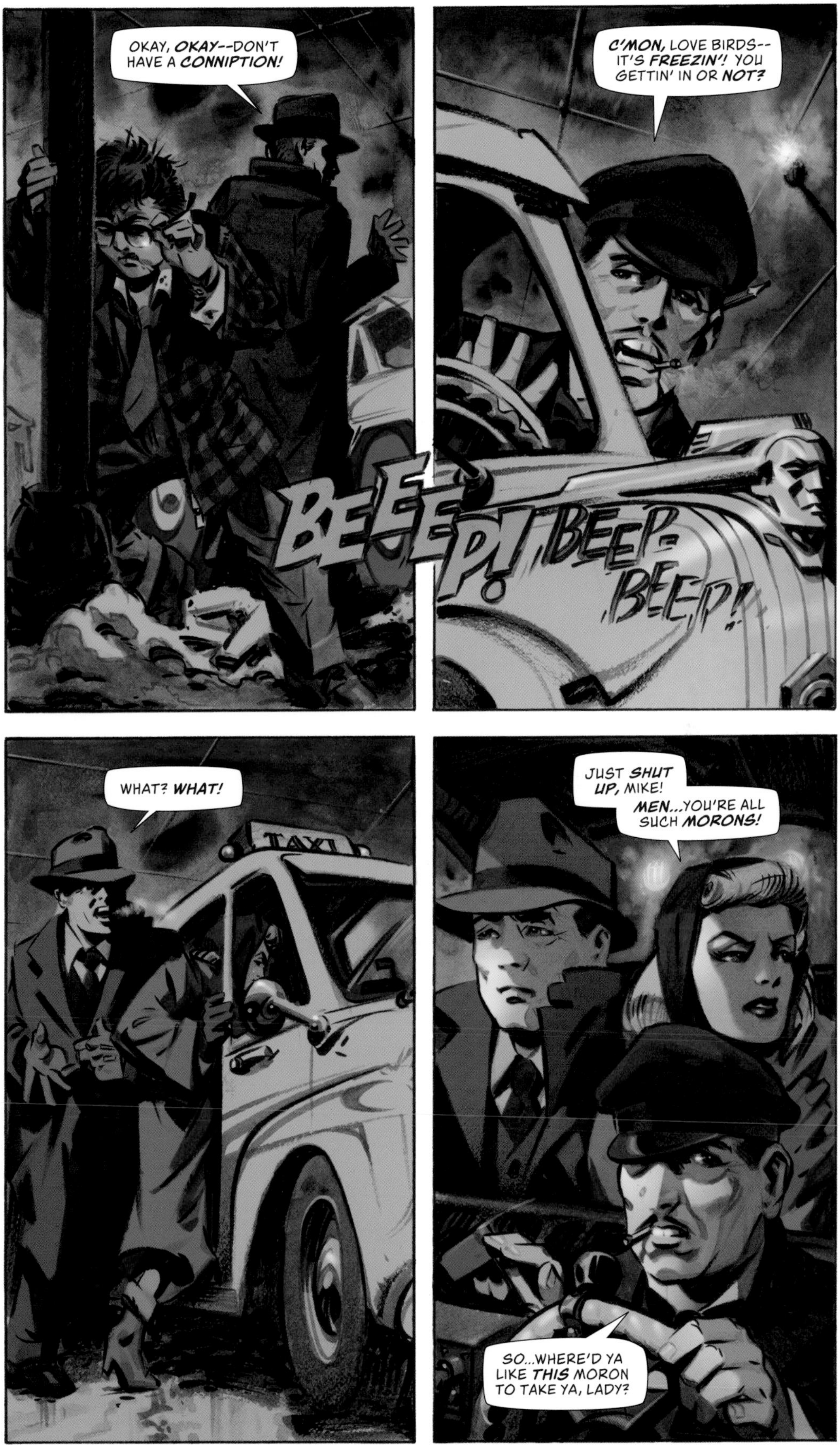
OKAY, OKAY--DON'T HAVE A CONNIPTION!
C'MON, LOVE BIRDS--IT'S FREEZIN'! YOU GETTIN' IN OR NOT?
BEEEP! BEEP-BEEP!
WHAT? WHAT!
TAXI
JUST SHUT UP, MIKE!
MEN...YOU'RE ALL SUCH MORONS!
SO...WHERE'D YA LIKE THIS MORON TO TAKE YA, LADY?

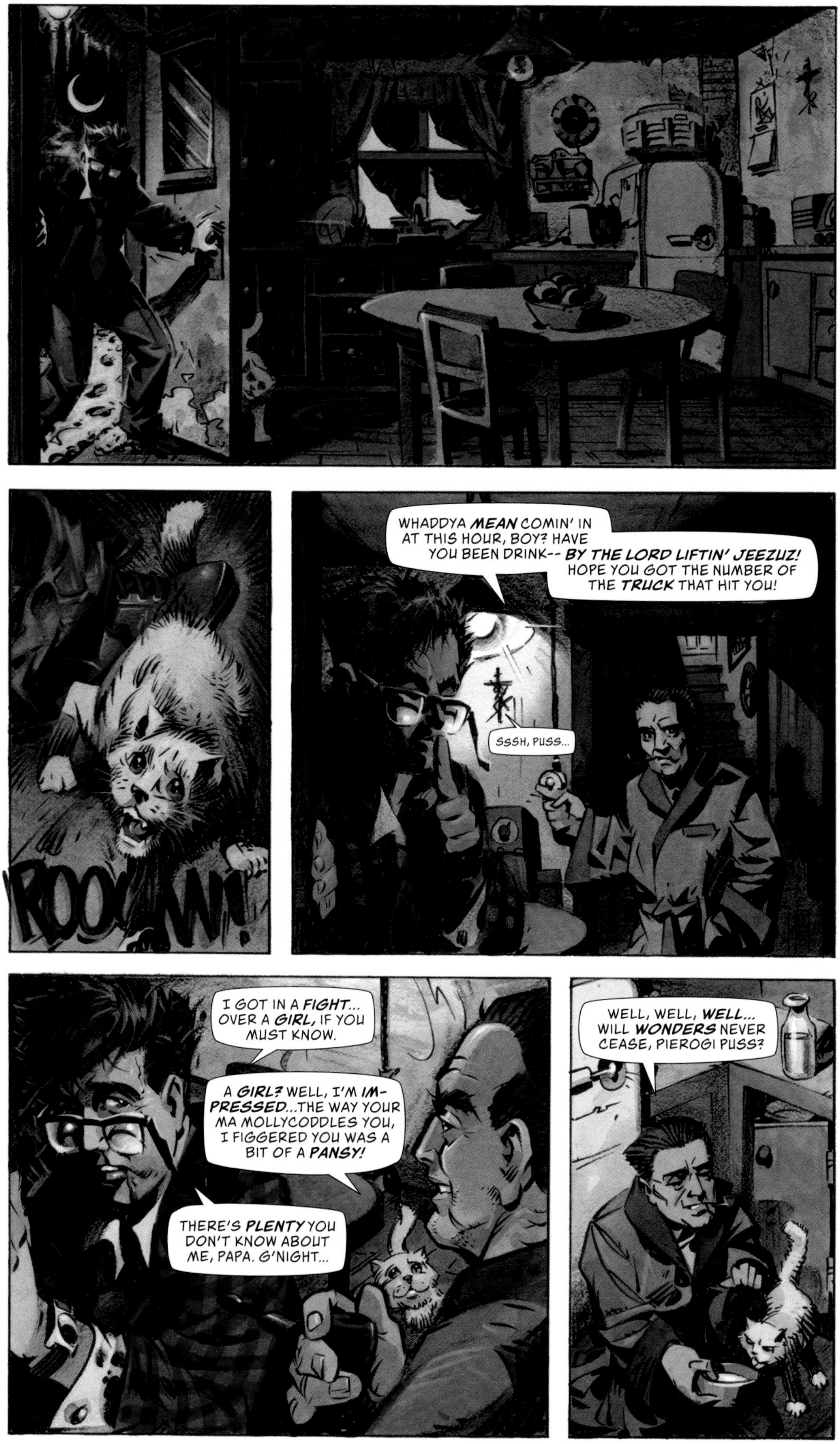
ROOWW!
WHADDYA MEAN COMIN' IN AT THIS HOUR, BOY? HAVE YOU BEEN DRINK-- BY THE LORD LIFTIN' JEEZUZ! HOPE YOU GOT THE NUMBER OF THE TRUCK THAT HIT YOU!
SSSH, PUSS...
I GOT IN A FIGHT... OVER A GIRL, IF YOU MUST KNOW.
A GIRL? WELL, I'M IMPRESSED...THE WAY YOUR MA MOLLYCODDLES YOU, I FIGGERED YOU WAS A BIT OF A PANSY!
THERE'S PLENTY YOU DON'T KNOW ABOUT ME, PAPA. G'NIGHT...
WELL, WELL, WELL... WILL WONDERS NEVER CEASE, PIEROGI PUSS?

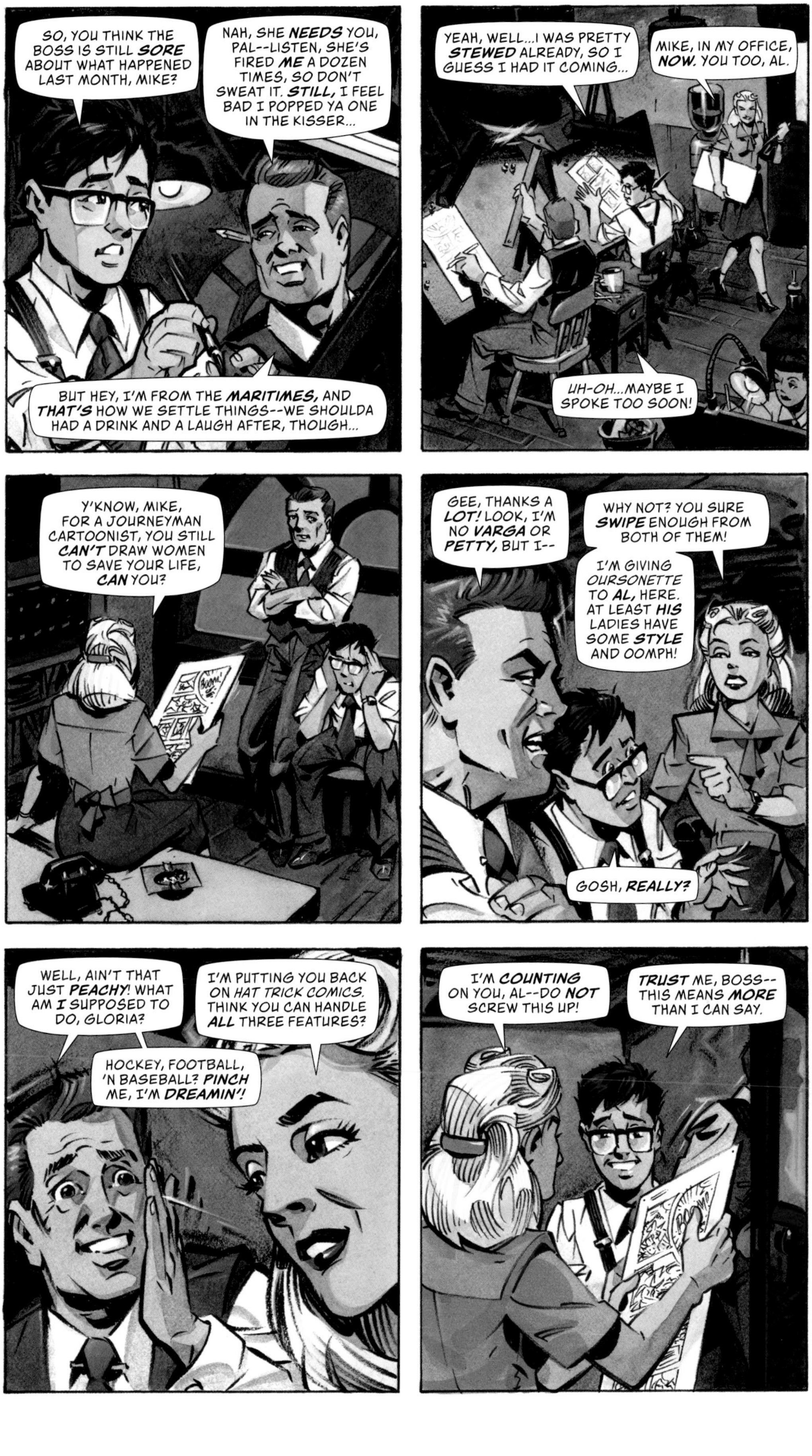

SO, YOU THINK THE BOSS IS STILL **SORE** ABOUT WHAT HAPPENED LAST MONTH, MIKE?
NAH, SHE **NEEDS** YOU, PAL--LISTEN, SHE'S FIRED **ME** A DOZEN TIMES, SO DON'T SWEAT IT. **STILL,** I FEEL BAD I POPPED YA ONE IN THE KISSER...
BUT HEY, I'M FROM THE **MARITIMES,** AND **THAT'S** HOW WE SETTLE THINGS--WE SHOULDA HAD A DRINK AND A LAUGH AFTER, THOUGH...
YEAH, WELL...I WAS PRETTY **STEWED** ALREADY, SO I GUESS I HAD IT COMING...
MIKE, IN MY OFFICE, **NOW.** YOU TOO, AL.
UH-OH...MAYBE I SPOKE TOO SOON!
Y'KNOW, MIKE, FOR A JOURNEYMAN CARTOONIST, YOU STILL **CAN'T** DRAW WOMEN TO SAVE YOUR LIFE, **CAN** YOU?
GEE, THANKS A **LOT!** LOOK, I'M NO **VARGA** OR **PETTY,** BUT I--
WHY NOT? YOU SURE **SWIPE** ENOUGH FROM BOTH OF THEM!
I'M GIVING *OURSONETTE* TO **AL,** HERE. AT LEAST **HIS** LADIES HAVE SOME **STYLE** AND OOMPH!
GOSH, **REALLY?**
WELL, AIN'T THAT JUST **PEACHY**! WHAT AM **I** SUPPOSED TO DO, GLORIA?
I'M PUTTING YOU BACK ON *HAT TRICK COMICS.* THINK YOU CAN HANDLE **ALL** THREE FEATURES?
HOCKEY, FOOTBALL, 'N BASEBALL? **PINCH** ME, I'M **DREAMIN'!**
I'M **COUNTING** ON YOU, AL--DO **NOT** SCREW THIS UP!
TRUST ME, BOSS--THIS MEANS **MORE** THAN I CAN SAY.

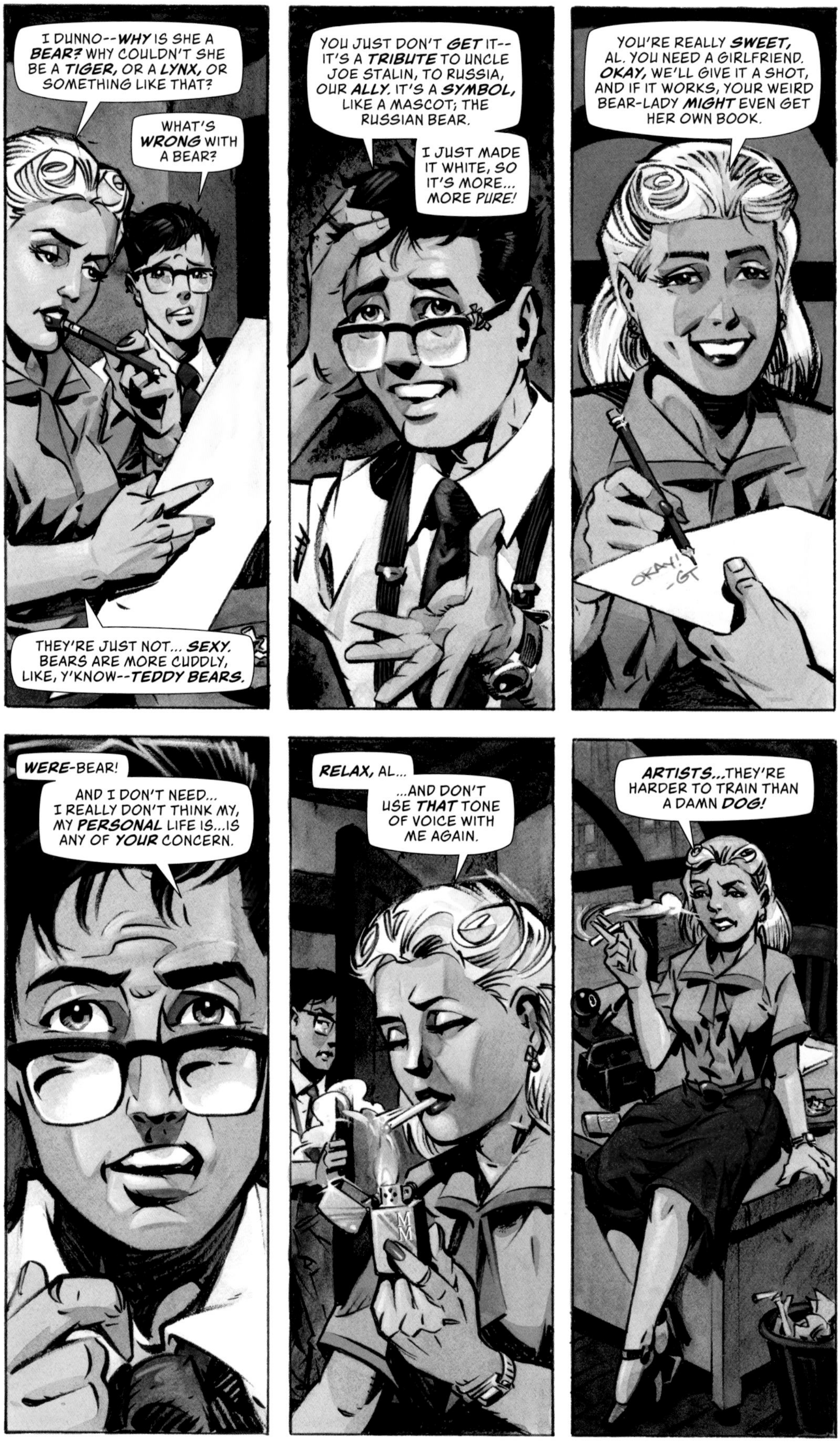
I DUNNO--WHY IS SHE A BEAR? WHY COULDN'T SHE BE A TIGER, OR A LYNX, OR SOMETHING LIKE THAT?
WHAT'S WRONG WITH A BEAR?
THEY'RE JUST NOT... SEXY. BEARS ARE MORE CUDDLY, LIKE, Y'KNOW--TEDDY BEARS.
YOU JUST DON'T GET IT--IT'S A TRIBUTE TO UNCLE JOE STALIN, TO RUSSIA, OUR ALLY. IT'S A SYMBOL, LIKE A MASCOT; THE RUSSIAN BEAR.
I JUST MADE IT WHITE, SO IT'S MORE... MORE PURE!
YOU'RE REALLY SWEET, AL. YOU NEED A GIRLFRIEND. OKAY, WE'LL GIVE IT A SHOT, AND IF IT WORKS, YOUR WEIRD BEAR-LADY MIGHT EVEN GET HER OWN BOOK.
OKAY! -GT
WERE-BEAR!
AND I DON'T NEED... I REALLY DON'T THINK MY, MY PERSONAL LIFE IS...IS ANY OF YOUR CONCERN.
RELAX, AL...
...AND DON'T USE THAT TONE OF VOICE WITH ME AGAIN.
MM
ARTISTS...THEY'RE HARDER TO TRAIN THAN A DAMN DOG!

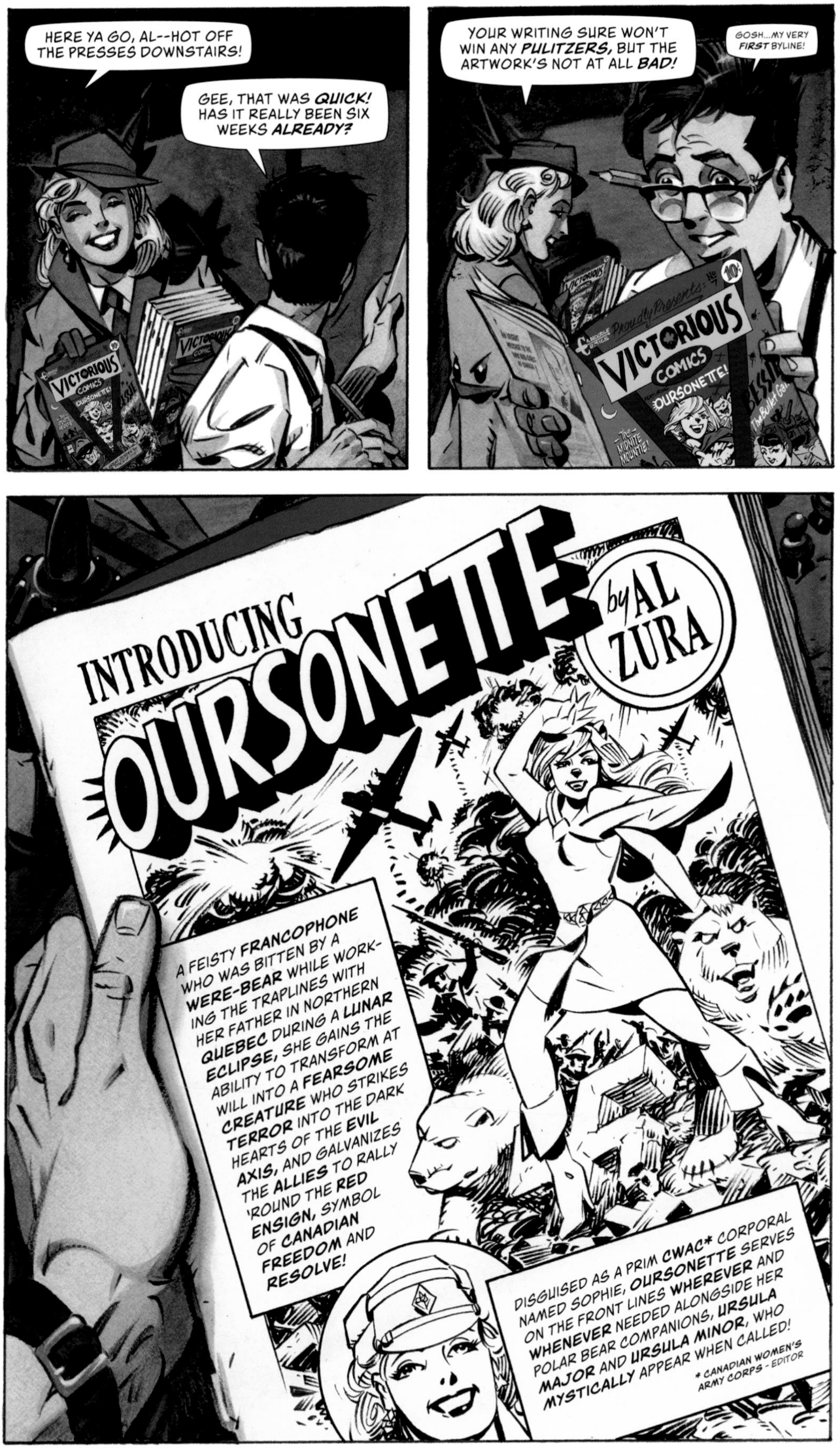
HERE YA GO, AL--HOT OFF THE PRESSES DOWNSTAIRS!
GEE, THAT WAS QUICK! HAS IT REALLY BEEN SIX WEEKS ALREADY?
VICTORIOUS COMICS
OURSONETTE!
YOUR WRITING SURE WON'T WIN ANY PULITZERS, BUT THE ARTWORK'S NOT AT ALL BAD!
GOSH...MY VERY FIRST BYLINE!
Proudly Presents
No 7
10¢
VICTORIOUS COMICS
OURSONETTE!
The Midnite Mountie!
The Bullet Gal
INTRODUCING OURSONETTE
by AL ZURA
A FEISTY FRANCOPHONE WHO WAS BITTEN BY A WERE-BEAR WHILE WORKING THE TRAPLINES WITH HER FATHER IN NORTHERN QUEBEC DURING A LUNAR ECLIPSE, SHE GAINS THE ABILITY TO TRANSFORM AT WILL INTO A FEARSOME CREATURE WHO STRIKES TERROR INTO THE DARK HEARTS OF THE EVIL AXIS, AND GALVANIZES THE ALLIES TO RALLY 'ROUND THE RED ENSIGN, SYMBOL OF CANADIAN FREEDOM AND RESOLVE!
DISGUISED AS A PRIM CWAC* CORPORAL NAMED SOPHIE, OURSONETTE SERVES ON THE FRONT LINES WHEREVER AND WHENEVER NEEDED ALONGSIDE HER POLAR BEAR COMPANIONS, URSULA MAJOR AND URSULA MINOR, WHO MYSTICALLY APPEAR WHEN CALLED!
* CANADIAN WOMEN'S ARMY CORPS - EDITOR

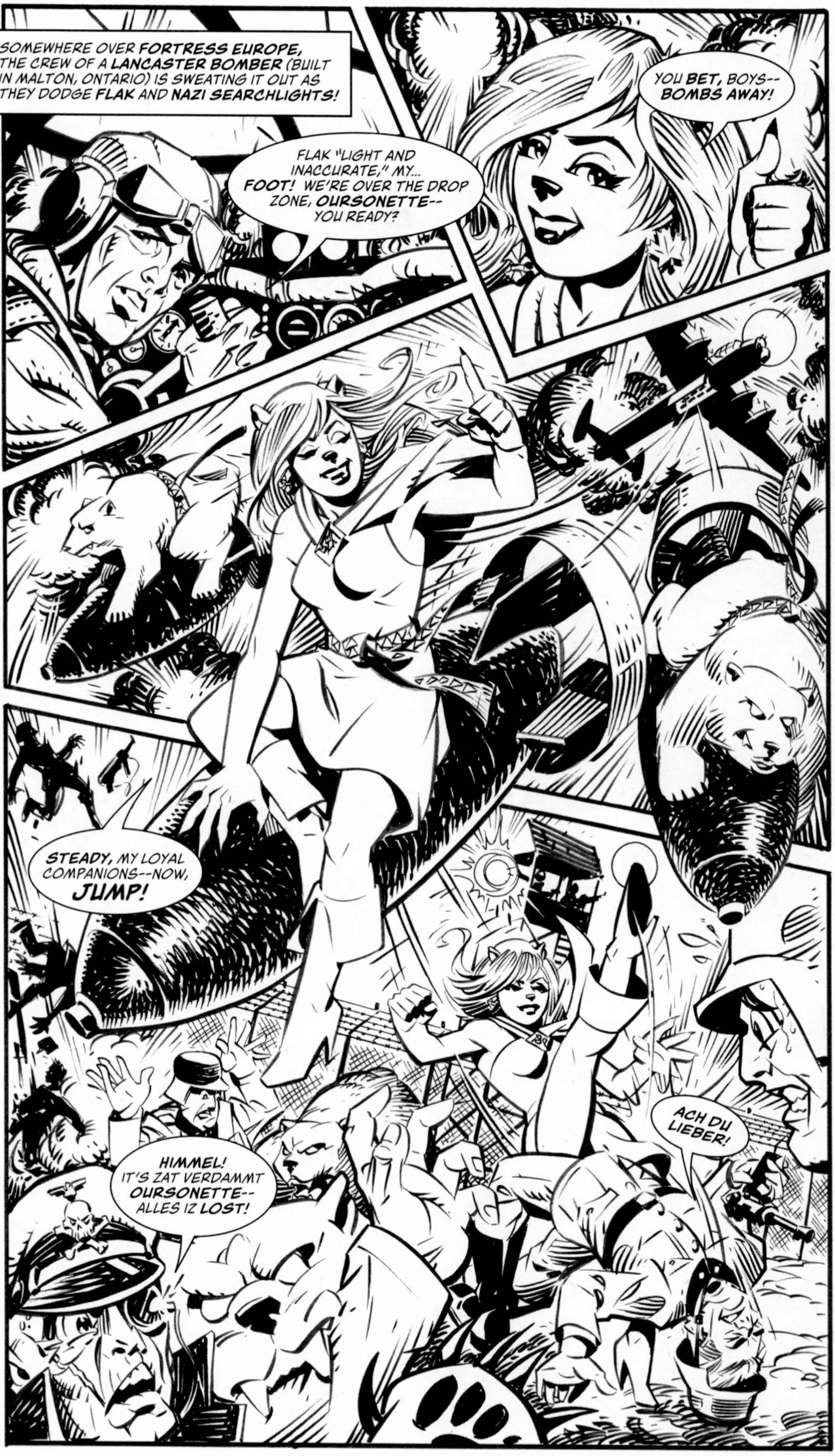
SOMEWHERE OVER FORTRESS EUROPE, THE CREW OF A LANCASTER BOMBER (BUILT IN MALTON, ONTARIO) IS SWEATING IT OUT AS THEY DODGE FLAK AND NAZI SEARCHLIGHTS!
FLAK "LIGHT AND INACCURATE," MY... FOOT! WE'RE OVER THE DROP ZONE, OURSONETTE-- YOU READY?
YOU BET, BOYS-- BOMBS AWAY!
STEADY, MY LOYAL COMPANIONS--NOW, JUMP!
HIMMEL! IT'S ZAT VERDAMMT OURSONETTE-- ALLES IZ LOST!
ACH DU LIEBER!

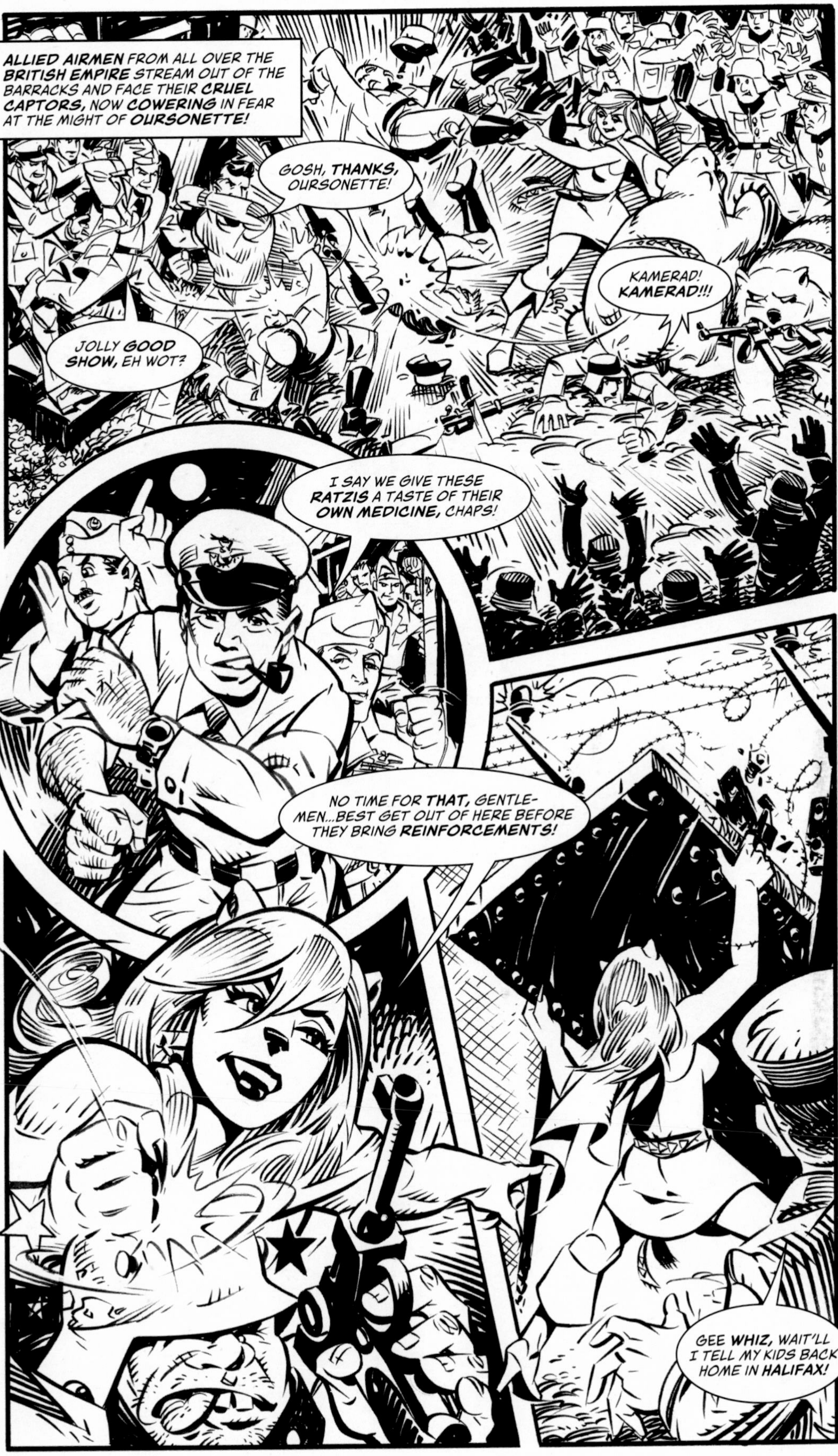
ALLIED AIRMEN FROM ALL OVER THE BRITISH EMPIRE STREAM OUT OF THE BARRACKS AND FACE THEIR CRUEL CAPTORS, NOW COWERING IN FEAR AT THE MIGHT OF OURSONETTE!
GOSH, THANKS, OURSONETTE!
KAMERAD! KAMERAD!!!
JOLLY GOOD SHOW, EH WOT?
I SAY WE GIVE THESE RATZIS A TASTE OF THEIR OWN MEDICINE, CHAPS!
NO TIME FOR THAT, GENTLE-MEN...BEST GET OUT OF HERE BEFORE THEY BRING REINFORCEMENTS!
GEE WHIZ, WAIT'LL I TELL MY KIDS BACK HOME IN HALIFAX!

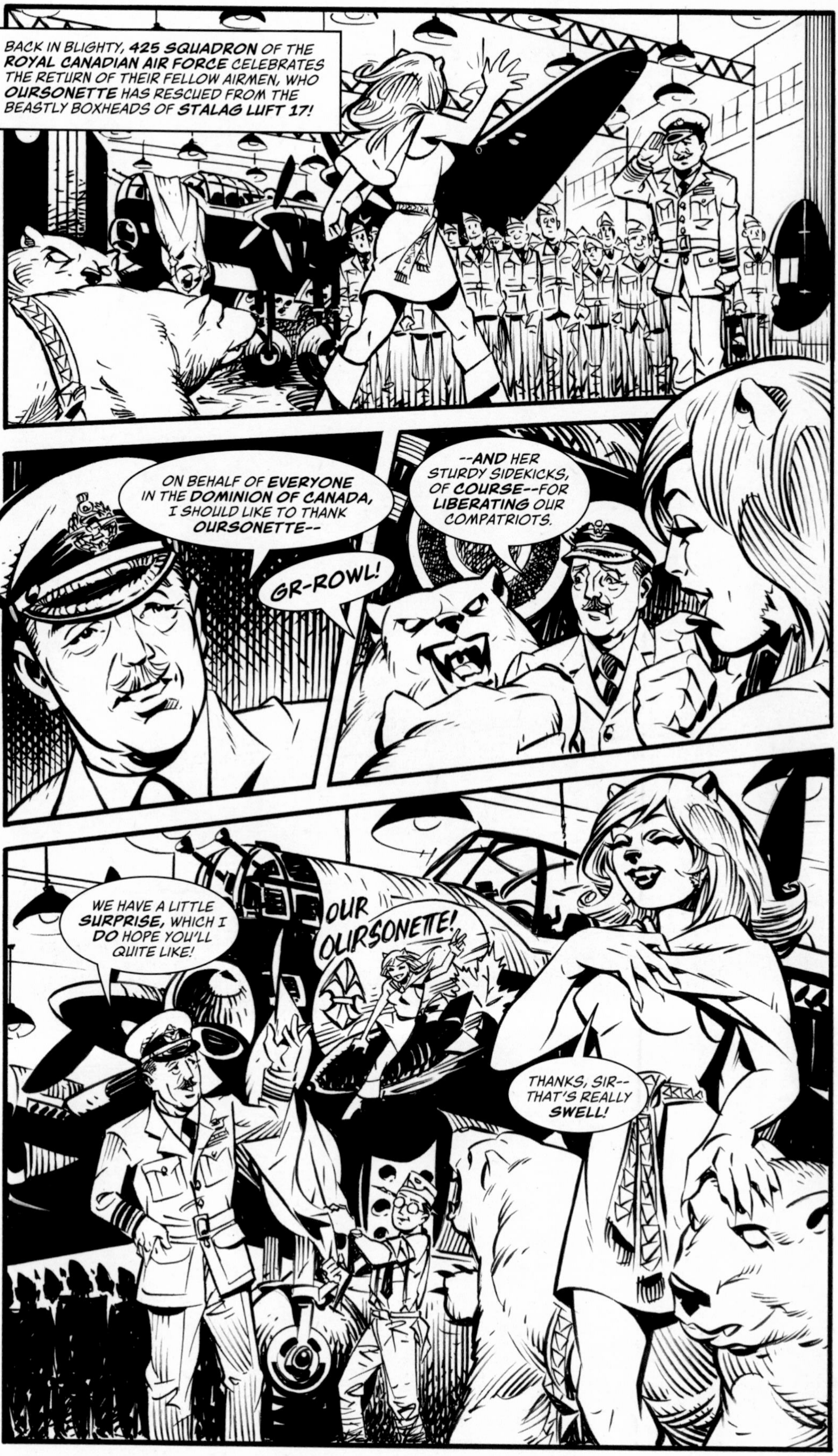
BACK IN BLIGHTY, 425 SQUADRON OF THE ROYAL CANADIAN AIR FORCE CELEBRATES THE RETURN OF THEIR FELLOW AIRMEN, WHO OURSONETTE HAS RESCUED FROM THE BEASTLY BOXHEADS OF STALAG LUFT 17!
ON BEHALF OF EVERYONE IN THE DOMINION OF CANADA, I SHOULD LIKE TO THANK OURSONETTE--
GR-ROWL!
--AND HER STURDY SIDEKICKS, OF COURSE--FOR LIBERATING OUR COMPATRIOTS.
WE HAVE A LITTLE SURPRISE, WHICH I DO HOPE YOU'LL QUITE LIKE!
OUR OURSONETTE!
THANKS, SIR--THAT'S REALLY SWELL!

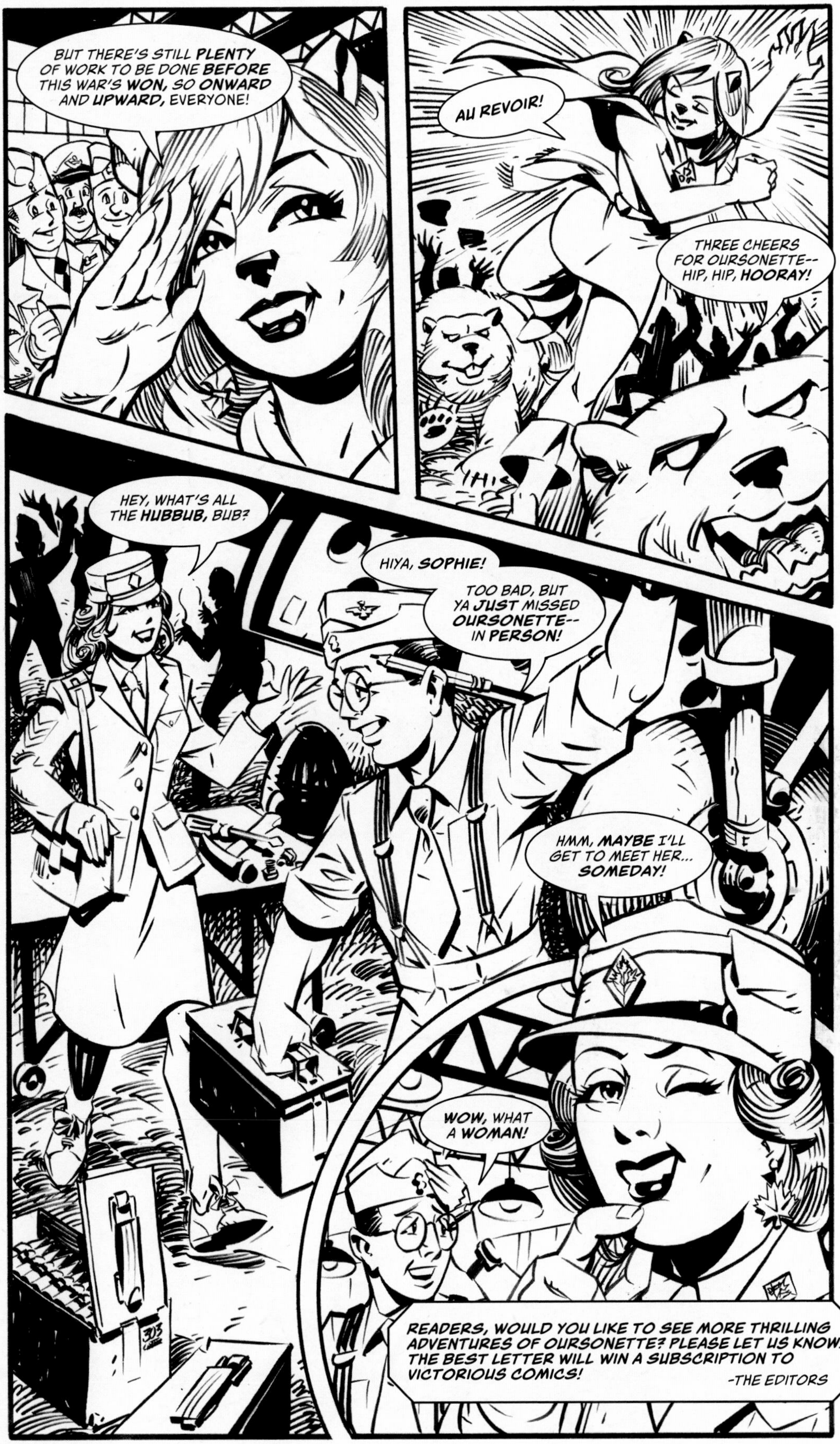
BUT THERE'S STILL PLENTY OF WORK TO BE DONE BEFORE THIS WAR'S WON, SO ONWARD AND UPWARD, EVERYONE!
AU REVOIR!
THREE CHEERS FOR OURSONETTE-- HIP, HIP, HOORAY!
HEY, WHAT'S ALL THE HUBBUB, BUB?
HIYA, SOPHIE!
TOO BAD, BUT YA JUST MISSED OURSONETTE-- IN PERSON!
HMM, MAYBE I'LL GET TO MEET HER... SOMEDAY!
WOW, WHAT A WOMAN!
READERS, WOULD YOU LIKE TO SEE MORE THRILLING ADVENTURES OF OURSONETTE? PLEASE LET US KNOW! THE BEST LETTER WILL WIN A SUBSCRIPTION TO VICTORIOUS COMICS!
-THE EDITORS

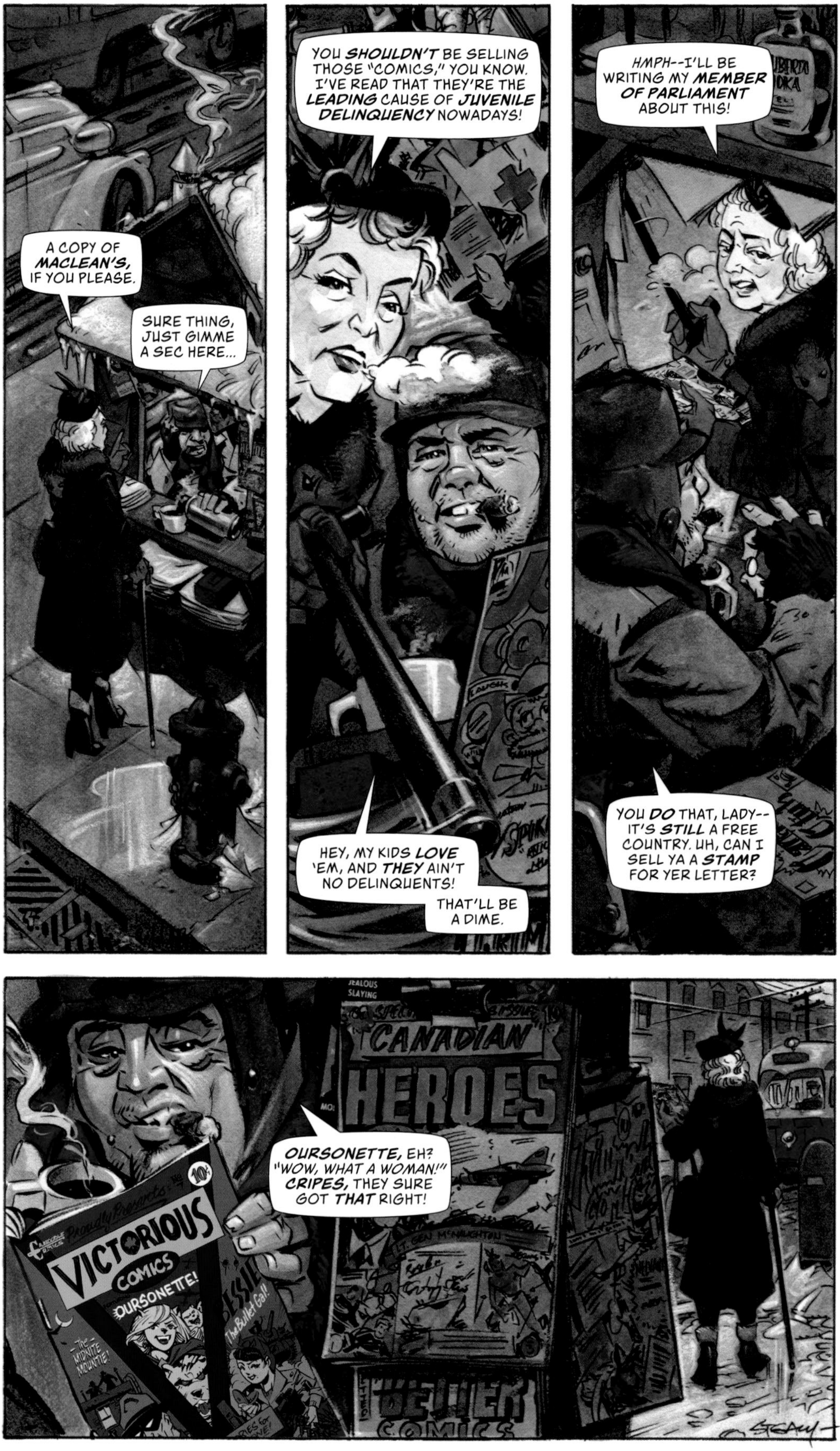
A COPY OF MACLEAN'S, IF YOU PLEASE.
SURE THING, JUST GIMME A SEC HERE...
YOU SHOULDN'T BE SELLING THOSE "COMICS," YOU KNOW. I'VE READ THAT THEY'RE THE LEADING CAUSE OF JUVENILE DELINQUENCY NOWADAYS!
HEY, MY KIDS LOVE 'EM, AND THEY AIN'T NO DELINQUENTS!
THAT'LL BE A DIME.
HMPH--I'LL BE WRITING MY MEMBER OF PARLIAMENT ABOUT THIS!
YOU DO THAT, LADY--IT'S STILL A FREE COUNTRY. UH, CAN I SELL YA A STAMP FOR YER LETTER?
JEALOUS SLAYING
CANADIAN HEROES
OURSONETTE, EH? "WOW, WHAT A WOMAN!" CRIPES, THEY SURE GOT THAT RIGHT!
10¢
VICTORIOUS COMICS
OURSONETTE!
COMICS

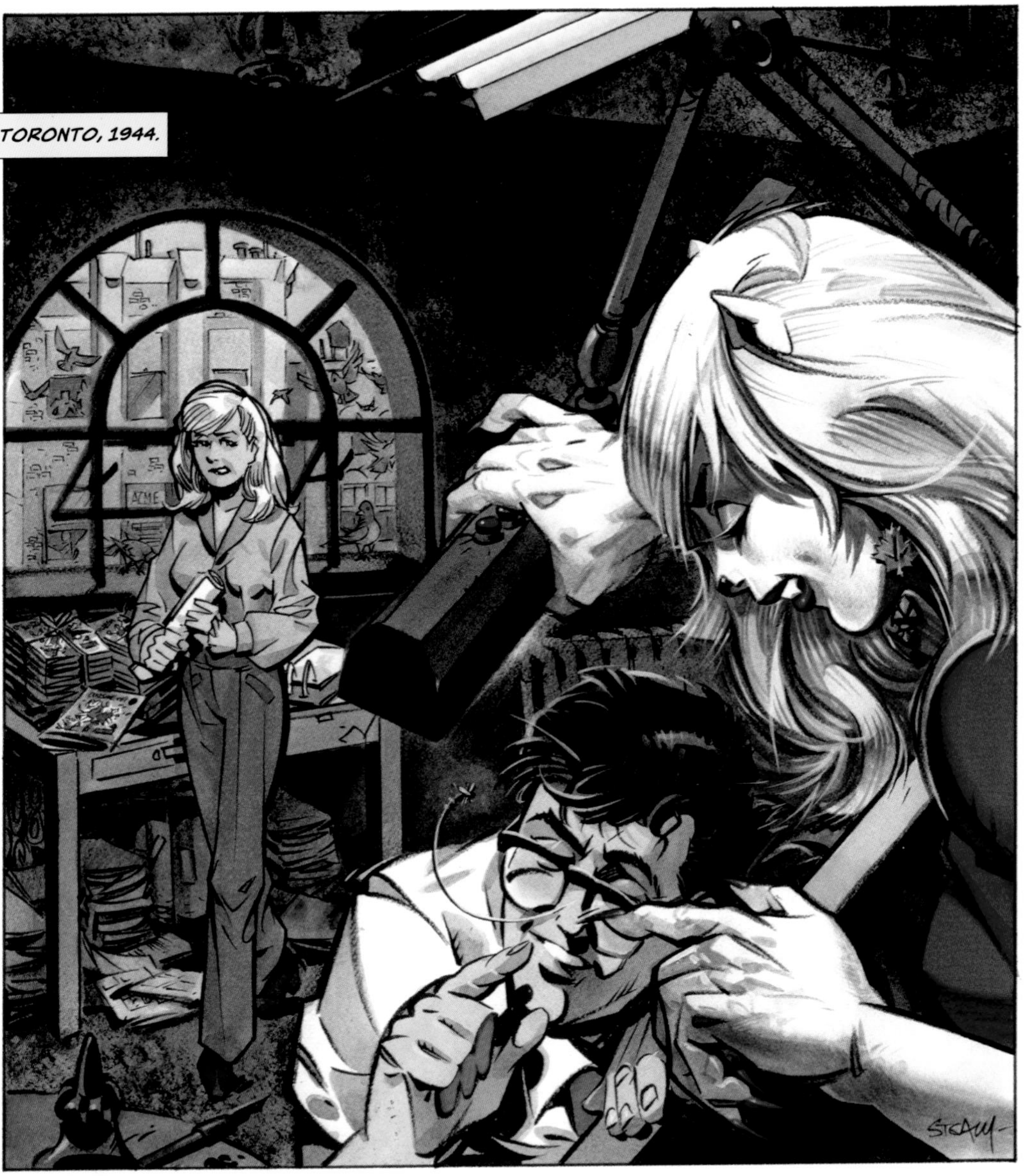
TORONTO, 1944.

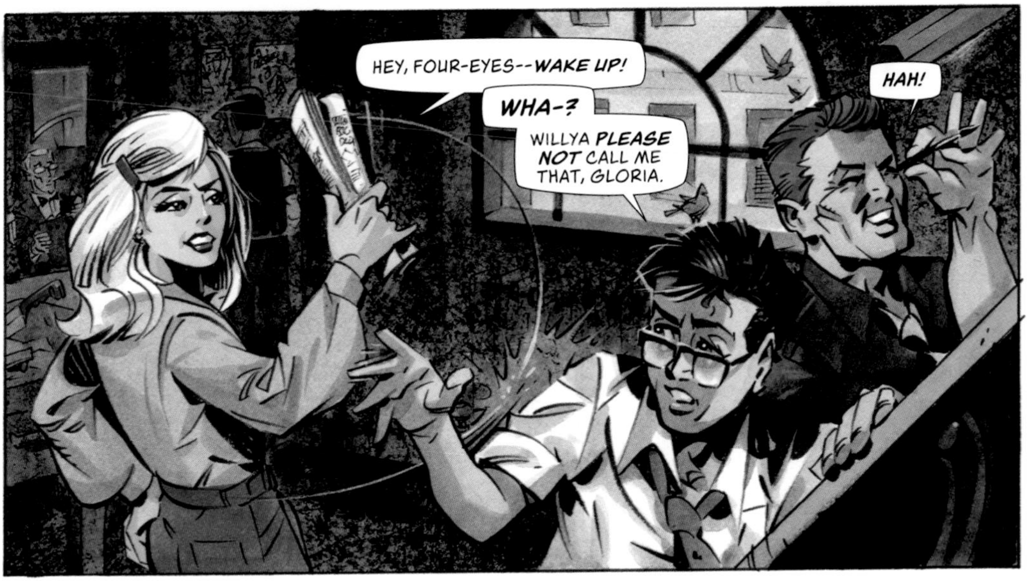
HEY, FOUR-EYES--WAKE UP!
WHA-?
WILLYA PLEASE NOT CALL ME THAT, GLORIA.
HAH!

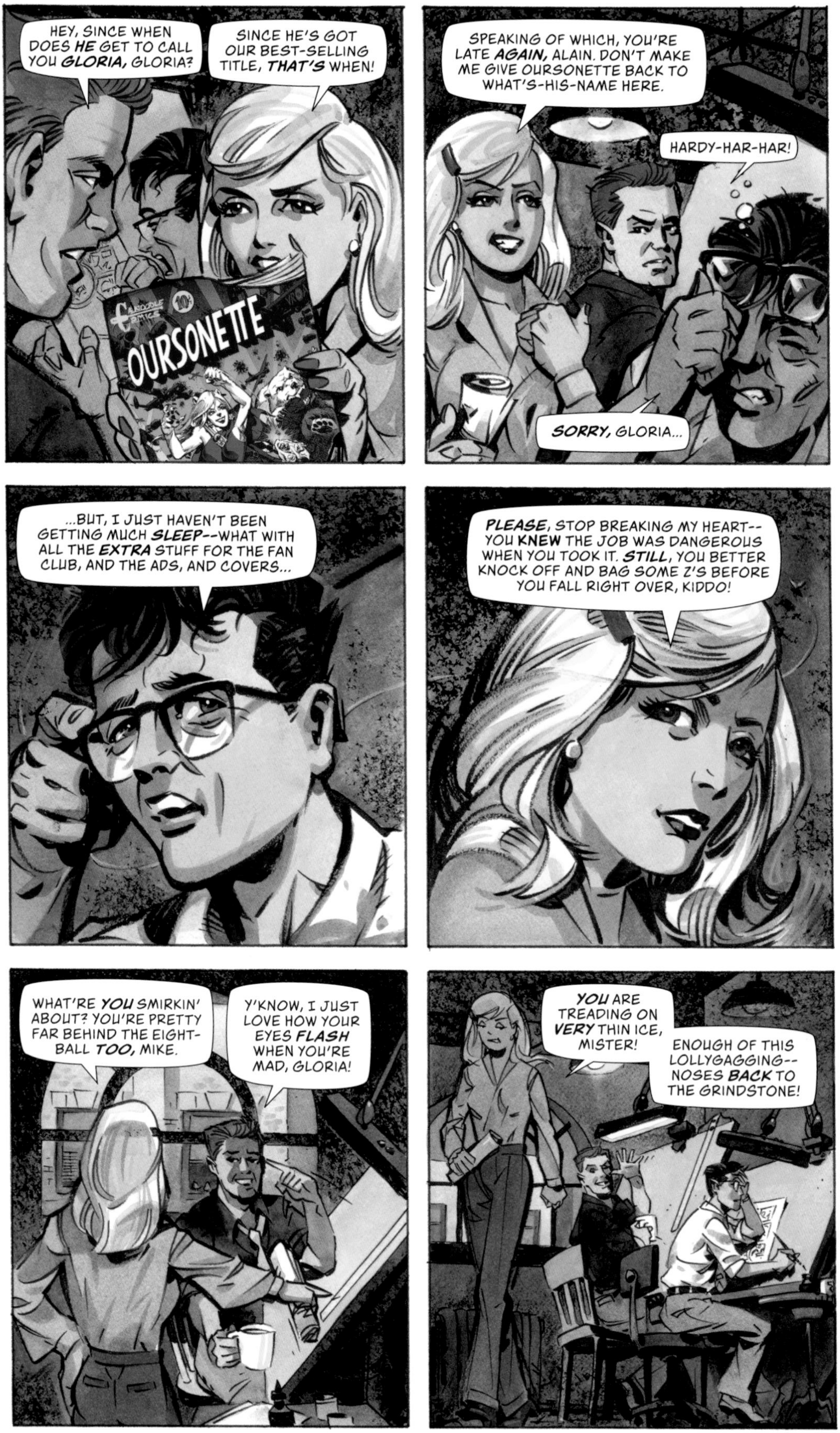
HEY, SINCE WHEN DOES HE GET TO CALL YOU GLORIA, GLORIA?
SINCE HE'S GOT OUR BEST-SELLING TITLE, THAT'S WHEN!
OURSONETTE
SPEAKING OF WHICH, YOU'RE LATE AGAIN, ALAIN. DON'T MAKE ME GIVE OURSONETTE BACK TO WHAT'S-HIS-NAME HERE.
HARDY-HAR-HAR!
SORRY, GLORIA...
...BUT, I JUST HAVEN'T BEEN GETTING MUCH SLEEP--WHAT WITH ALL THE EXTRA STUFF FOR THE FAN CLUB, AND THE ADS, AND COVERS...
PLEASE, STOP BREAKING MY HEART--YOU KNEW THE JOB WAS DANGEROUS WHEN YOU TOOK IT. STILL, YOU BETTER KNOCK OFF AND BAG SOME Z'S BEFORE YOU FALL RIGHT OVER, KIDDO!
WHAT'RE YOU SMIRKIN' ABOUT? YOU'RE PRETTY FAR BEHIND THE EIGHT-BALL TOO, MIKE.
Y'KNOW, I JUST LOVE HOW YOUR EYES FLASH WHEN YOU'RE MAD, GLORIA!
YOU ARE TREADING ON VERY THIN ICE, MISTER!
ENOUGH OF THIS LOLLYGAGGING--NOSES BACK TO THE GRINDSTONE!

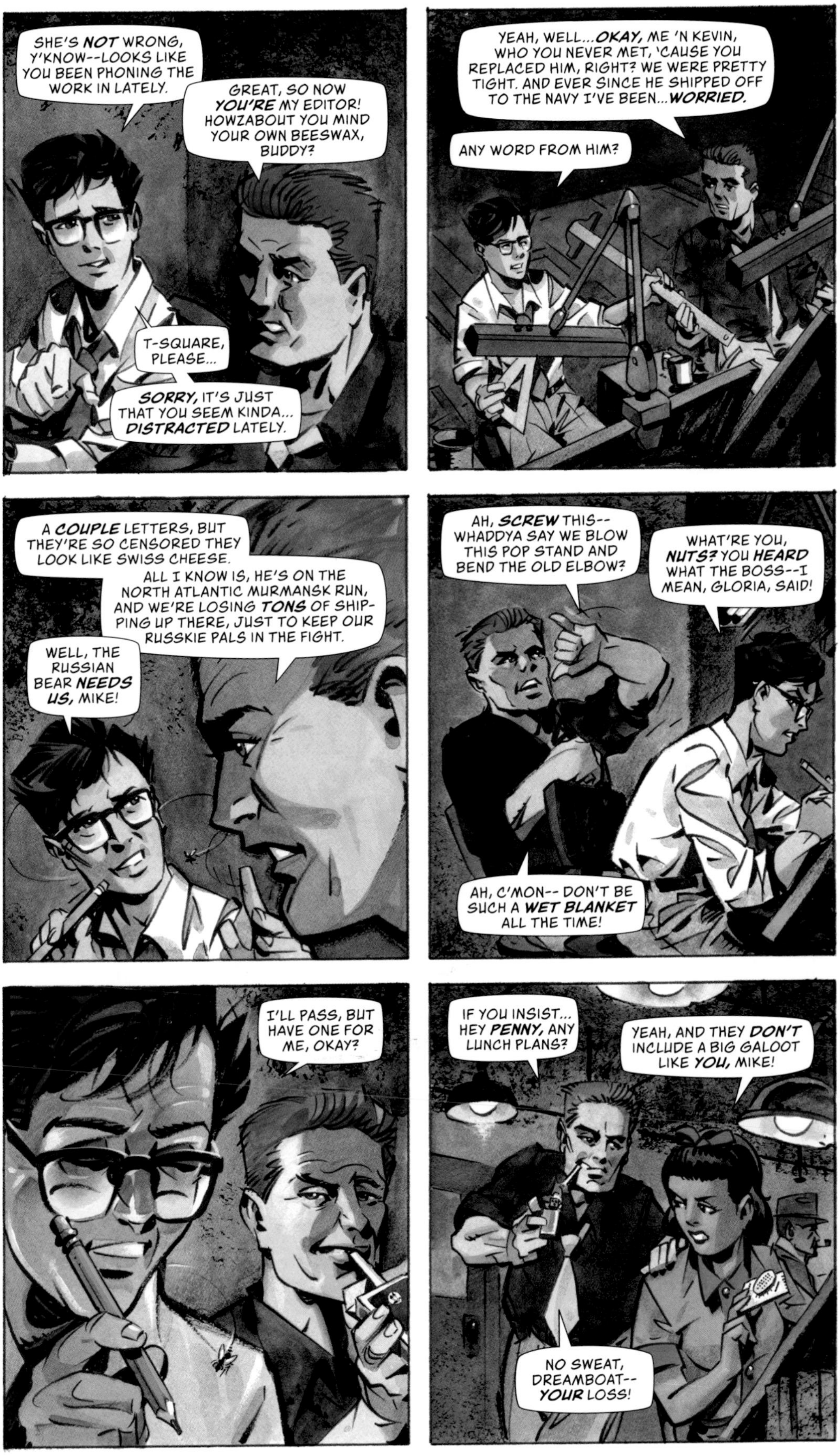
SHE'S NOT WRONG, Y'KNOW--LOOKS LIKE YOU BEEN PHONING THE WORK IN LATELY.
GREAT, SO NOW YOU'RE MY EDITOR! HOWZABOUT YOU MIND YOUR OWN BEESWAX, BUDDY?
T-SQUARE, PLEASE...
SORRY, IT'S JUST THAT YOU SEEM KINDA... DISTRACTED LATELY.
YEAH, WELL...OKAY, ME 'N KEVIN, WHO YOU NEVER MET, 'CAUSE YOU REPLACED HIM, RIGHT? WE WERE PRETTY TIGHT. AND EVER SINCE HE SHIPPED OFF TO THE NAVY I'VE BEEN...WORRIED.
ANY WORD FROM HIM?
A COUPLE LETTERS, BUT THEY'RE SO CENSORED THEY LOOK LIKE SWISS CHEESE.
ALL I KNOW IS, HE'S ON THE NORTH ATLANTIC MURMANSK RUN, AND WE'RE LOSING TONS OF SHIPPING UP THERE, JUST TO KEEP OUR RUSSKIE PALS IN THE FIGHT.
WELL, THE RUSSIAN BEAR NEEDS US, MIKE!
AH, SCREW THIS--WHADDYA SAY WE BLOW THIS POP STAND AND BEND THE OLD ELBOW?
WHAT'RE YOU, NUTS? YOU HEARD WHAT THE BOSS--I MEAN, GLORIA, SAID!
AH, C'MON-- DON'T BE SUCH A WET BLANKET ALL THE TIME!
I'LL PASS, BUT HAVE ONE FOR ME, OKAY?
IF YOU INSIST... HEY PENNY, ANY LUNCH PLANS?
YEAH, AND THEY DON'T INCLUDE A BIG GALOOT LIKE YOU, MIKE!
NO SWEAT, DREAMBOAT--YOUR LOSS!

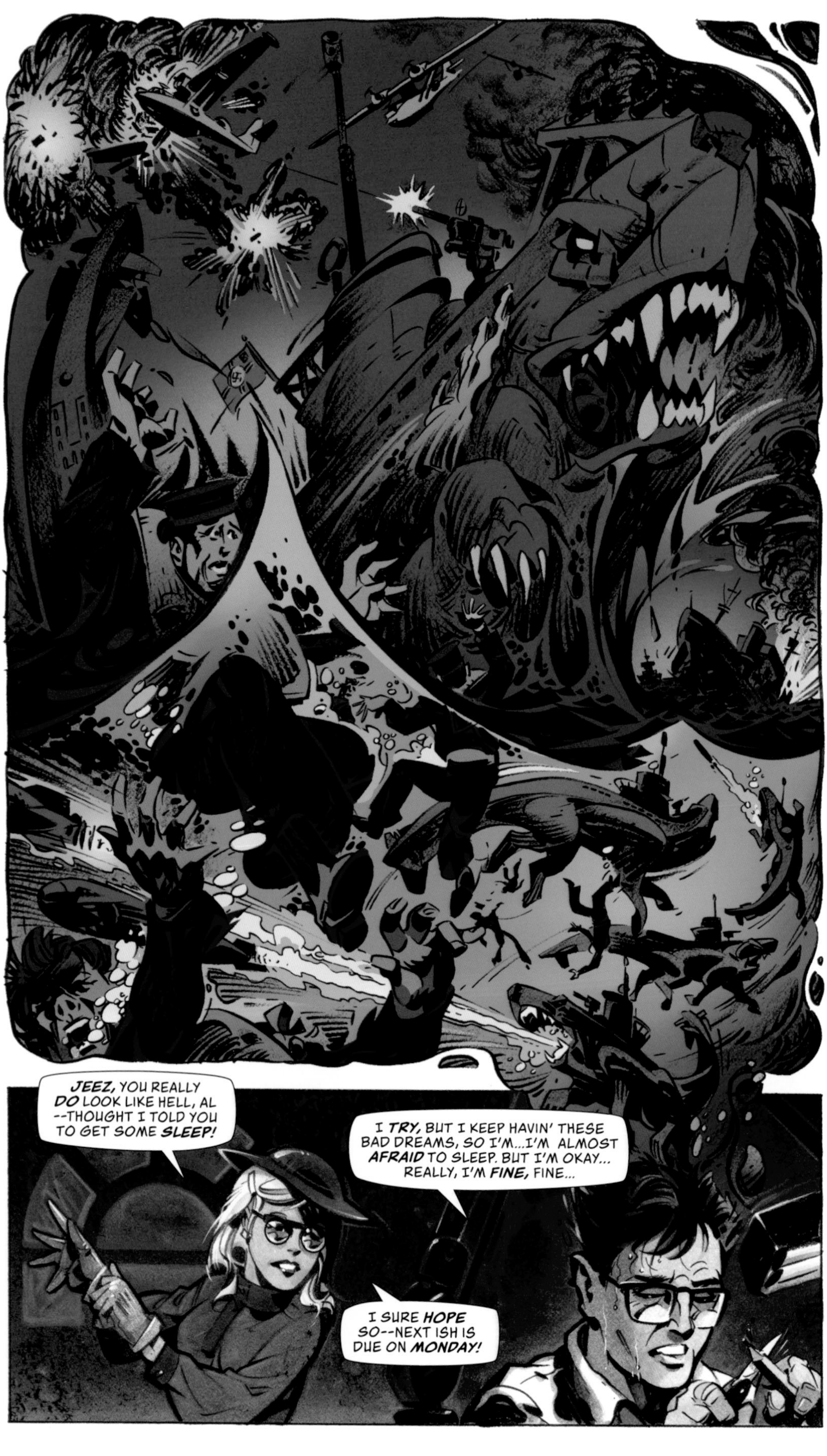
JEEZ, YOU REALLY DO LOOK LIKE HELL, AL --THOUGHT I TOLD YOU TO GET SOME SLEEP!
I TRY, BUT I KEEP HAVIN' THESE BAD DREAMS, SO I'M...I'M ALMOST AFRAID TO SLEEP. BUT I'M OKAY... REALLY, I'M FINE, FINE...
I SURE HOPE SO--NEXT ISH IS DUE ON MONDAY!

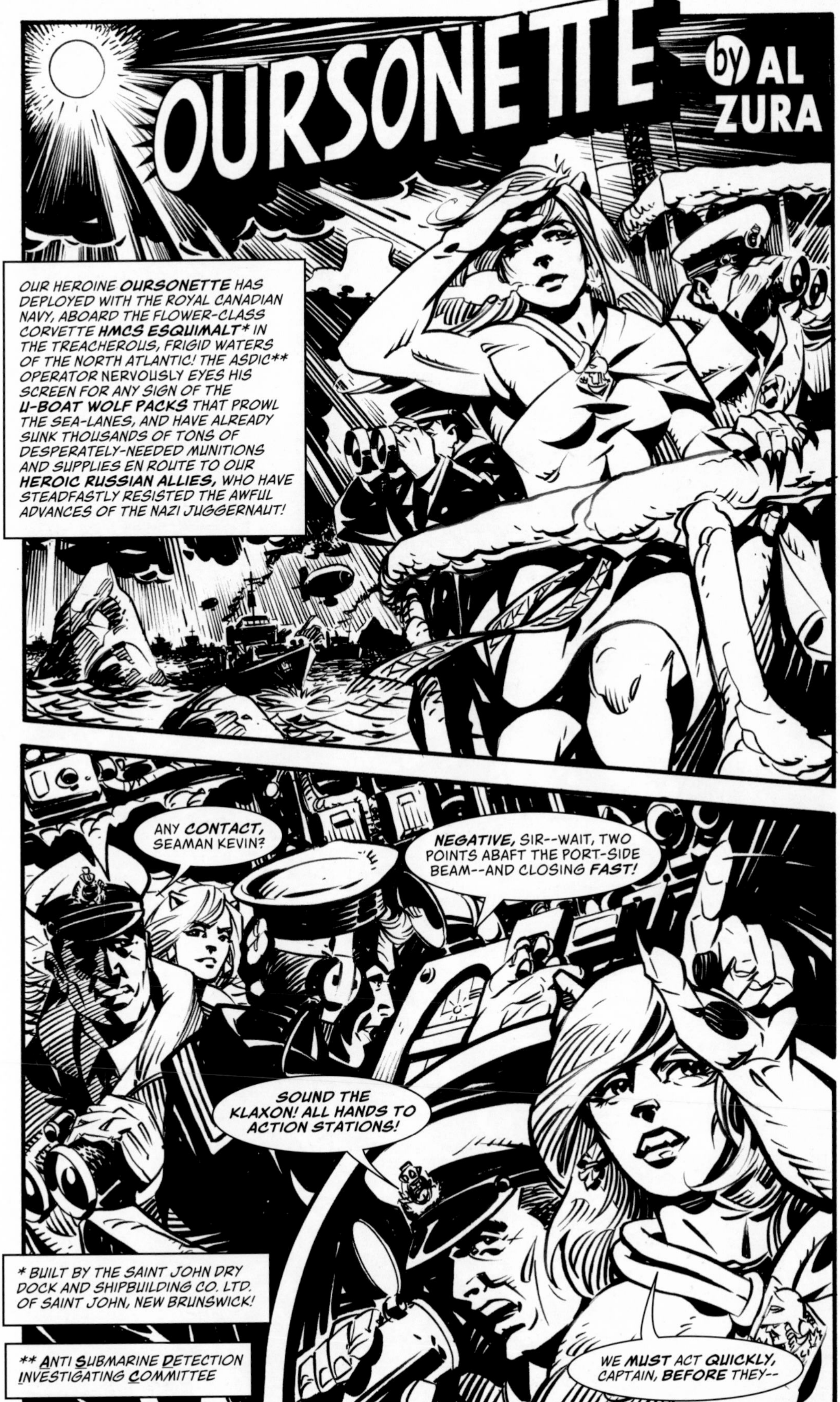
OURSONETTE
by AL ZURA
OUR HEROINE OURSONETTE HAS DEPLOYED WITH THE ROYAL CANADIAN NAVY, ABOARD THE FLOWER-CLASS CORVETTE HMCS ESQUIMALT* IN THE TREACHEROUS, FRIGID WATERS OF THE NORTH ATLANTIC! THE ASDIC** OPERATOR NERVOUSLY EYES HIS SCREEN FOR ANY SIGN OF THE U-BOAT WOLF PACKS THAT PROWL THE SEA-LANES, AND HAVE ALREADY SUNK THOUSANDS OF TONS OF DESPERATELY-NEEDED MUNITIONS AND SUPPLIES EN ROUTE TO OUR HEROIC RUSSIAN ALLIES, WHO HAVE STEADFASTLY RESISTED THE AWFUL ADVANCES OF THE NAZI JUGGERNAUT!
ANY CONTACT, SEAMAN KEVIN?
NEGATIVE, SIR--WAIT, TWO POINTS ABAFT THE PORT-SIDE BEAM--AND CLOSING FAST!
SOUND THE KLAXON! ALL HANDS TO ACTION STATIONS!
* BUILT BY THE SAINT JOHN DRY DOCK AND SHIPBUILDING CO. LTD. OF SAINT JOHN, NEW BRUNSWICK!
** ANTI SUBMARINE DETECTION INVESTIGATING COMMITTEE
WE MUST ACT QUICKLY, CAPTAIN, BEFORE THEY--

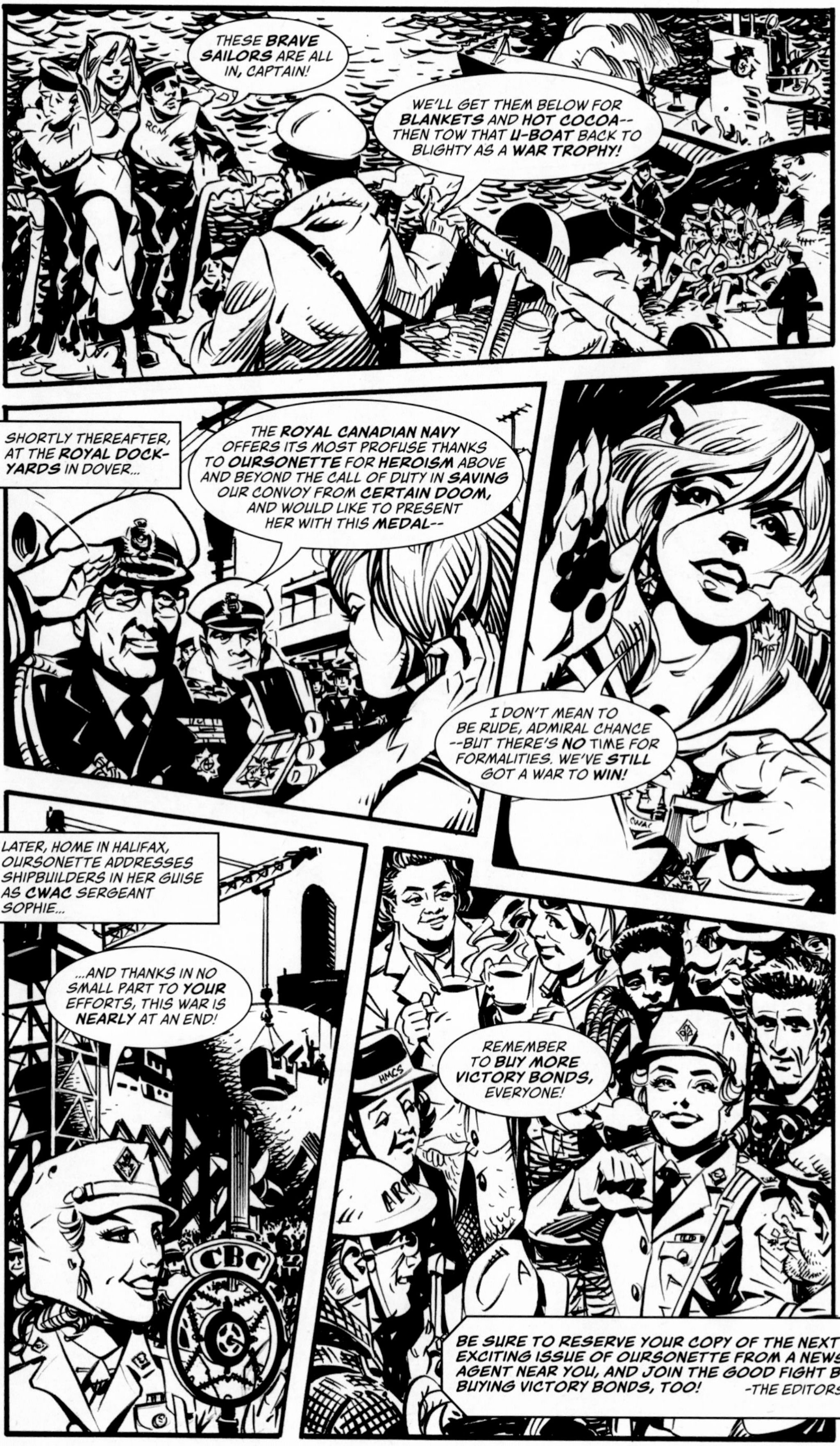
THESE BRAVE SAILORS ARE ALL IN, CAPTAIN!
WE'LL GET THEM BELOW FOR BLANKETS AND HOT COCOA-- THEN TOW THAT U-BOAT BACK TO BLIGHTY AS A WAR TROPHY!
SHORTLY THEREAFTER, AT THE ROYAL DOCKYARDS IN DOVER...
THE ROYAL CANADIAN NAVY OFFERS ITS MOST PROFUSE THANKS TO OURSONETTE FOR HEROISM ABOVE AND BEYOND THE CALL OF DUTY IN SAVING OUR CONVOY FROM CERTAIN DOOM, AND WOULD LIKE TO PRESENT HER WITH THIS MEDAL--
I DON'T MEAN TO BE RUDE, ADMIRAL CHANCE --BUT THERE'S NO TIME FOR FORMALITIES. WE'VE STILL GOT A WAR TO WIN!
LATER, HOME IN HALIFAX, OURSONETTE ADDRESSES SHIPBUILDERS IN HER GUISE AS CWAC SERGEANT SOPHIE...
...AND THANKS IN NO SMALL PART TO YOUR EFFORTS, THIS WAR IS NEARLY AT AN END!
CBC
REMEMBER TO BUY MORE VICTORY BONDS, EVERYONE!
BE SURE TO RESERVE YOUR COPY OF THE NEXT EXCITING ISSUE OF OURSONETTE FROM A NEWS-AGENT NEAR YOU, AND JOIN THE GOOD FIGHT BY BUYING VICTORY BONDS, TOO! -THE EDITORS

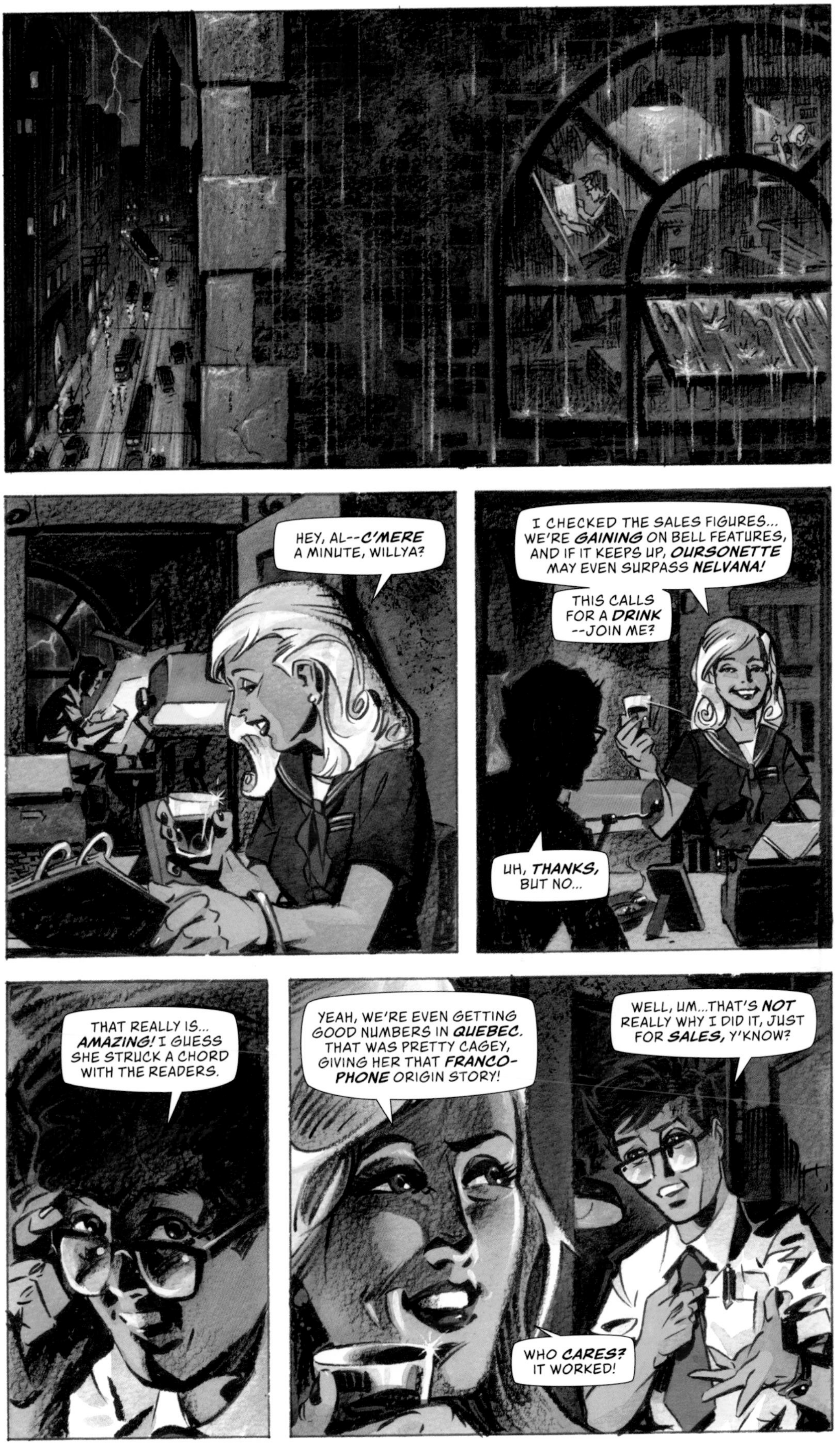
HEY, AL--C'MERE A MINUTE, WILLYA?
I CHECKED THE SALES FIGURES... WE'RE GAINING ON BELL FEATURES, AND IF IT KEEPS UP, OURSONETTE MAY EVEN SURPASS NELVANA!
THIS CALLS FOR A DRINK --JOIN ME?
UH, THANKS, BUT NO...
THAT REALLY IS... AMAZING! I GUESS SHE STRUCK A CHORD WITH THE READERS.
YEAH, WE'RE EVEN GETTING GOOD NUMBERS IN QUEBEC. THAT WAS PRETTY CAGEY, GIVING HER THAT FRANCOPHONE ORIGIN STORY!
WELL, UM...THAT'S NOT REALLY WHY I DID IT, JUST FOR SALES, Y'KNOW?
WHO CARES? IT WORKED!

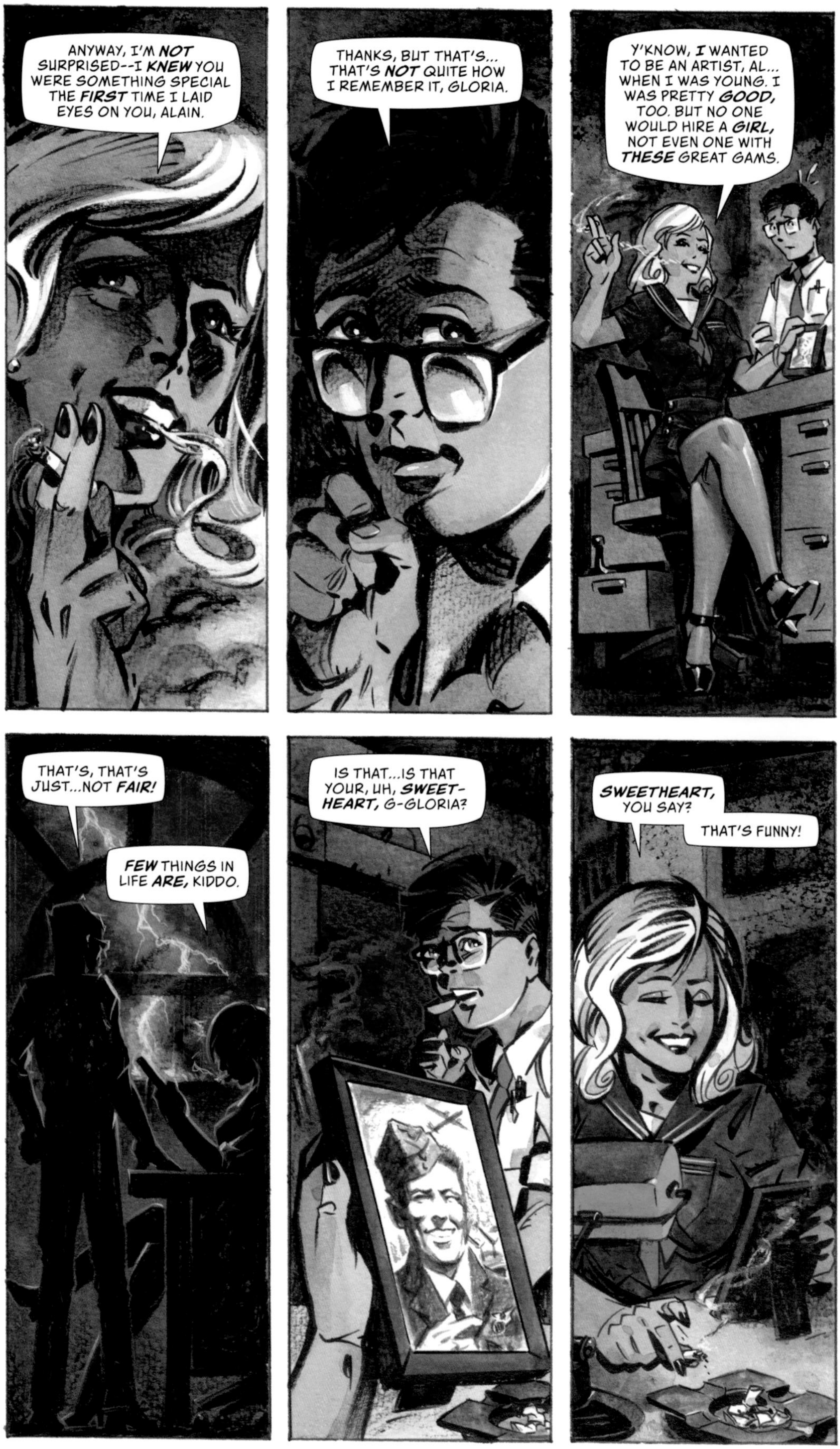
ANYWAY, I'M NOT SURPRISED--I KNEW YOU WERE SOMETHING SPECIAL THE FIRST TIME I LAID EYES ON YOU, ALAIN.
THANKS, BUT THAT'S... THAT'S NOT QUITE HOW I REMEMBER IT, GLORIA.
Y'KNOW, I WANTED TO BE AN ARTIST, AL... WHEN I WAS YOUNG. I WAS PRETTY GOOD, TOO. BUT NO ONE WOULD HIRE A GIRL, NOT EVEN ONE WITH THESE GREAT GAMS.
THAT'S, THAT'S JUST...NOT FAIR!
FEW THINGS IN LIFE ARE, KIDDO.
IS THAT...IS THAT YOUR, UH, SWEET-HEART, G-GLORIA?
SWEETHEART, YOU SAY?
THAT'S FUNNY!

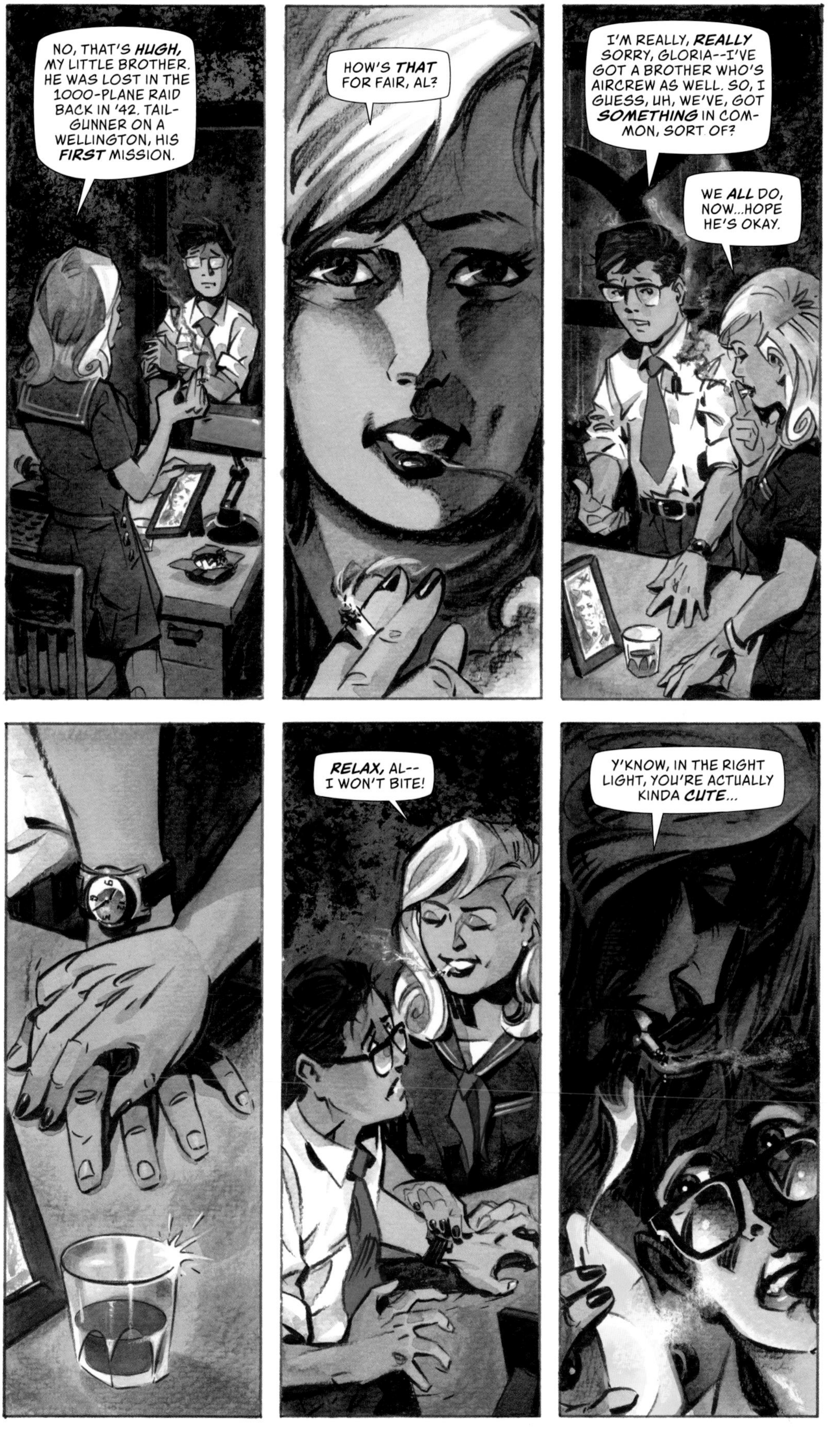
NO, THAT'S HUGH, MY LITTLE BROTHER. HE WAS LOST IN THE 1000-PLANE RAID BACK IN '42. TAIL-GUNNER ON A WELLINGTON, HIS FIRST MISSION.
HOW'S THAT FOR FAIR, AL?
I'M REALLY, REALLY SORRY, GLORIA--I'VE GOT A BROTHER WHO'S AIRCREW AS WELL. SO, I GUESS, UH, WE'VE, GOT SOMETHING IN COMMON, SORT OF?
WE ALL DO, NOW...HOPE HE'S OKAY.
RELAX, AL--I WON'T BITE!
Y'KNOW, IN THE RIGHT LIGHT, YOU'RE ACTUALLY KINDA CUTE...

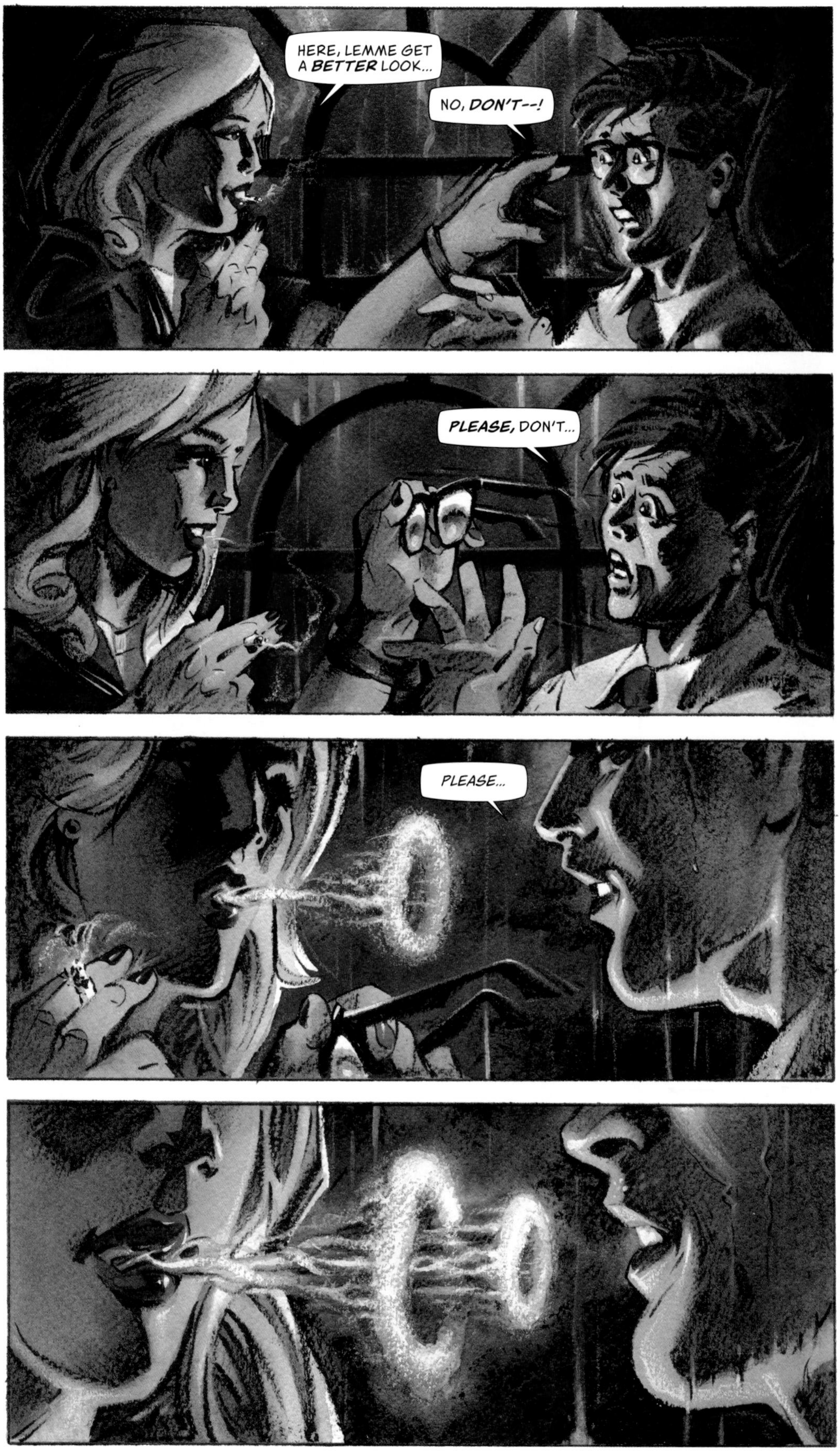
HERE, LEMME GET A BETTER LOOK...
NO, DON'T--!
PLEASE, DON'T...
PLEASE...

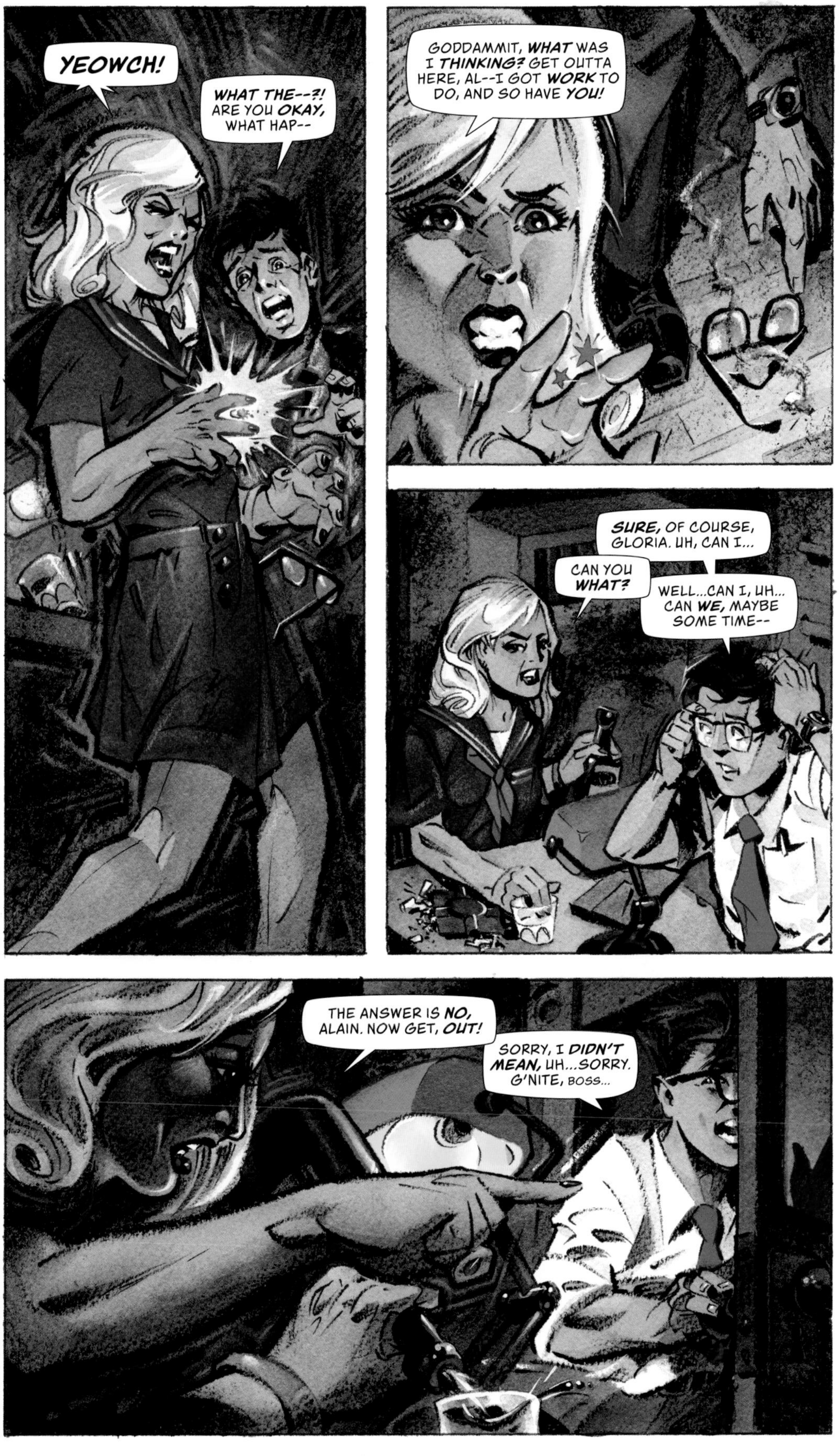
YEOWCH!
WHAT THE--?! ARE YOU OKAY, WHAT HAP--
GODDAMMIT, WHAT WAS I THINKING? GET OUTTA HERE, AL--I GOT WORK TO DO, AND SO HAVE YOU!
SURE, OF COURSE, GLORIA. UH, CAN I...
CAN YOU WHAT?
WELL...CAN I, UH... CAN WE, MAYBE SOME TIME--
THE ANSWER IS NO, ALAIN. NOW GET, OUT!
SORRY, I DIDN'T MEAN, UH...SORRY. G'NITE, BOSS...

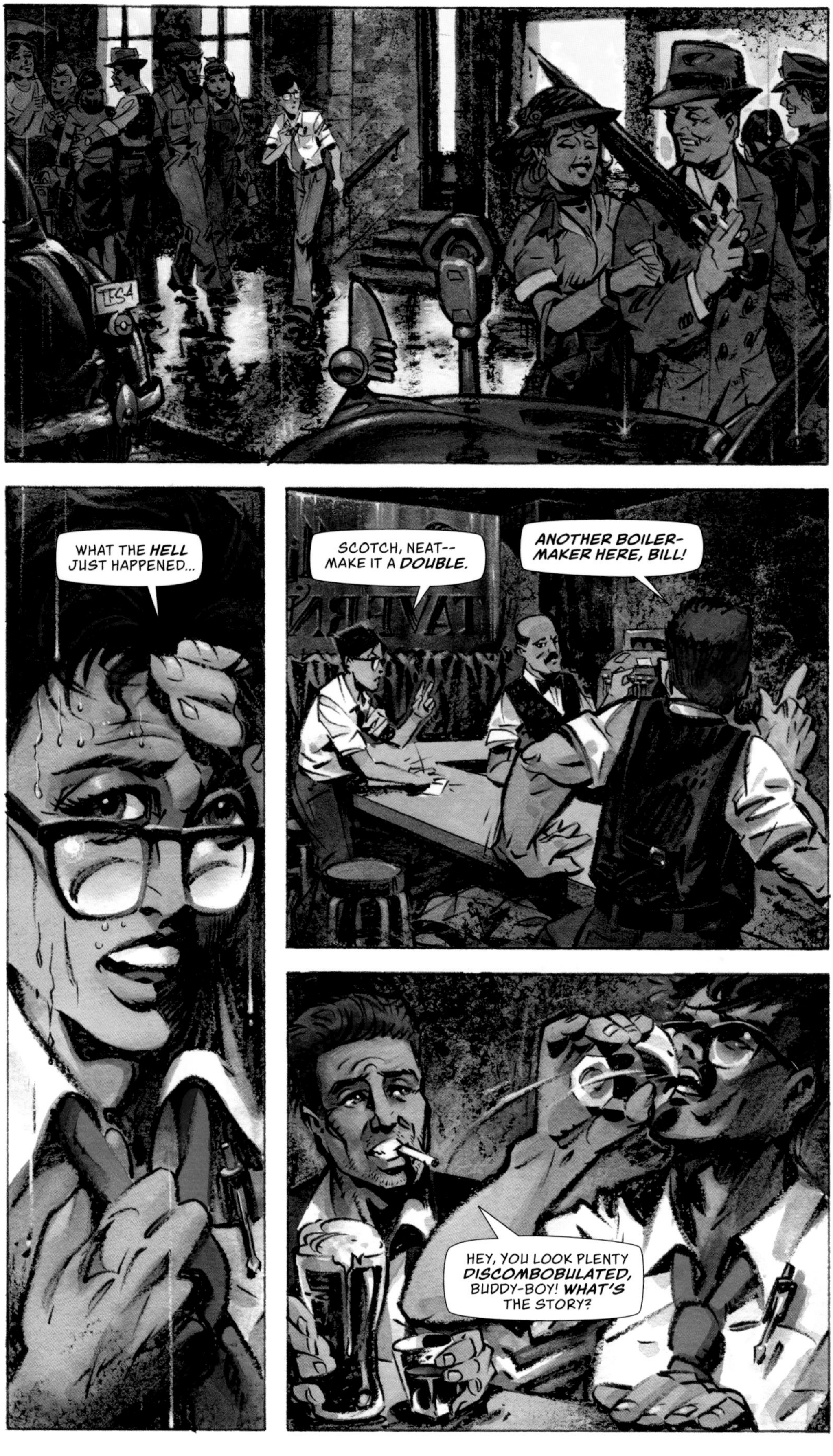
WHAT THE HELL JUST HAPPENED...
SCOTCH, NEAT-- MAKE IT A DOUBLE.
ANOTHER BOILER-MAKER HERE, BILL!
HEY, YOU LOOK PLENTY DISCOMBOBULATED, BUDDY-BOY! WHAT'S THE STORY?

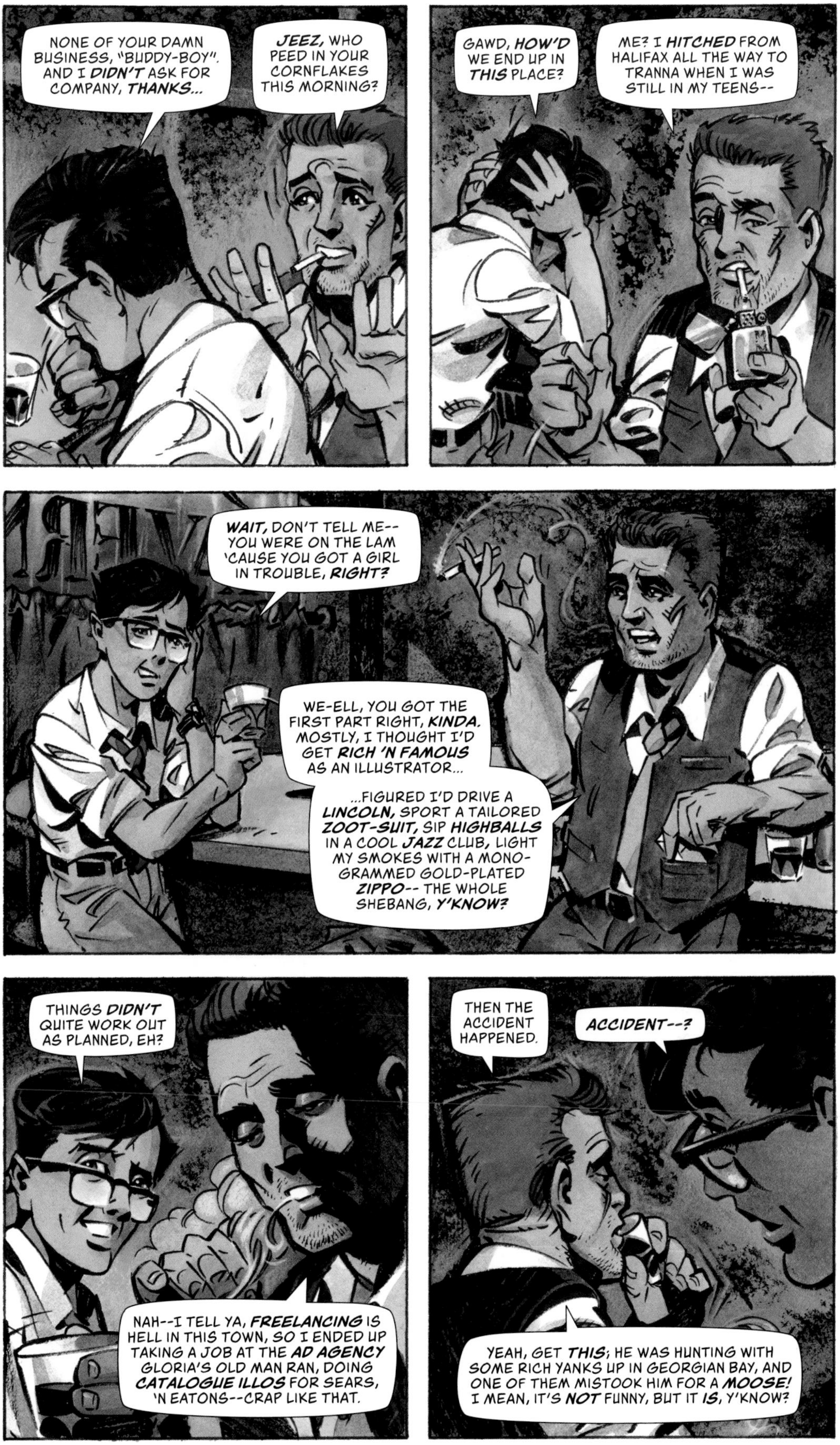

NONE OF YOUR DAMN BUSINESS, "BUDDY-BOY". AND I DIDN'T ASK FOR COMPANY, THANKS...
JEEZ, WHO PEED IN YOUR CORNFLAKES THIS MORNING?
GAWD, HOW'D WE END UP IN THIS PLACE?
ME? I HITCHED FROM HALIFAX ALL THE WAY TO TRANNA WHEN I WAS STILL IN MY TEENS--
WAIT, DON'T TELL ME-- YOU WERE ON THE LAM 'CAUSE YOU GOT A GIRL IN TROUBLE, RIGHT?
WE-ELL, YOU GOT THE FIRST PART RIGHT, KINDA. MOSTLY, I THOUGHT I'D GET RICH 'N FAMOUS AS AN ILLUSTRATOR...
...FIGURED I'D DRIVE A LINCOLN, SPORT A TAILORED ZOOT-SUIT, SIP HIGHBALLS IN A COOL JAZZ CLUB, LIGHT MY SMOKES WITH A MONO-GRAMMED GOLD-PLATED ZIPPO-- THE WHOLE SHEBANG, Y'KNOW?
THINGS DIDN'T QUITE WORK OUT AS PLANNED, EH?
NAH--I TELL YA, FREELANCING IS HELL IN THIS TOWN, SO I ENDED UP TAKING A JOB AT THE AD AGENCY GLORIA'S OLD MAN RAN, DOING CATALOGUE ILLOS FOR SEARS, 'N EATONS--CRAP LIKE THAT.
THEN THE ACCIDENT HAPPENED.
ACCIDENT--?
YEAH, GET THIS; HE WAS HUNTING WITH SOME RICH YANKS UP IN GEORGIAN BAY, AND ONE OF THEM MISTOOK HIM FOR A MOOSE! I MEAN, IT'S NOT FUNNY, BUT IT IS, Y'KNOW?

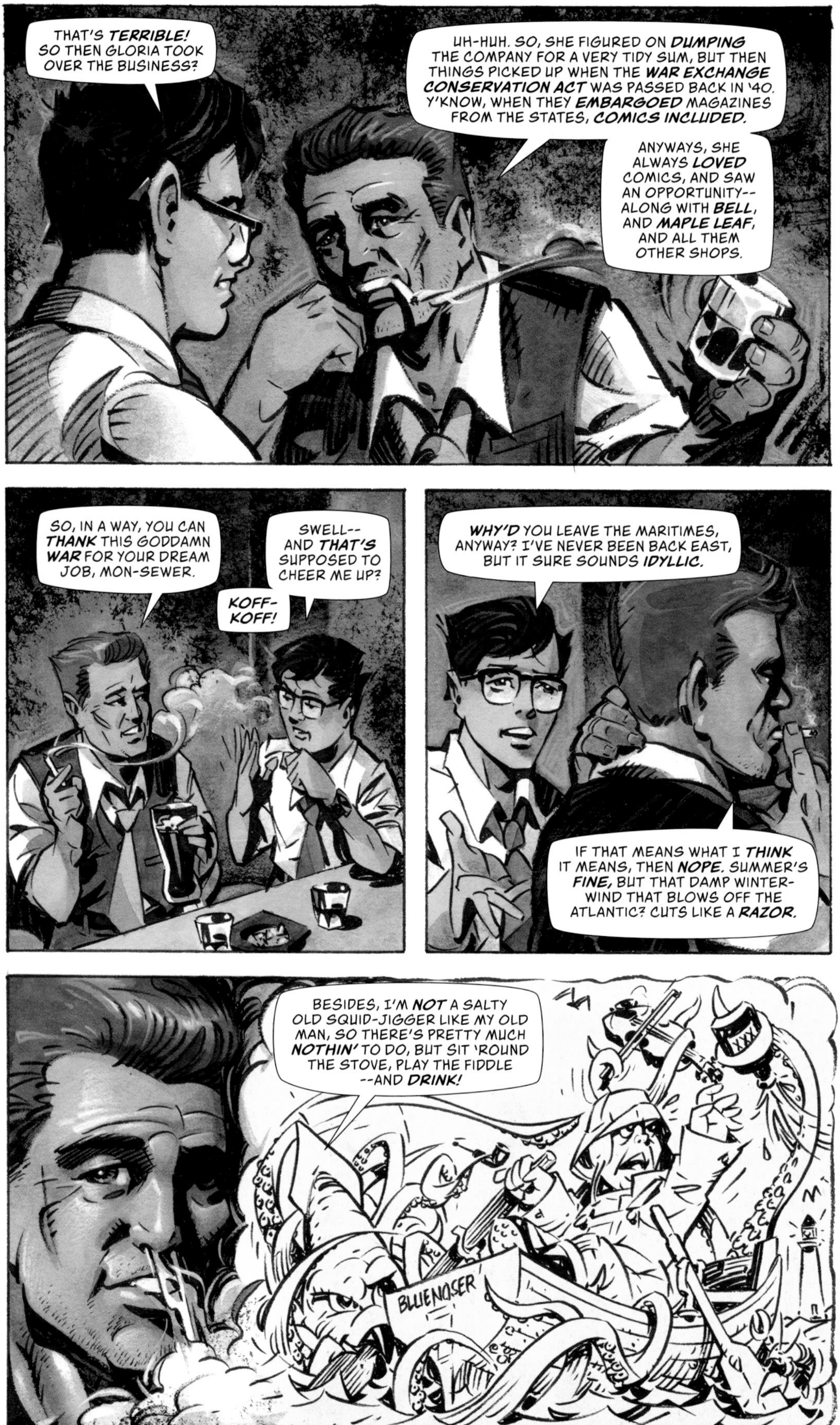
THAT'S TERRIBLE! SO THEN GLORIA TOOK OVER THE BUSINESS?
UH-HUH. SO, SHE FIGURED ON DUMPING THE COMPANY FOR A VERY TIDY SUM, BUT THEN THINGS PICKED UP WHEN THE WAR EXCHANGE CONSERVATION ACT WAS PASSED BACK IN '40. Y'KNOW, WHEN THEY EMBARGOED MAGAZINES FROM THE STATES, COMICS INCLUDED.
ANYWAYS, SHE ALWAYS LOVED COMICS, AND SAW AN OPPORTUNITY-- ALONG WITH BELL, AND MAPLE LEAF, AND ALL THEM OTHER SHOPS.
SO, IN A WAY, YOU CAN THANK THIS GODDAMN WAR FOR YOUR DREAM JOB, MON-SEWER.
KOFF-KOFF!
SWELL-- AND THAT'S SUPPOSED TO CHEER ME UP?
WHY'D YOU LEAVE THE MARITIMES, ANYWAY? I'VE NEVER BEEN BACK EAST, BUT IT SURE SOUNDS IDYLLIC.
IF THAT MEANS WHAT I THINK IT MEANS, THEN NOPE. SUMMER'S FINE, BUT THAT DAMP WINTER-WIND THAT BLOWS OFF THE ATLANTIC? CUTS LIKE A RAZOR.
BESIDES, I'M NOT A SALTY OLD SQUID-JIGGER LIKE MY OLD MAN, SO THERE'S PRETTY MUCH NOTHIN' TO DO, BUT SIT 'ROUND THE STOVE, PLAY THE FIDDLE --AND DRINK!
XXX
BLUENOSER

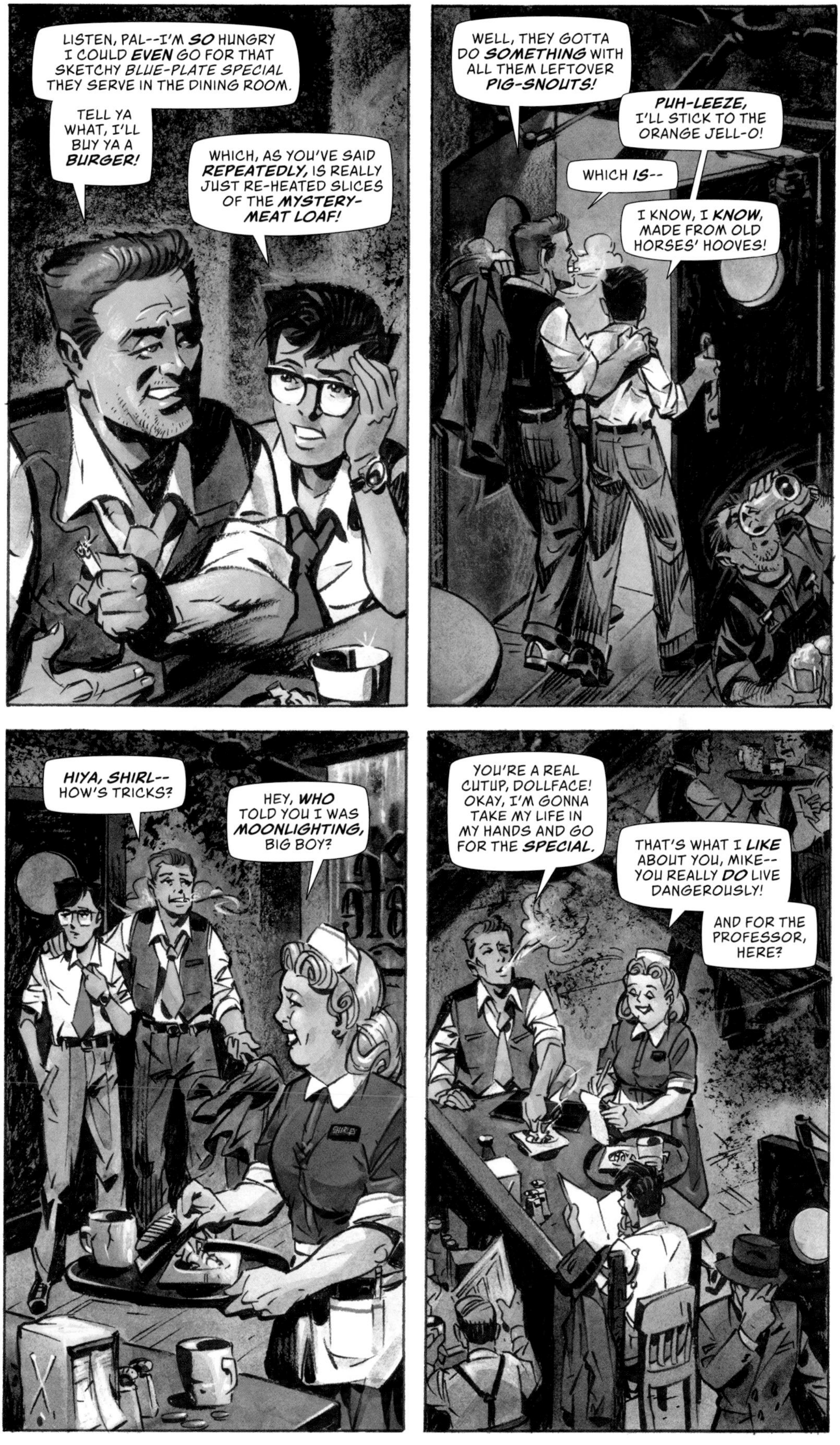
LISTEN, PAL--I'M SO HUNGRY I COULD EVEN GO FOR THAT SKETCHY BLUE-PLATE SPECIAL THEY SERVE IN THE DINING ROOM.
TELL YA WHAT, I'LL BUY YA A BURGER!
WHICH, AS YOU'VE SAID REPEATEDLY, IS REALLY JUST RE-HEATED SLICES OF THE MYSTERY-MEAT LOAF!
WELL, THEY GOTTA DO SOMETHING WITH ALL THEM LEFTOVER PIG-SNOUTS!
PUH-LEEZE, I'LL STICK TO THE ORANGE JELL-O!
WHICH IS--
I KNOW, I KNOW, MADE FROM OLD HORSES' HOOVES!
HIYA, SHIRL-- HOW'S TRICKS?
HEY, WHO TOLD YOU I WAS MOONLIGHTING, BIG BOY?
YOU'RE A REAL CUTUP, DOLLFACE! OKAY, I'M GONNA TAKE MY LIFE IN MY HANDS AND GO FOR THE SPECIAL.
THAT'S WHAT I LIKE ABOUT YOU, MIKE-- YOU REALLY DO LIVE DANGEROUSLY!
AND FOR THE PROFESSOR, HERE?

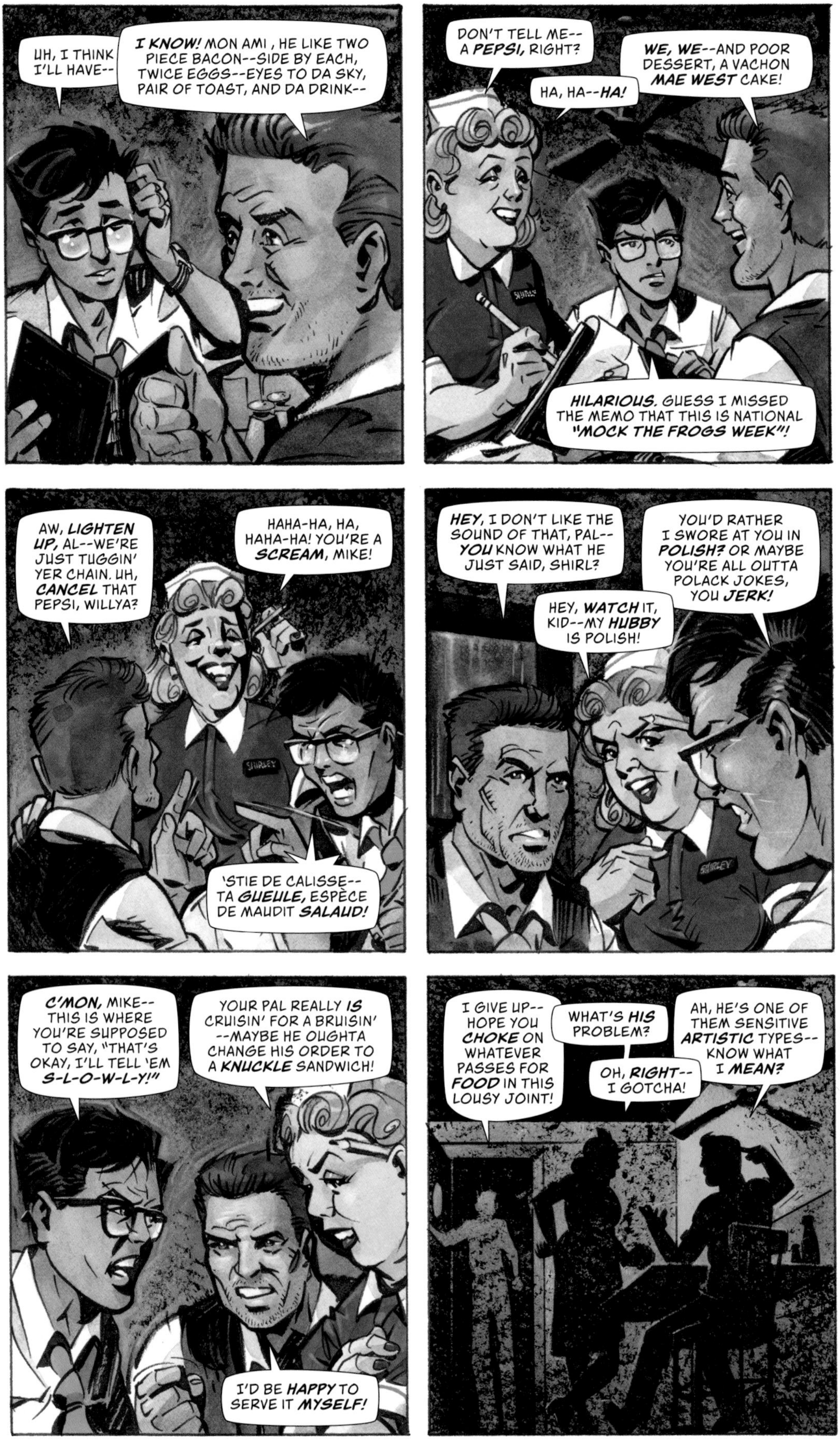
UH, I THINK I'LL HAVE--
I KNOW! MON AMI , HE LIKE TWO PIECE BACON--SIDE BY EACH, TWICE EGGS--EYES TO DA SKY, PAIR OF TOAST, AND DA DRINK--
DON'T TELL ME-- A PEPSI, RIGHT?
HA, HA--HA!
WE, WE--AND POOR DESSERT, A VACHON MAE WEST CAKE!
HILARIOUS. GUESS I MISSED THE MEMO THAT THIS IS NATIONAL "MOCK THE FROGS WEEK"!
AW, LIGHTEN UP, AL--WE'RE JUST TUGGIN' YER CHAIN. UH, CANCEL THAT PEPSI, WILLYA?
HAHA-HA, HA, HAHA-HA! YOU'RE A SCREAM, MIKE!
SHIRLEY
'STIE DE CALISSE-- TA GUEULE, ESPÈCE DE MAUDIT SALAUD!
HEY, I DON'T LIKE THE SOUND OF THAT, PAL-- YOU KNOW WHAT HE JUST SAID, SHIRL?
HEY, WATCH IT, KID--MY HUBBY IS POLISH!
YOU'D RATHER I SWORE AT YOU IN POLISH? OR MAYBE YOU'RE ALL OUTTA POLACK JOKES, YOU JERK!
C'MON, MIKE-- THIS IS WHERE YOU'RE SUPPOSED TO SAY, "THAT'S OKAY, I'LL TELL 'EM S-L-O-W-L-Y!"
YOUR PAL REALLY IS CRUISIN' FOR A BRUISIN' --MAYBE HE OUGHTA CHANGE HIS ORDER TO A KNUCKLE SANDWICH!
I'D BE HAPPY TO SERVE IT MYSELF!
I GIVE UP-- HOPE YOU CHOKE ON WHATEVER PASSES FOR FOOD IN THIS LOUSY JOINT!
WHAT'S HIS PROBLEM?
OH, RIGHT-- I GOTCHA!
AH, HE'S ONE OF THEM SENSITIVE ARTISTIC TYPES-- KNOW WHAT I MEAN?

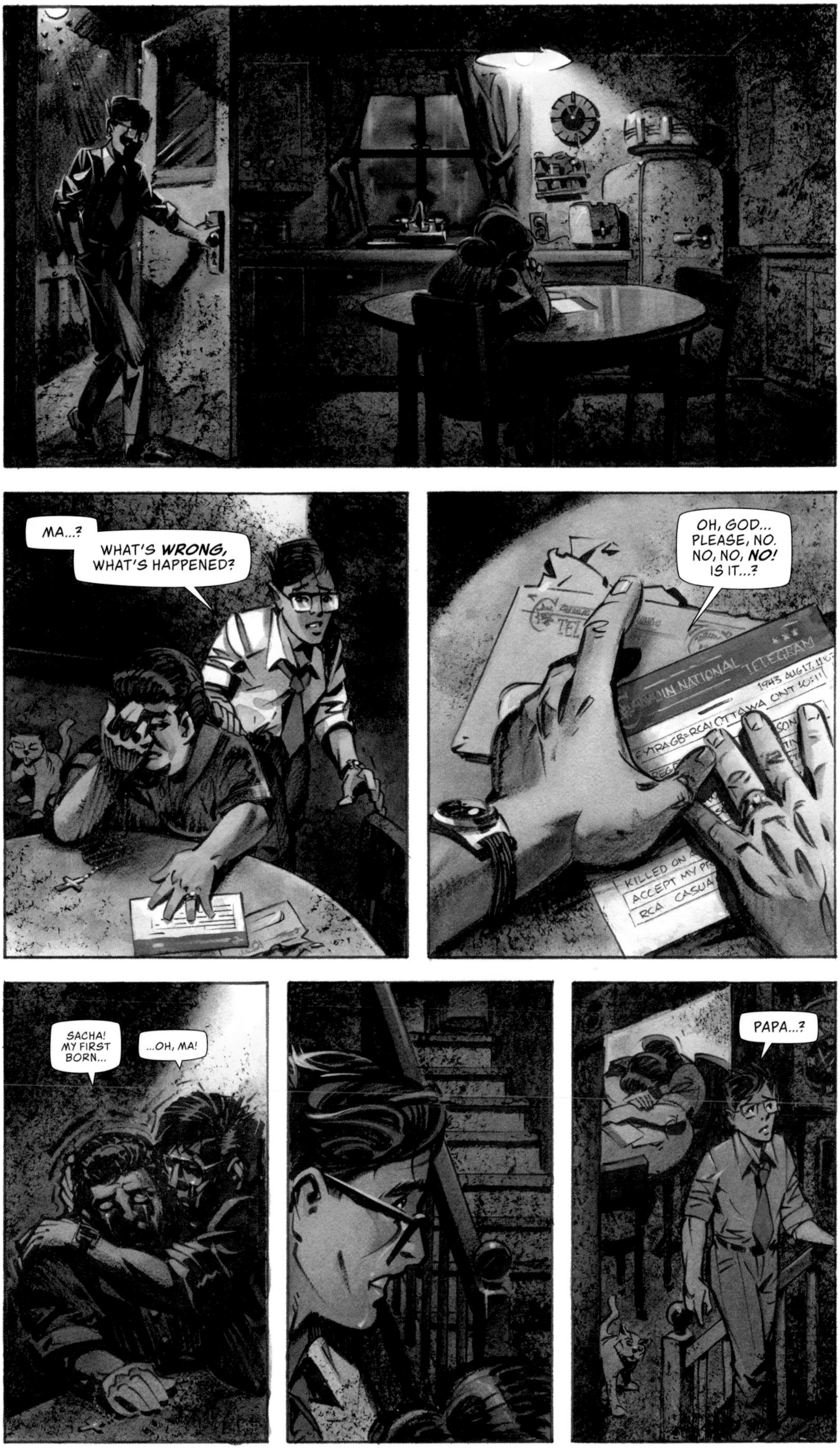
MA...?
WHAT'S WRONG, WHAT'S HAPPENED?
OH, GOD... PLEASE, NO. NO, NO, NO! IS IT...?
TELEGRAM
KILLED ON
ACCEPT MY
RCA CASUA
SACHA! MY FIRST BORN...
...OH, MA!
PAPA...?

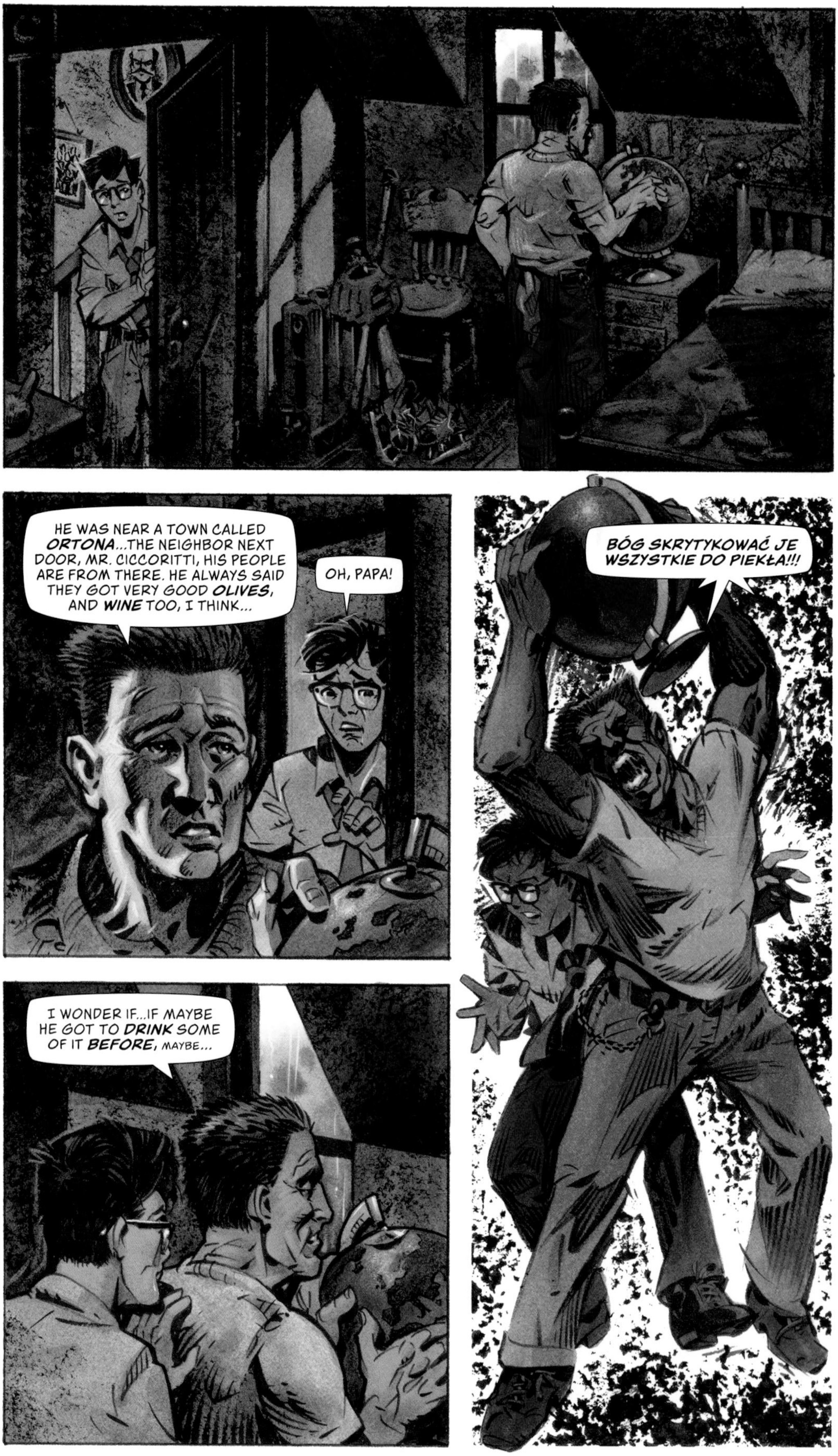
HE WAS NEAR A TOWN CALLED ORTONA...THE NEIGHBOR NEXT DOOR, MR. CICCORITTI, HIS PEOPLE ARE FROM THERE. HE ALWAYS SAID THEY GOT VERY GOOD OLIVES, AND WINE TOO, I THINK...
OH, PAPA!
I WONDER IF...IF MAYBE HE GOT TO DRINK SOME OF IT BEFORE, MAYBE...
BÓG SKRYTYKOWAĆ JE WSZYSTKIE DO PIEKŁA!!!

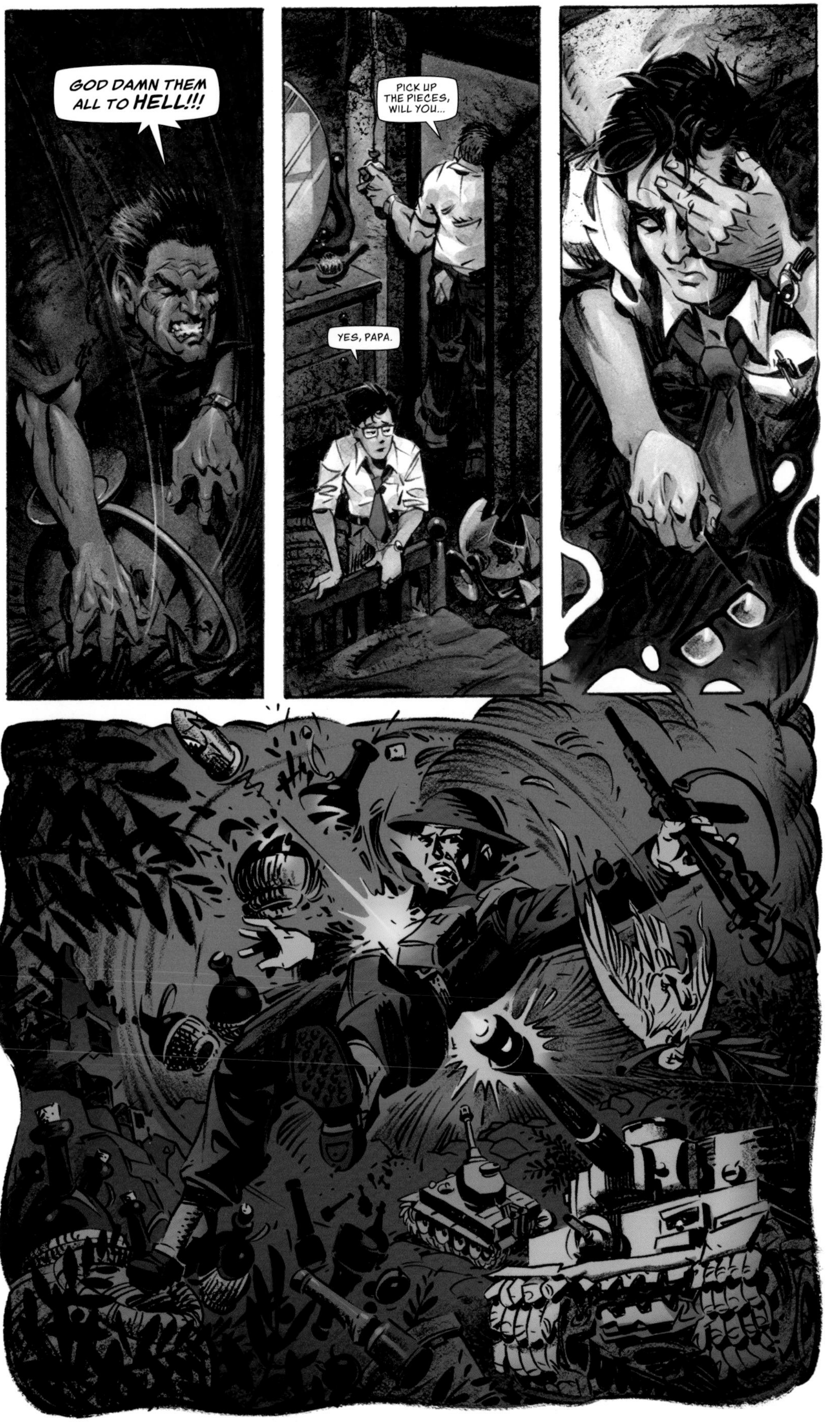
GOD DAMN THEM ALL TO HELL!!!
PICK UP THE PIECES, WILL YOU...
YES, PAPA.

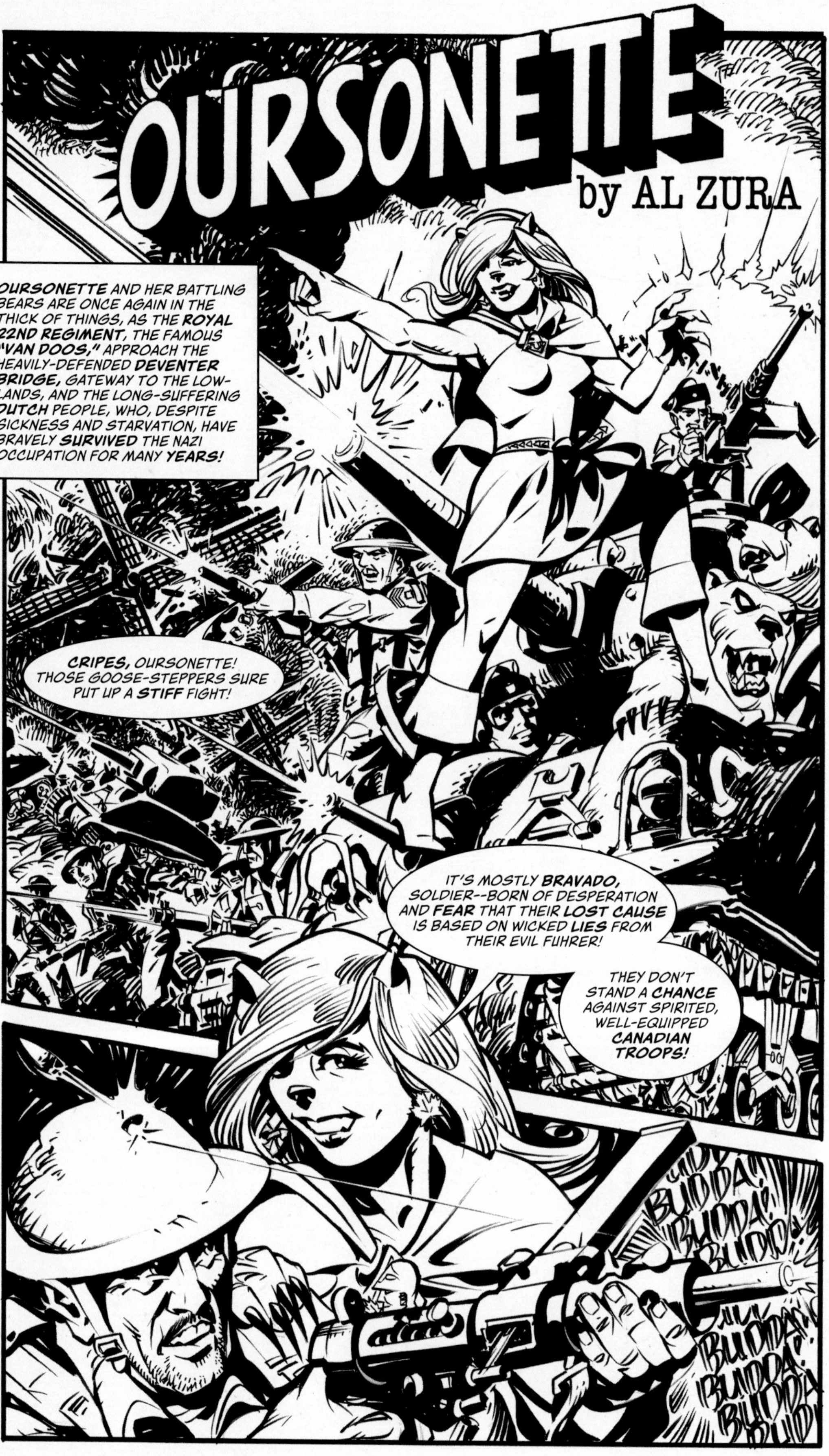
OURSONETTE
by AL ZURA
OURSONETTE AND HER BATTLING BEARS ARE ONCE AGAIN IN THE THICK OF THINGS, AS THE ROYAL 22ND REGIMENT, THE FAMOUS "VAN DOOS," APPROACH THE HEAVILY-DEFENDED DEVENTER BRIDGE, GATEWAY TO THE LOW-LANDS, AND THE LONG-SUFFERING DUTCH PEOPLE, WHO, DESPITE SICKNESS AND STARVATION, HAVE BRAVELY SURVIVED THE NAZI OCCUPATION FOR MANY YEARS!
CRIPES, OURSONETTE! THOSE GOOSE-STEPPERS SURE PUT UP A STIFF FIGHT!
IT'S MOSTLY BRAVADO, SOLDIER--BORN OF DESPERATION AND FEAR THAT THEIR LOST CAUSE IS BASED ON WICKED LIES FROM THEIR EVIL FUHRER!
THEY DON'T STAND A CHANCE AGAINST SPIRITED, WELL-EQUIPPED CANADIAN TROOPS!
BUDDA! BUDDA! BUDD!
BUDDA! BUDDA! BUDDA! BUDD!

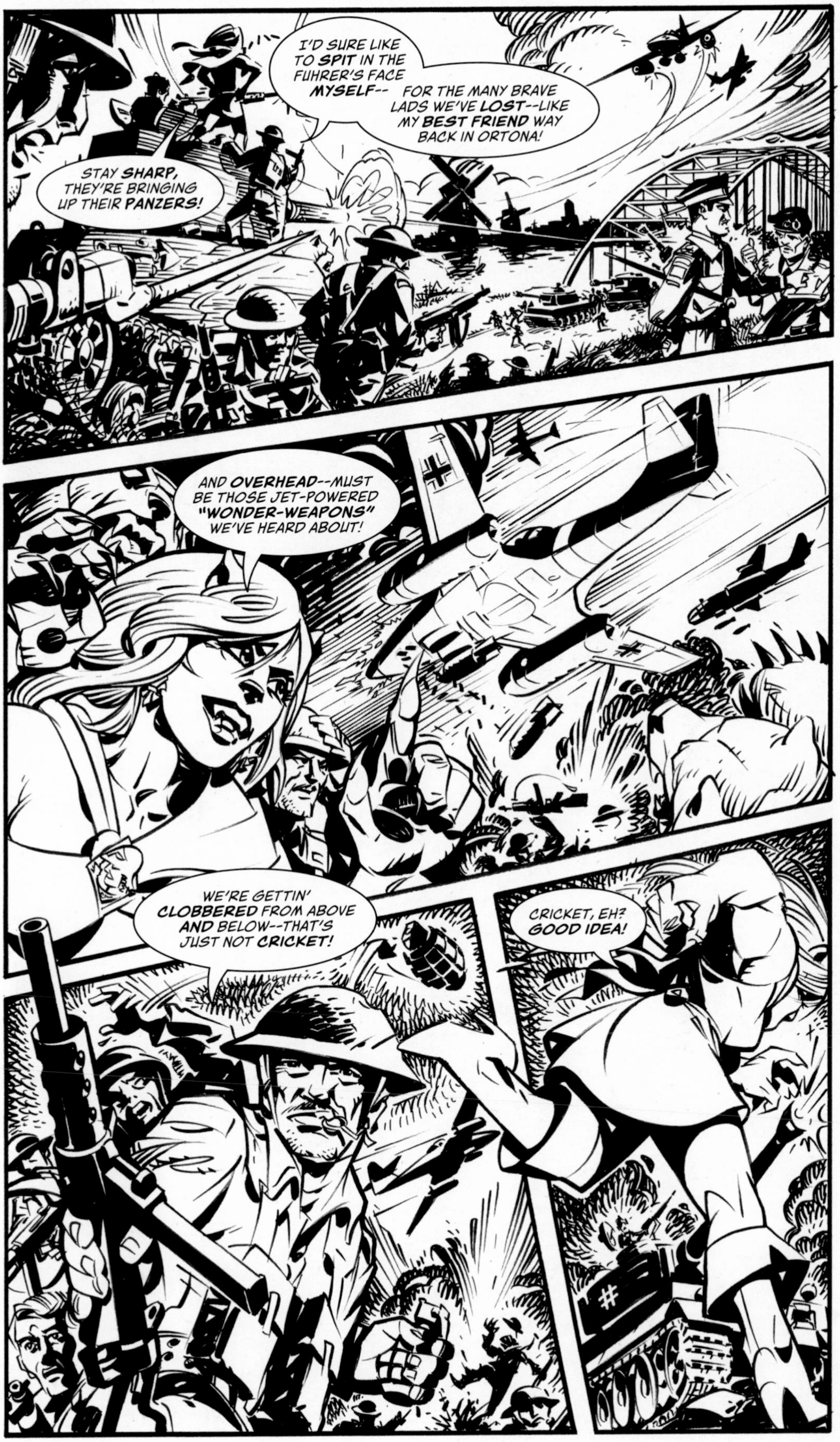
I'D SURE LIKE TO SPIT IN THE FUHRER'S FACE MYSELF-- FOR THE MANY BRAVE LADS WE'VE LOST--LIKE MY BEST FRIEND WAY BACK IN ORTONA!
STAY SHARP, THEY'RE BRINGING UP THEIR PANZERS!
AND OVERHEAD--MUST BE THOSE JET-POWERED "WONDER-WEAPONS" WE'VE HEARD ABOUT!
WE'RE GETTIN' CLOBBERED FROM ABOVE AND BELOW--THAT'S JUST NOT CRICKET!
CRICKET, EH? GOOD IDEA!

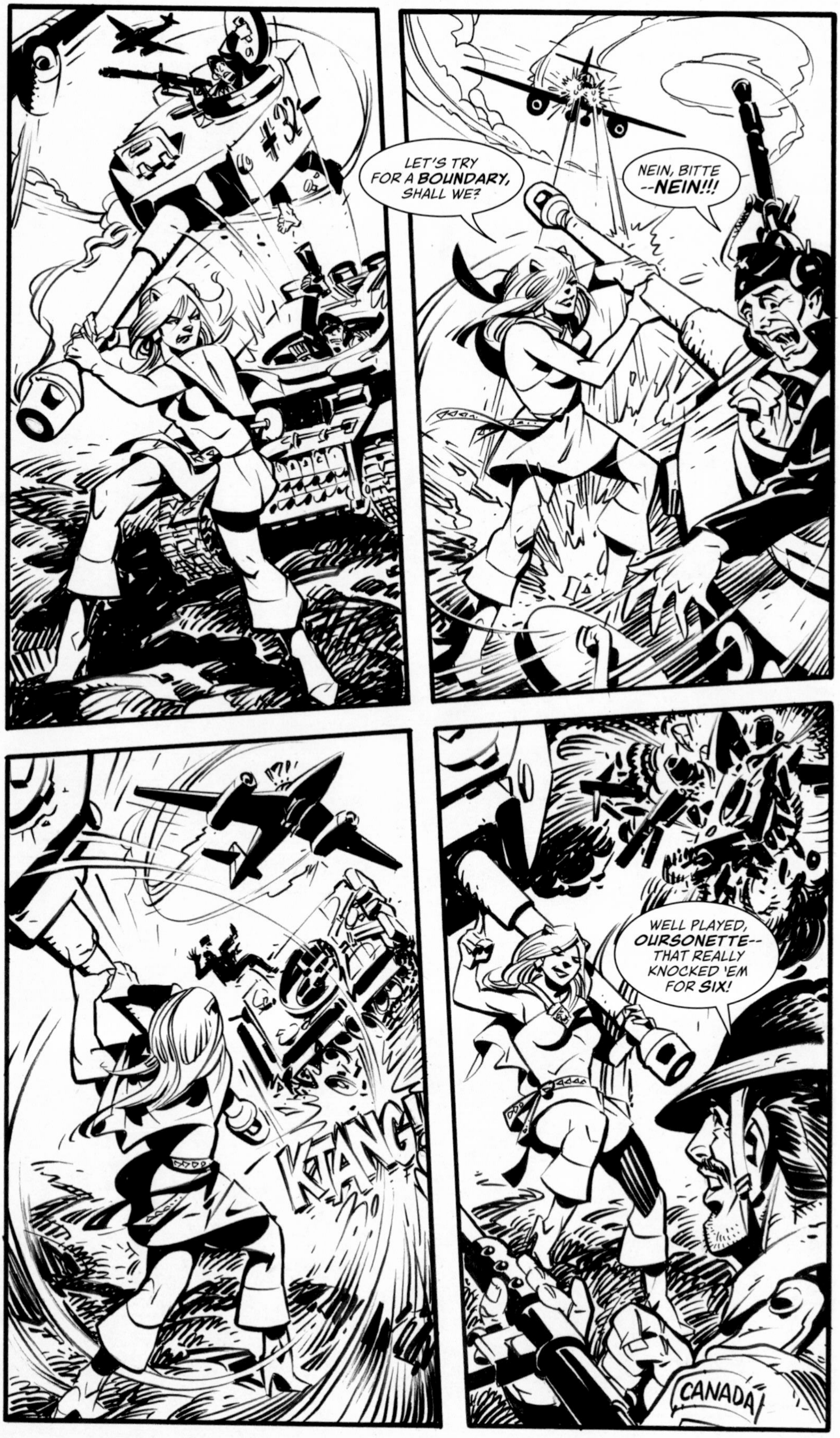
LET'S TRY FOR A **BOUNDARY,** SHALL WE?
NEIN, BITTE --**NEIN!!!**
KTANG!
WELL PLAYED, **OURSONETTE**-- THAT REALLY KNOCKED 'EM FOR **SIX!**
CANADA

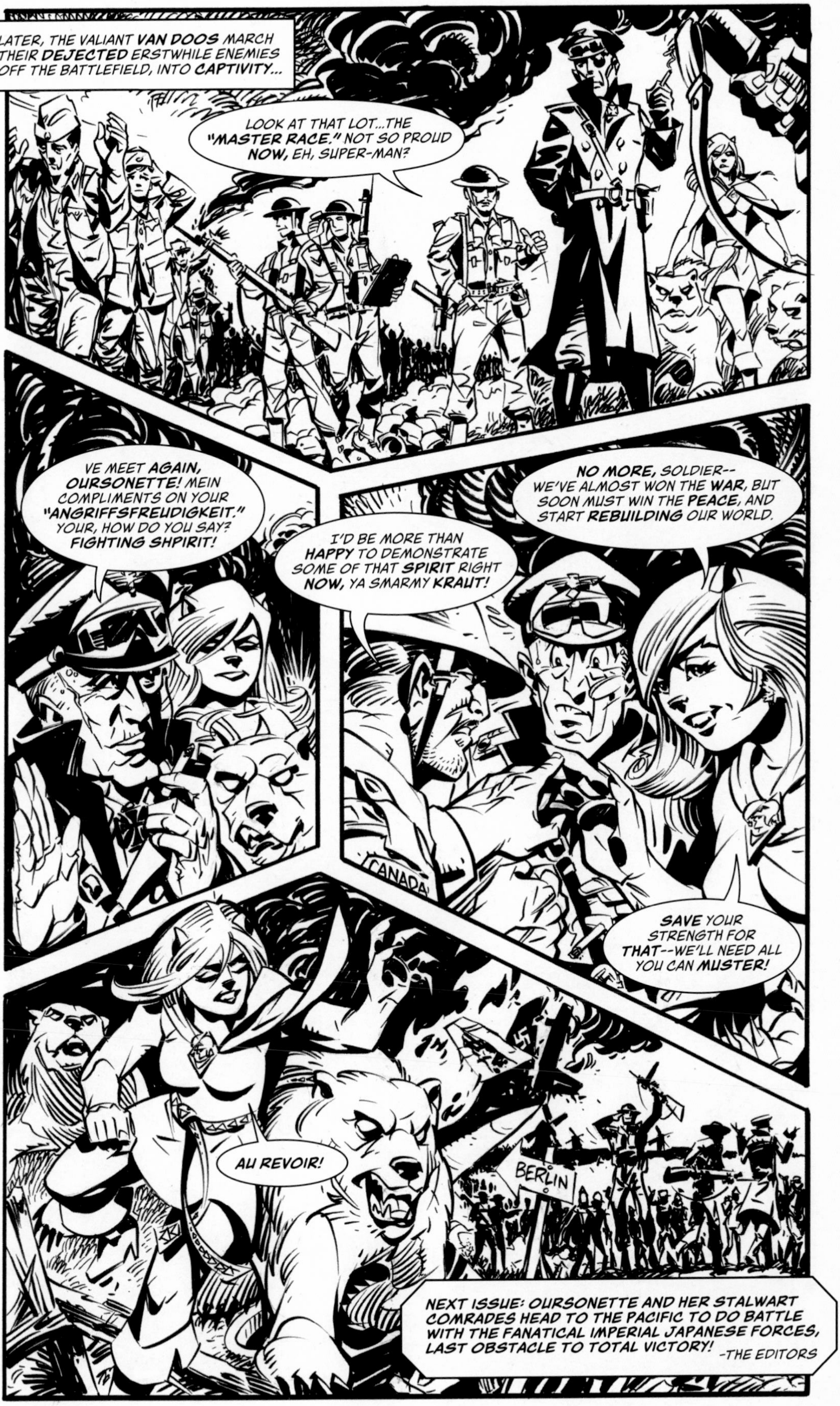
LATER, THE VALIANT VAN DOOS MARCH THEIR DEJECTED ERSTWHILE ENEMIES OFF THE BATTLEFIELD, INTO CAPTIVITY...
LOOK AT THAT LOT...THE "MASTER RACE." NOT SO PROUD NOW, EH, SUPER-MAN?
VE MEET AGAIN, OURSONETTE! MEIN COMPLIMENTS ON YOUR "ANGRIFFSFREUDIGKEIT." YOUR, HOW DO YOU SAY? FIGHTING SHPIRIT!
I'D BE MORE THAN HAPPY TO DEMONSTRATE SOME OF THAT SPIRIT RIGHT NOW, YA SMARMY KRAUT!
NO MORE, SOLDIER-- WE'VE ALMOST WON THE WAR, BUT SOON MUST WIN THE PEACE, AND START REBUILDING OUR WORLD.
CANADA
SAVE YOUR STRENGTH FOR THAT--WE'LL NEED ALL YOU CAN MUSTER!
AU REVOIR!
BERLIN
NEXT ISSUE: OURSONETTE AND HER STALWART COMRADES HEAD TO THE PACIFIC TO DO BATTLE WITH THE FANATICAL IMPERIAL JAPANESE FORCES, LAST OBSTACLE TO TOTAL VICTORY! -THE EDITORS

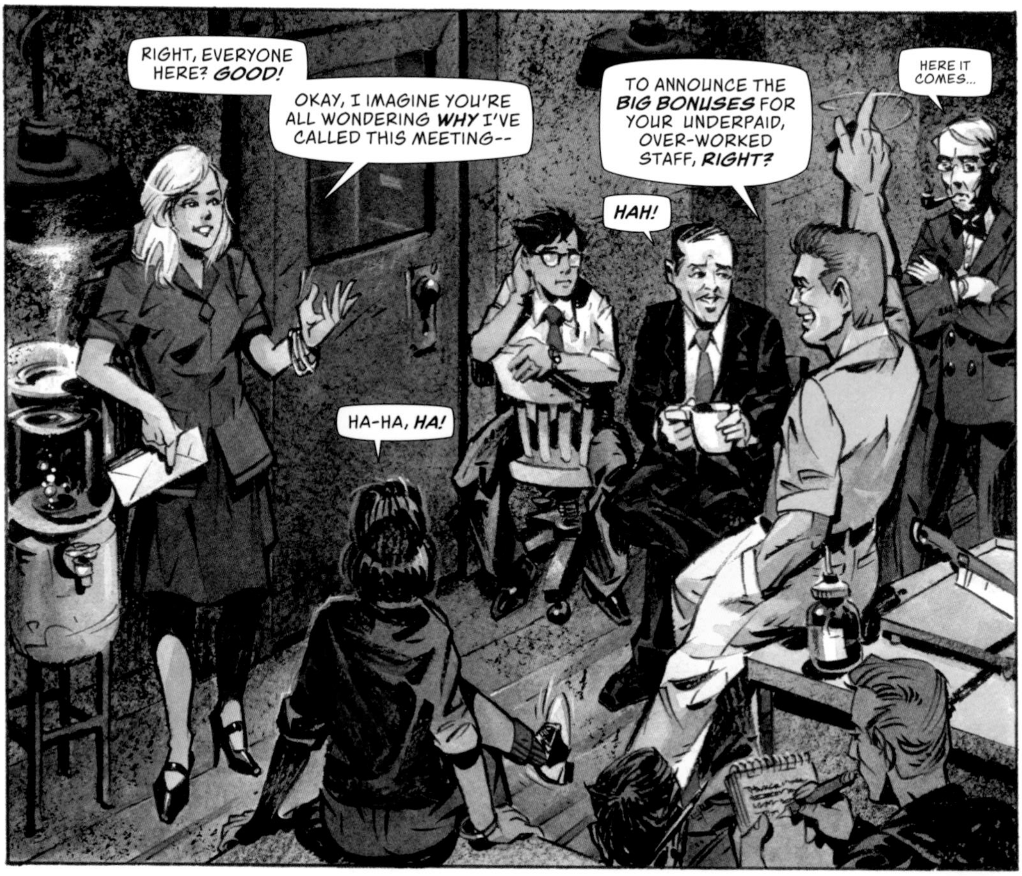
RIGHT, EVERYONE HERE? GOOD!
OKAY, I IMAGINE YOU'RE ALL WONDERING WHY I'VE CALLED THIS MEETING--
TO ANNOUNCE THE BIG BONUSES FOR YOUR UNDERPAID, OVER-WORKED STAFF, RIGHT?
HERE IT COMES...
HAH!
HA-HA, HA!

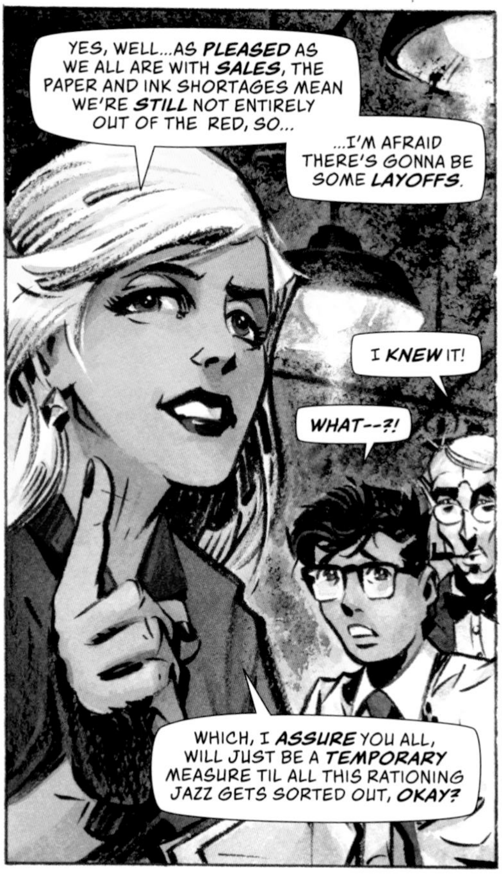
YES, WELL...AS PLEASED AS WE ALL ARE WITH SALES, THE PAPER AND INK SHORTAGES MEAN WE'RE STILL NOT ENTIRELY OUT OF THE RED, SO...
...I'M AFRAID THERE'S GONNA BE SOME LAYOFFS.
I KNEW IT!
WHAT--?!
WHICH, I ASSURE YOU ALL, WILL JUST BE A TEMPORARY MEASURE TIL ALL THIS RATIONING JAZZ GETS SORTED OUT, OKAY?

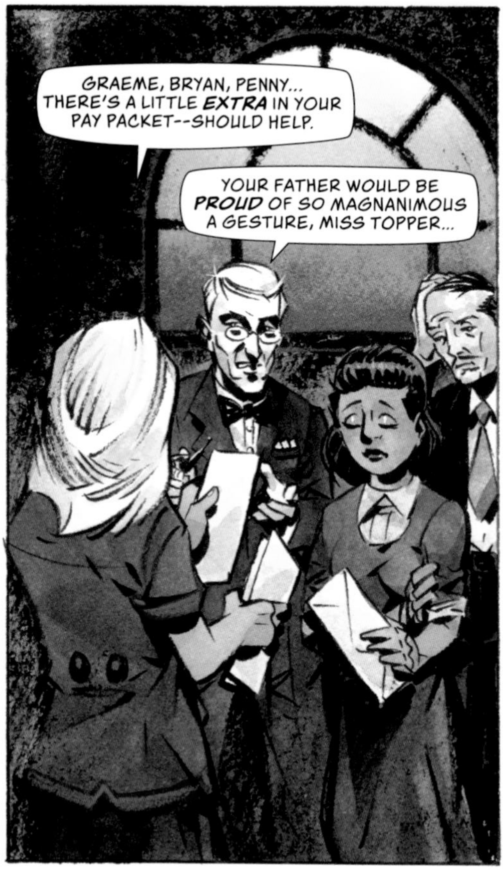
GRAEME, BRYAN, PENNY... THERE'S A LITTLE EXTRA IN YOUR PAY PACKET--SHOULD HELP.
YOUR FATHER WOULD BE PROUD OF SO MAGNANIMOUS A GESTURE, MISS TOPPER...

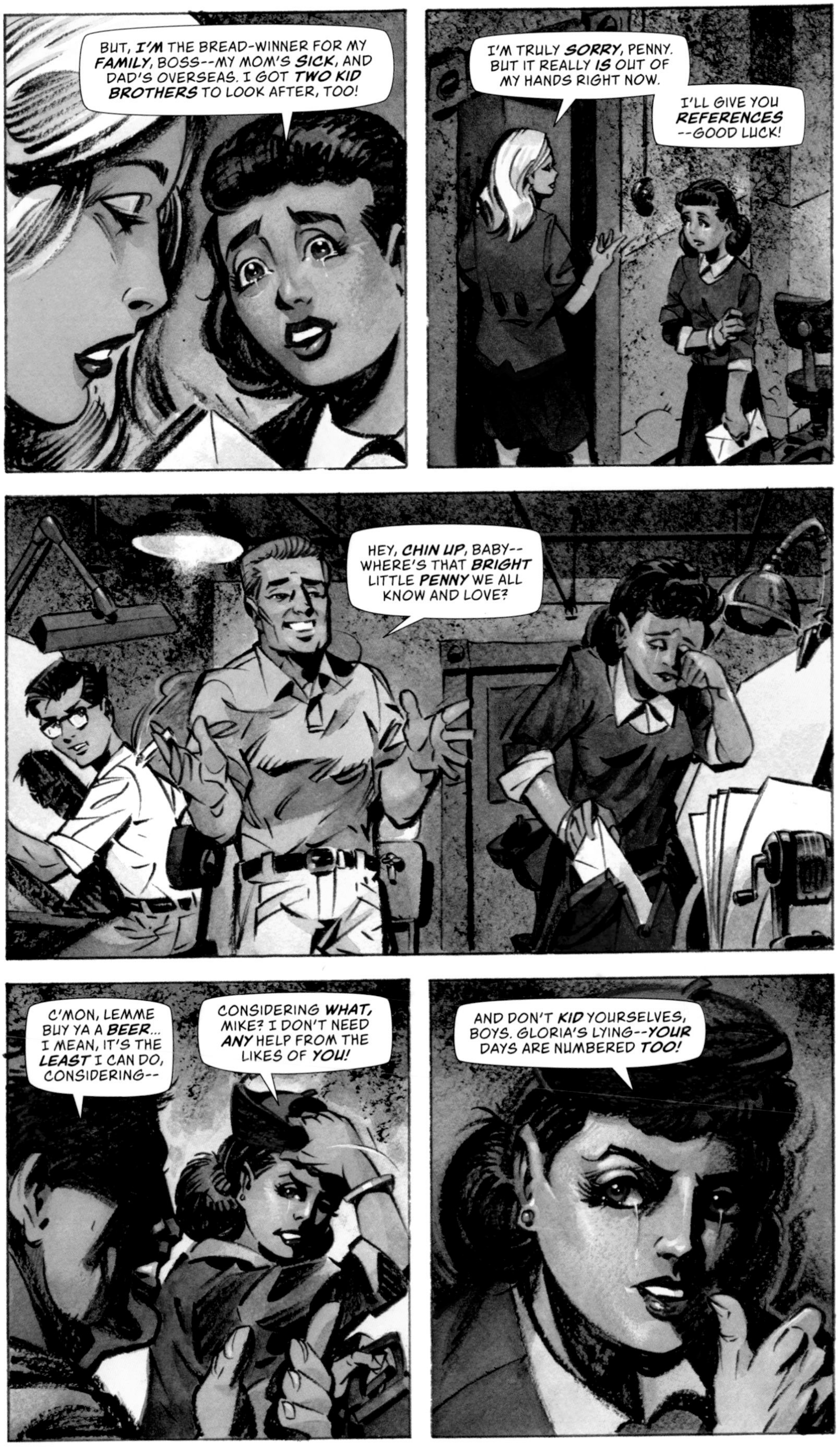
BUT, I'M THE BREAD-WINNER FOR MY FAMILY, BOSS--MY MOM'S SICK, AND DAD'S OVERSEAS. I GOT TWO KID BROTHERS TO LOOK AFTER, TOO!
I'M TRULY SORRY, PENNY. BUT IT REALLY IS OUT OF MY HANDS RIGHT NOW.
I'LL GIVE YOU REFERENCES --GOOD LUCK!
HEY, CHIN UP, BABY-- WHERE'S THAT BRIGHT LITTLE PENNY WE ALL KNOW AND LOVE?
C'MON, LEMME BUY YA A BEER... I MEAN, IT'S THE LEAST I CAN DO, CONSIDERING--
CONSIDERING WHAT, MIKE? I DON'T NEED ANY HELP FROM THE LIKES OF YOU!
AND DON'T KID YOURSELVES, BOYS. GLORIA'S LYING--YOUR DAYS ARE NUMBERED TOO!

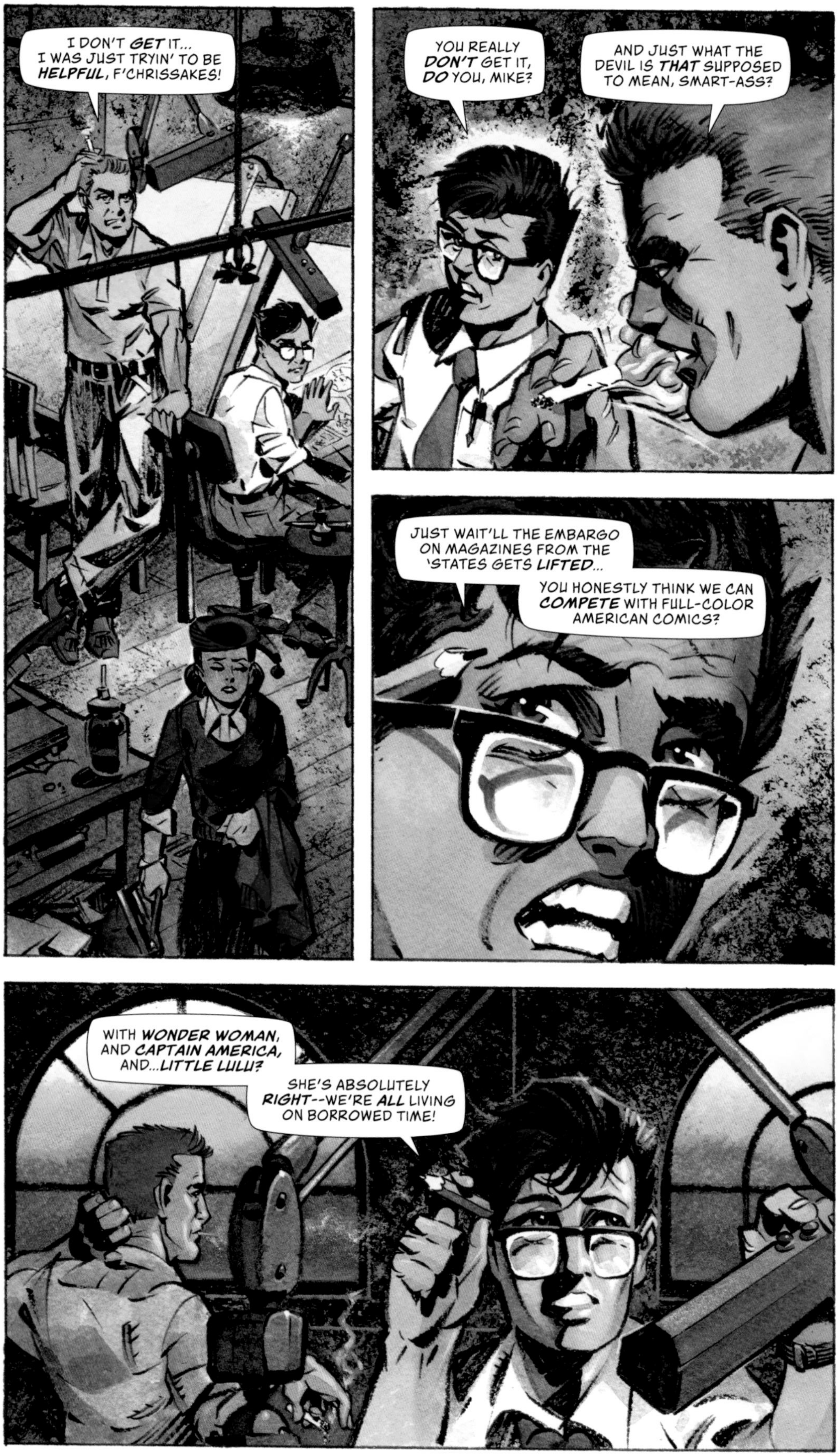
I DON'T GET IT... I WAS JUST TRYIN' TO BE HELPFUL, F'CHRISSAKES!
YOU REALLY DON'T GET IT, DO YOU, MIKE?
AND JUST WHAT THE DEVIL IS THAT SUPPOSED TO MEAN, SMART-ASS?
JUST WAIT'LL THE EMBARGO ON MAGAZINES FROM THE 'STATES GETS LIFTED...
YOU HONESTLY THINK WE CAN COMPETE WITH FULL-COLOR AMERICAN COMICS?
WITH WONDER WOMAN, AND CAPTAIN AMERICA, AND...LITTLE LULU?
SHE'S ABSOLUTELY RIGHT--WE'RE ALL LIVING ON BORROWED TIME!

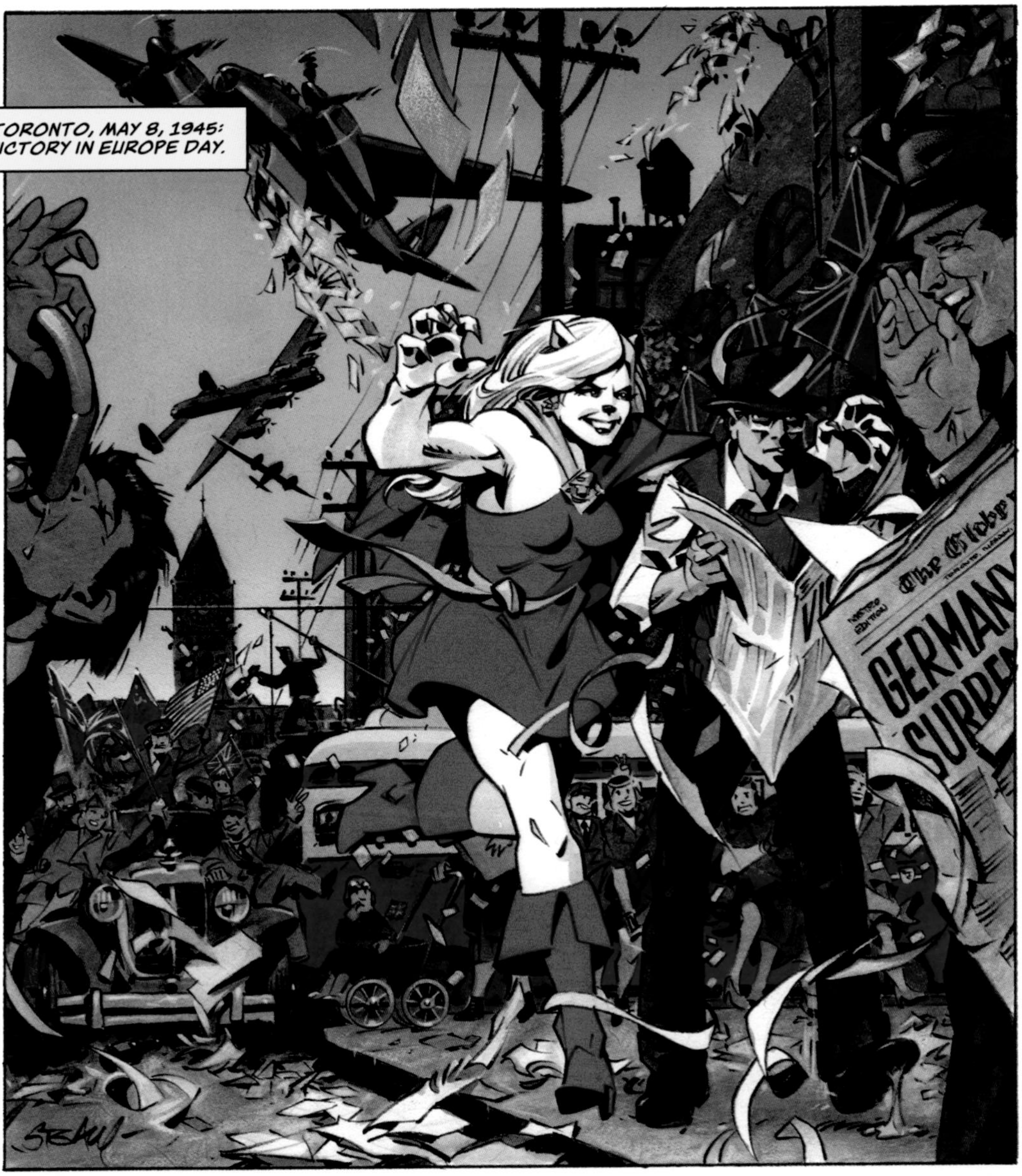
TORONTO, MAY 8, 1945:
VICTORY IN EUROPE DAY.

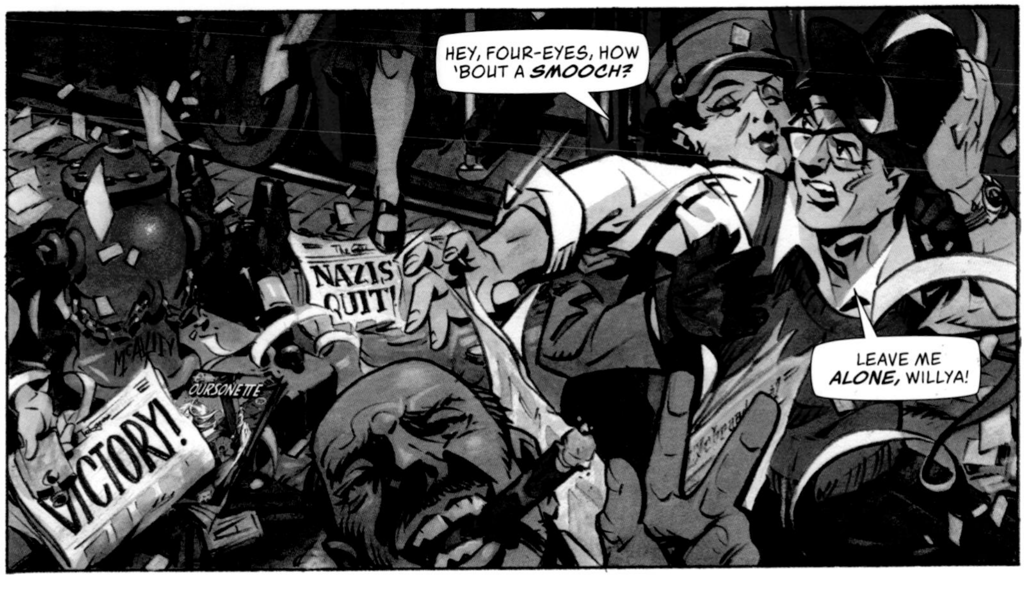
HEY, FOUR-EYES, HOW 'BOUT A *SMOOCH?*
LEAVE ME *ALONE,* WILLYA!
NAZIS QUIT!
VICTORY!

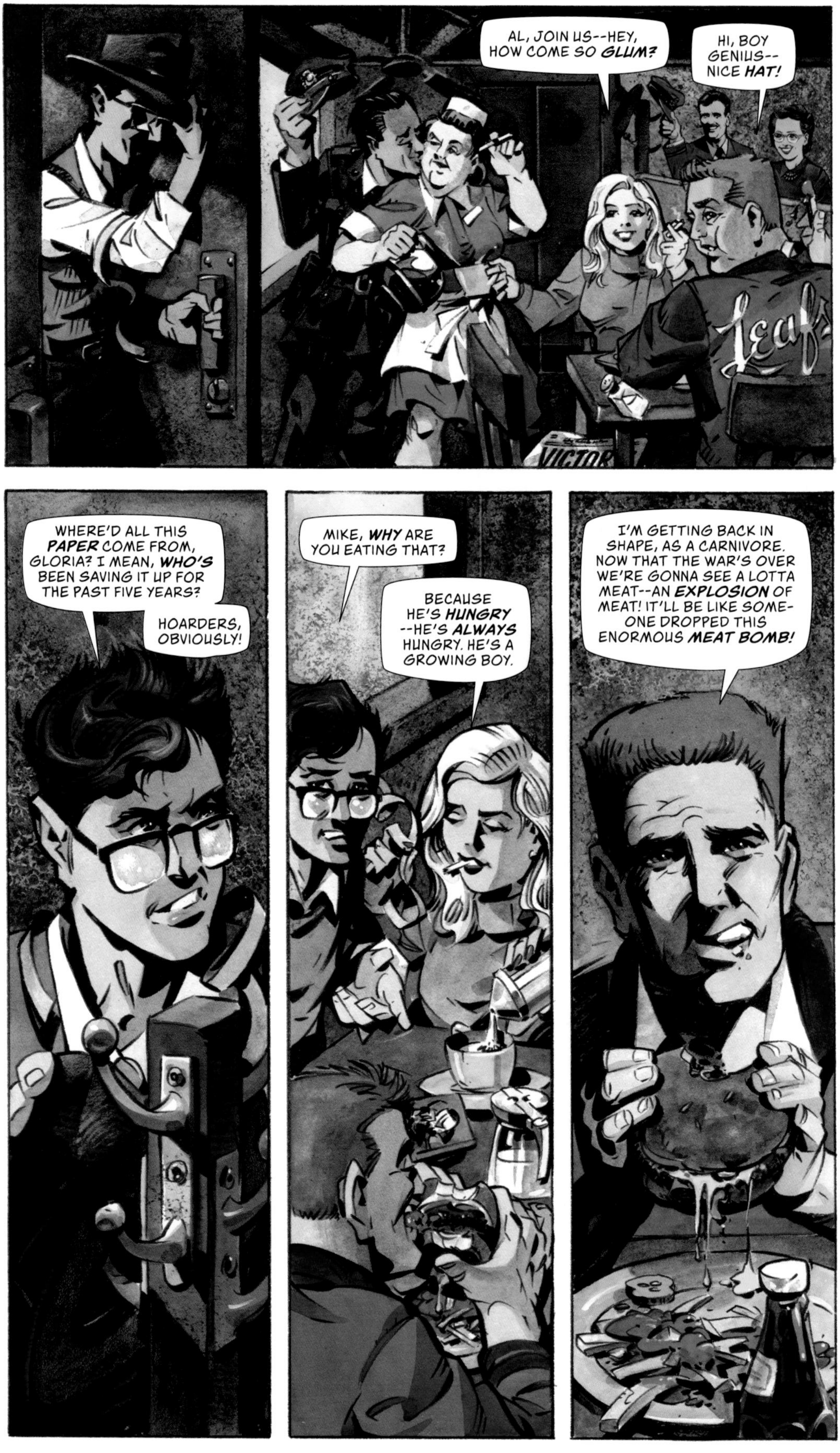
AL, JOIN US--HEY, HOW COME SO GLUM?
HI, BOY GENIUS--NICE HAT!
WHERE'D ALL THIS PAPER COME FROM, GLORIA? I MEAN, WHO'S BEEN SAVING IT UP FOR THE PAST FIVE YEARS?
HOARDERS, OBVIOUSLY!
MIKE, WHY ARE YOU EATING THAT?
BECAUSE HE'S HUNGRY--HE'S ALWAYS HUNGRY. HE'S A GROWING BOY.
I'M GETTING BACK IN SHAPE, AS A CARNIVORE. NOW THAT THE WAR'S OVER WE'RE GONNA SEE A LOTTA MEAT--AN EXPLOSION OF MEAT! IT'LL BE LIKE SOME-ONE DROPPED THIS ENORMOUS MEAT BOMB!

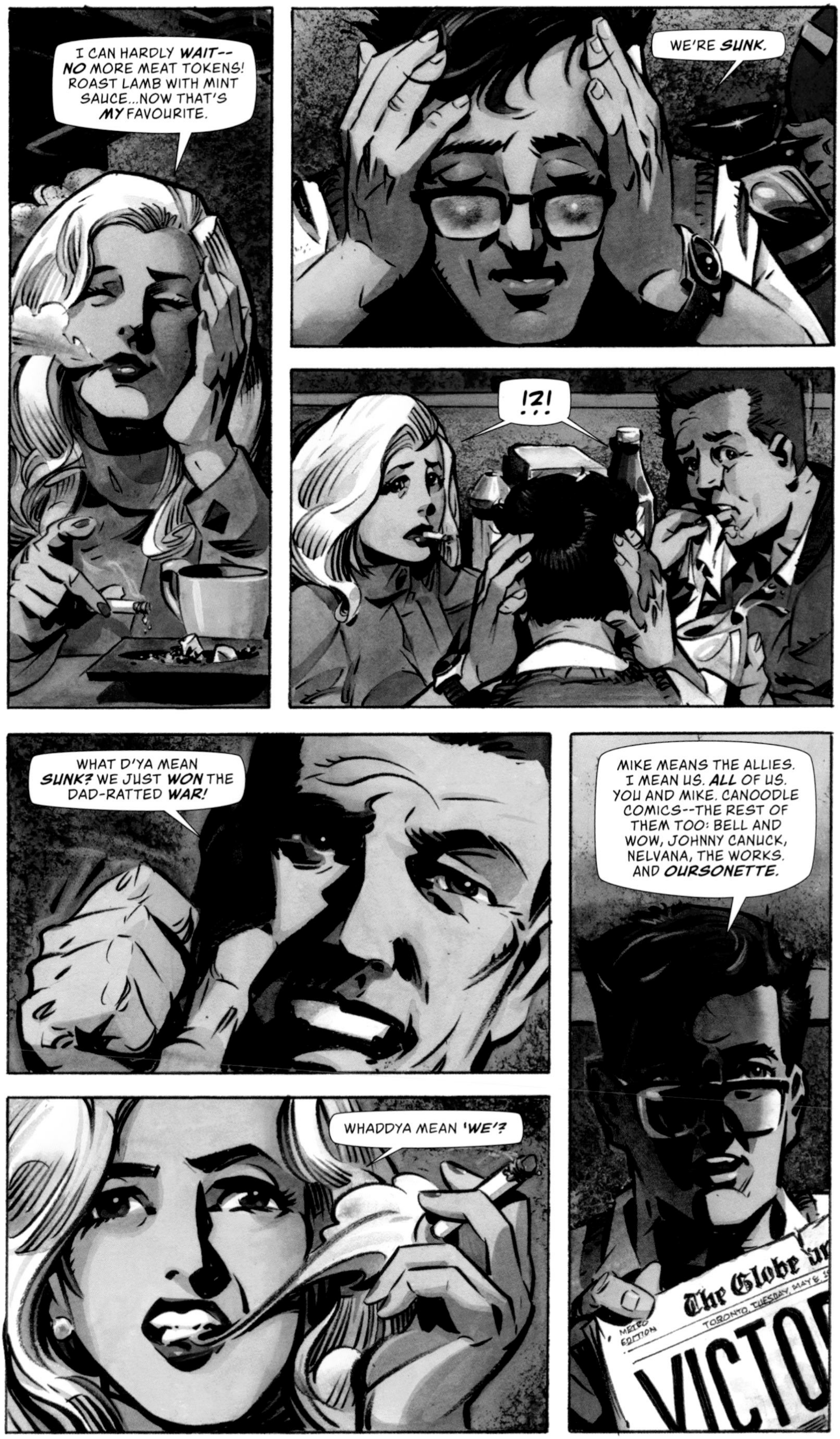
I CAN HARDLY WAIT-- NO MORE MEAT TOKENS! ROAST LAMB WITH MINT SAUCE...NOW THAT'S MY FAVOURITE.
WE'RE SUNK.
!?!
WHAT D'YA MEAN SUNK? WE JUST WON THE DAD-RATTED WAR!
MIKE MEANS THE ALLIES. I MEAN US. ALL OF US. YOU AND MIKE. CANOODLE COMICS--THE REST OF THEM TOO: BELL AND WOW, JOHNNY CANUCK, NELVANA, THE WORKS. AND OURSONETTE.
WHADDYA MEAN 'WE'?

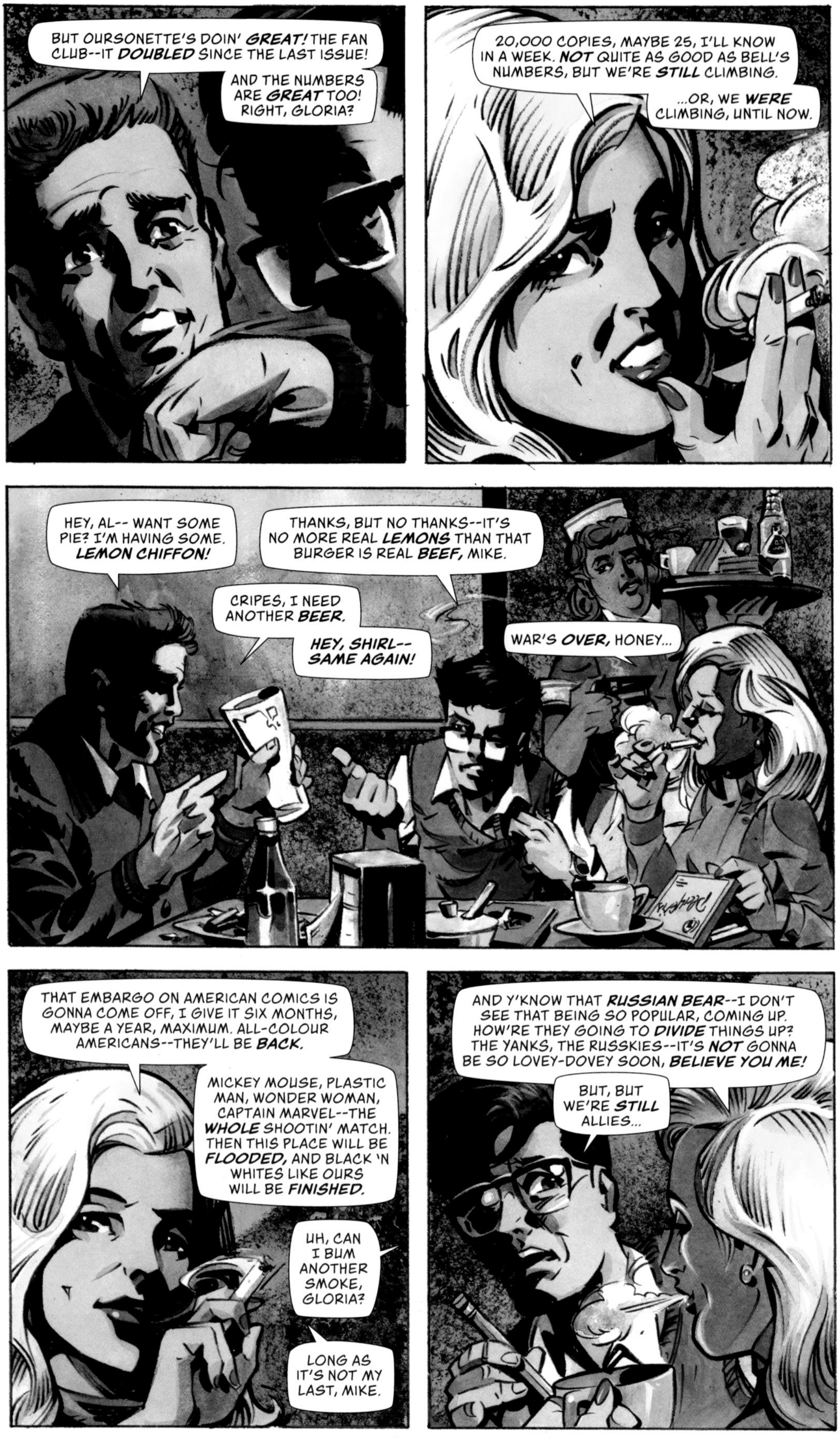

BUT OURSONETTE'S DOIN' GREAT! THE FAN CLUB--IT DOUBLED SINCE THE LAST ISSUE!
AND THE NUMBERS ARE GREAT TOO! RIGHT, GLORIA?
20,000 COPIES, MAYBE 25, I'LL KNOW IN A WEEK. NOT QUITE AS GOOD AS BELL'S NUMBERS, BUT WE'RE STILL CLIMBING.
...OR, WE WERE CLIMBING, UNTIL NOW.
HEY, AL-- WANT SOME PIE? I'M HAVING SOME. LEMON CHIFFON!
THANKS, BUT NO THANKS--IT'S NO MORE REAL LEMONS THAN THAT BURGER IS REAL BEEF, MIKE.
CRIPES, I NEED ANOTHER BEER.
HEY, SHIRL-- SAME AGAIN!
WAR'S OVER, HONEY...
THAT EMBARGO ON AMERICAN COMICS IS GONNA COME OFF, I GIVE IT SIX MONTHS, MAYBE A YEAR, MAXIMUM. ALL-COLOUR AMERICANS--THEY'LL BE BACK.
MICKEY MOUSE, PLASTIC MAN, WONDER WOMAN, CAPTAIN MARVEL--THE WHOLE SHOOTIN' MATCH. THEN THIS PLACE WILL BE FLOODED, AND BLACK 'N WHITES LIKE OURS WILL BE FINISHED.
UH, CAN I BUM ANOTHER SMOKE, GLORIA?
LONG AS IT'S NOT MY LAST, MIKE.
AND Y'KNOW THAT RUSSIAN BEAR--I DON'T SEE THAT BEING SO POPULAR, COMING UP. HOW'RE THEY GOING TO DIVIDE THINGS UP? THE YANKS, THE RUSSKIES--IT'S NOT GONNA BE SO LOVEY-DOVEY SOON, BELIEVE YOU ME!
BUT, BUT WE'RE STILL ALLIES...

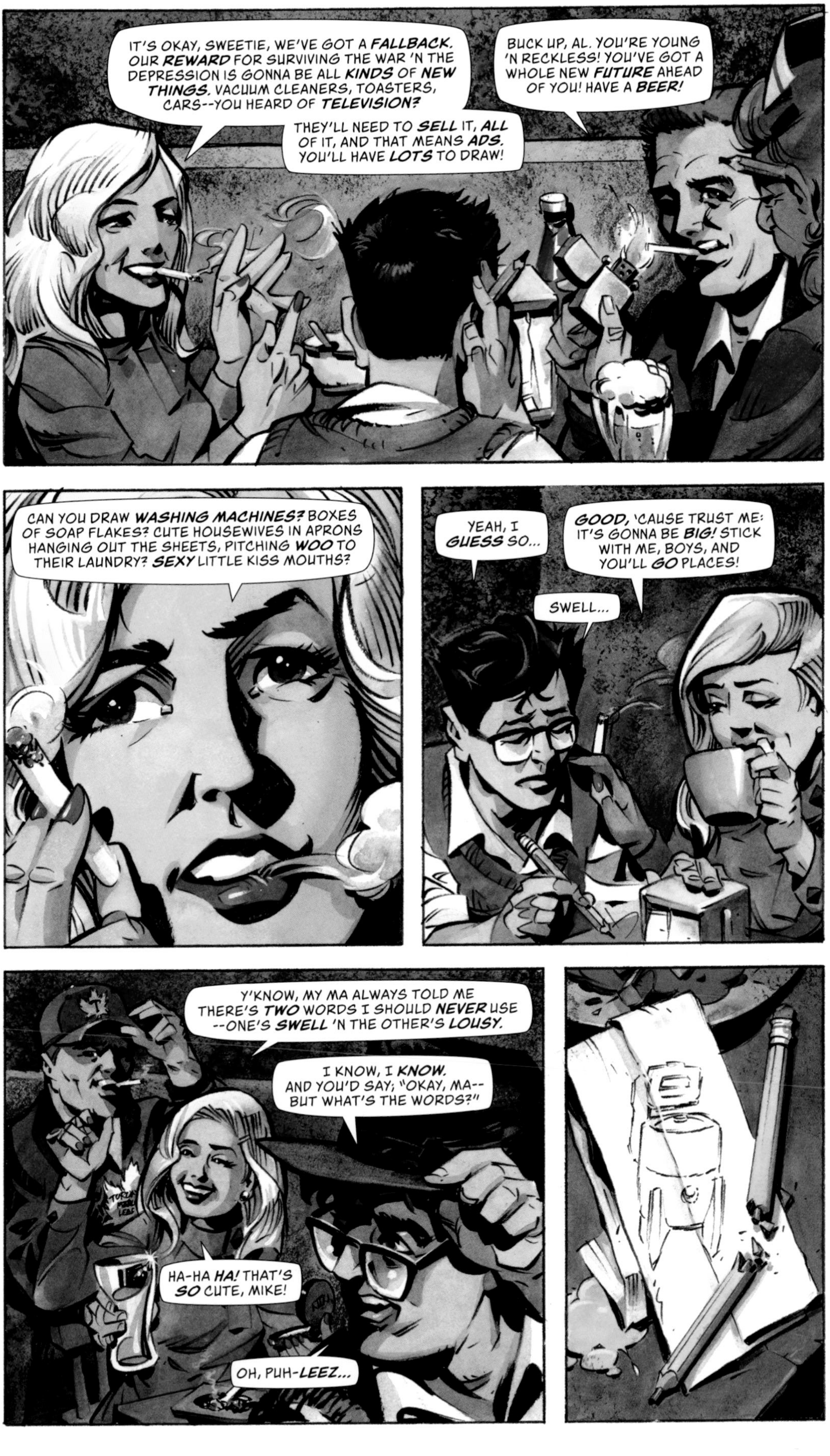
IT'S OKAY, SWEETIE, WE'VE GOT A FALLBACK. OUR REWARD FOR SURVIVING THE WAR 'N THE DEPRESSION IS GONNA BE ALL KINDS OF NEW THINGS. VACUUM CLEANERS, TOASTERS, CARS--YOU HEARD OF TELEVISION?
THEY'LL NEED TO SELL IT, ALL OF IT, AND THAT MEANS ADS. YOU'LL HAVE LOTS TO DRAW!
BUCK UP, AL. YOU'RE YOUNG 'N RECKLESS! YOU'VE GOT A WHOLE NEW FUTURE AHEAD OF YOU! HAVE A BEER!
CAN YOU DRAW WASHING MACHINES? BOXES OF SOAP FLAKES? CUTE HOUSEWIVES IN APRONS HANGING OUT THE SHEETS, PITCHING WOO TO THEIR LAUNDRY? SEXY LITTLE KISS MOUTHS?
YEAH, I GUESS SO...
GOOD, 'CAUSE TRUST ME: IT'S GONNA BE BIG! STICK WITH ME, BOYS, AND YOU'LL GO PLACES!
SWELL...
Y'KNOW, MY MA ALWAYS TOLD ME THERE'S TWO WORDS I SHOULD NEVER USE --ONE'S SWELL 'N THE OTHER'S LOUSY.
I KNOW, I KNOW. AND YOU'D SAY; "OKAY, MA-- BUT WHAT'S THE WORDS?"
HA-HA HA! THAT'S SO CUTE, MIKE!
OH, PUH-LEEZ...

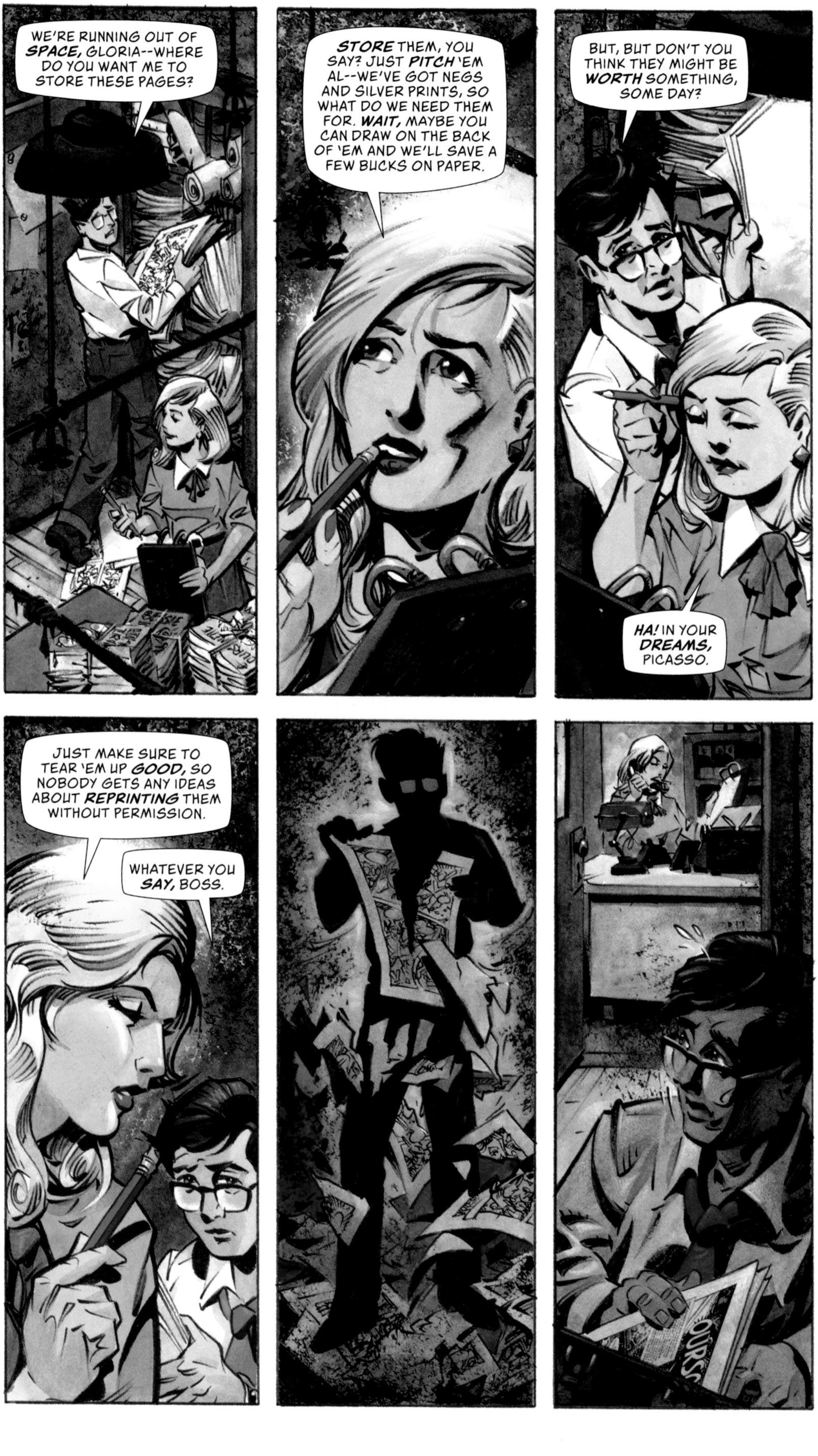
WE'RE RUNNING OUT OF SPACE, GLORIA--WHERE DO YOU WANT ME TO STORE THESE PAGES?
STORE THEM, YOU SAY? JUST PITCH 'EM AL--WE'VE GOT NEGS AND SILVER PRINTS, SO WHAT DO WE NEED THEM FOR. WAIT, MAYBE YOU CAN DRAW ON THE BACK OF 'EM AND WE'LL SAVE A FEW BUCKS ON PAPER.
BUT, BUT DON'T YOU THINK THEY MIGHT BE WORTH SOMETHING, SOME DAY?
HA! IN YOUR DREAMS, PICASSO.
JUST MAKE SURE TO TEAR 'EM UP GOOD, SO NOBODY GETS ANY IDEAS ABOUT REPRINTING THEM WITHOUT PERMISSION.
WHATEVER YOU SAY, BOSS.

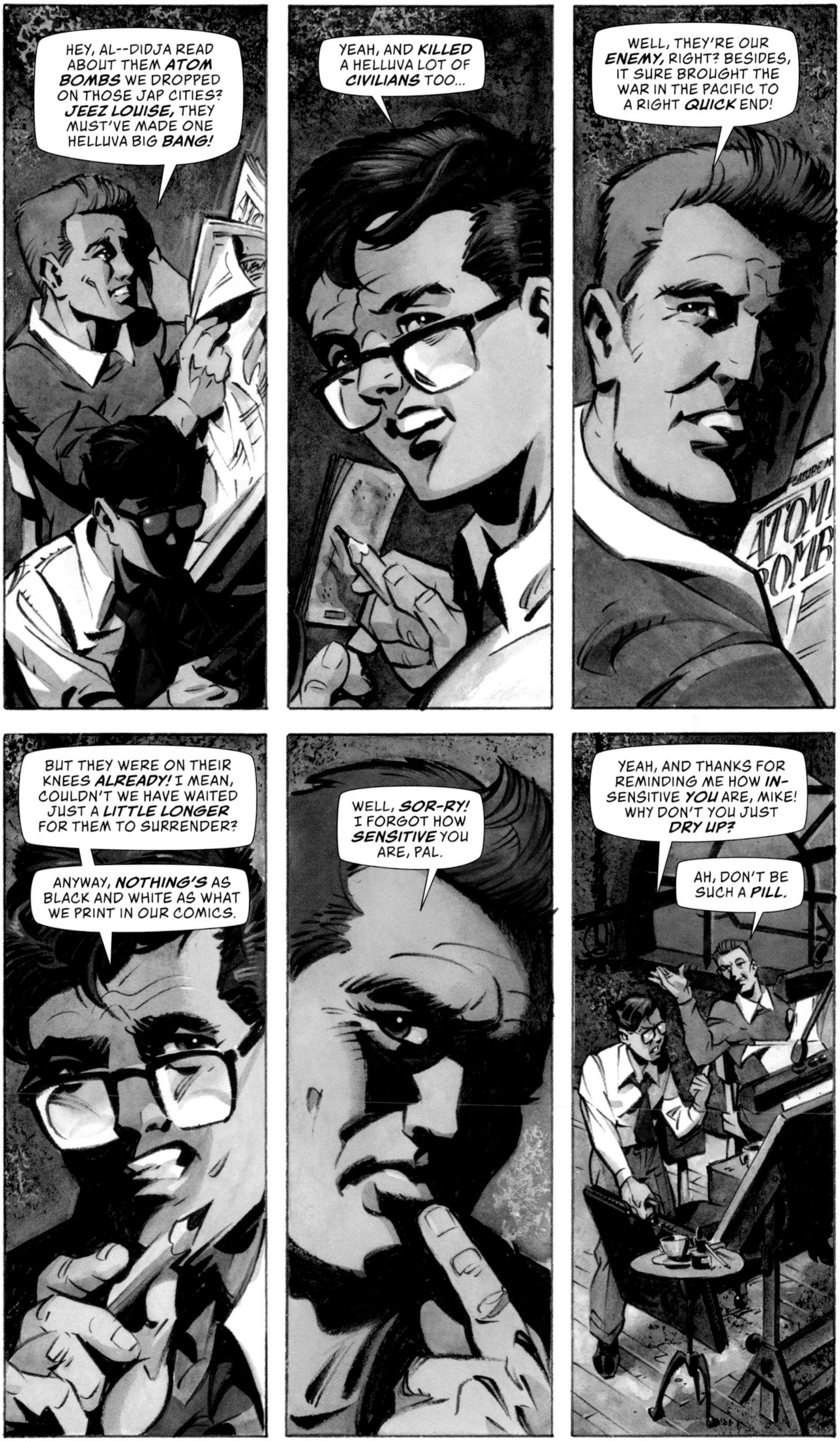
HEY, AL--DIDJA READ ABOUT THEM ATOM BOMBS WE DROPPED ON THOSE JAP CITIES? JEEZ LOUISE, THEY MUST'VE MADE ONE HELLUVA BIG BANG!
YEAH, AND KILLED A HELLUVA LOT OF CIVILIANS TOO...
WELL, THEY'RE OUR ENEMY, RIGHT? BESIDES, IT SURE BROUGHT THE WAR IN THE PACIFIC TO A RIGHT QUICK END!
ATOM BOMB
BUT THEY WERE ON THEIR KNEES ALREADY! I MEAN, COULDN'T WE HAVE WAITED JUST A LITTLE LONGER FOR THEM TO SURRENDER?
ANYWAY, NOTHING'S AS BLACK AND WHITE AS WHAT WE PRINT IN OUR COMICS.
WELL, SOR-RY! I FORGOT HOW SENSITIVE YOU ARE, PAL.
YEAH, AND THANKS FOR REMINDING ME HOW IN-SENSITIVE YOU ARE, MIKE! WHY DON'T YOU JUST DRY UP?
AH, DON'T BE SUCH A PILL.

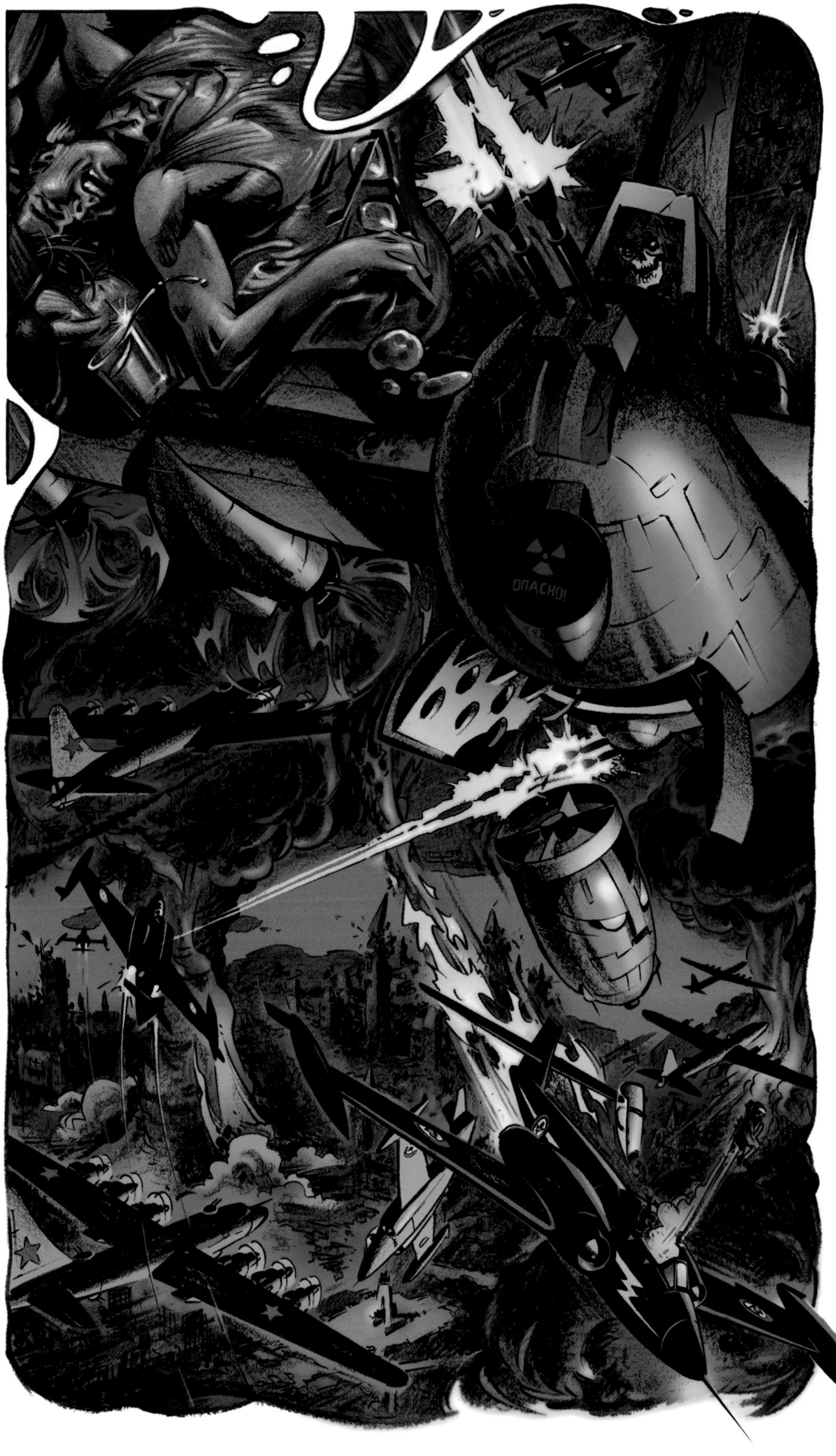
ОПАСНО!

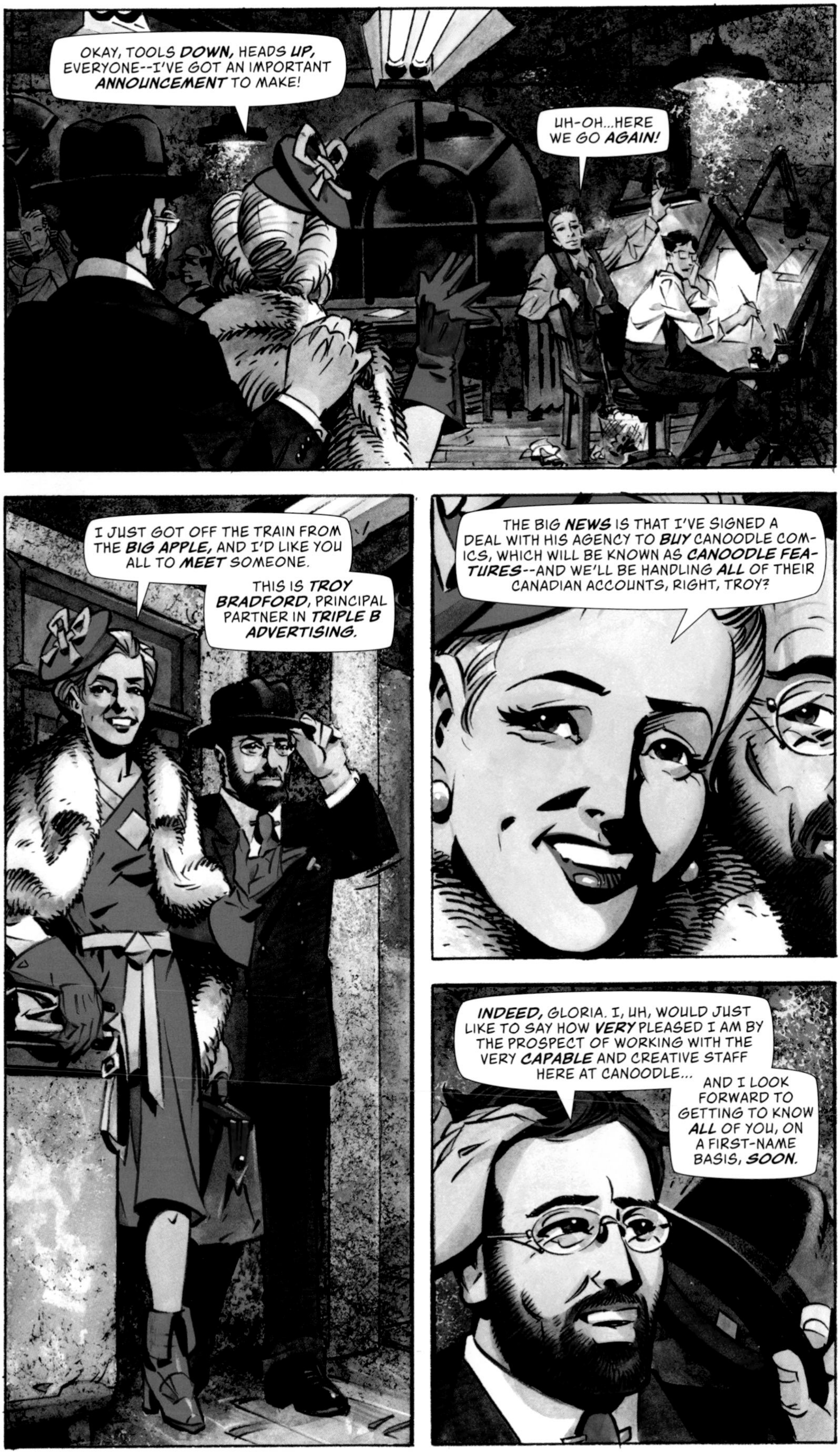

OKAY, TOOLS DOWN, HEADS UP, EVERYONE--I'VE GOT AN IMPORTANT ANNOUNCEMENT TO MAKE!
UH-OH...HERE WE GO AGAIN!
I JUST GOT OFF THE TRAIN FROM THE BIG APPLE, AND I'D LIKE YOU ALL TO MEET SOMEONE.
THIS IS TROY BRADFORD, PRINCIPAL PARTNER IN TRIPLE B ADVERTISING.
THE BIG NEWS IS THAT I'VE SIGNED A DEAL WITH HIS AGENCY TO BUY CANOODLE COMICS, WHICH WILL BE KNOWN AS CANOODLE FEATURES--AND WE'LL BE HANDLING ALL OF THEIR CANADIAN ACCOUNTS, RIGHT, TROY?
INDEED, GLORIA. I, UH, WOULD JUST LIKE TO SAY HOW VERY PLEASED I AM BY THE PROSPECT OF WORKING WITH THE VERY CAPABLE AND CREATIVE STAFF HERE AT CANOODLE...
AND I LOOK FORWARD TO GETTING TO KNOW ALL OF YOU, ON A FIRST-NAME BASIS, SOON.

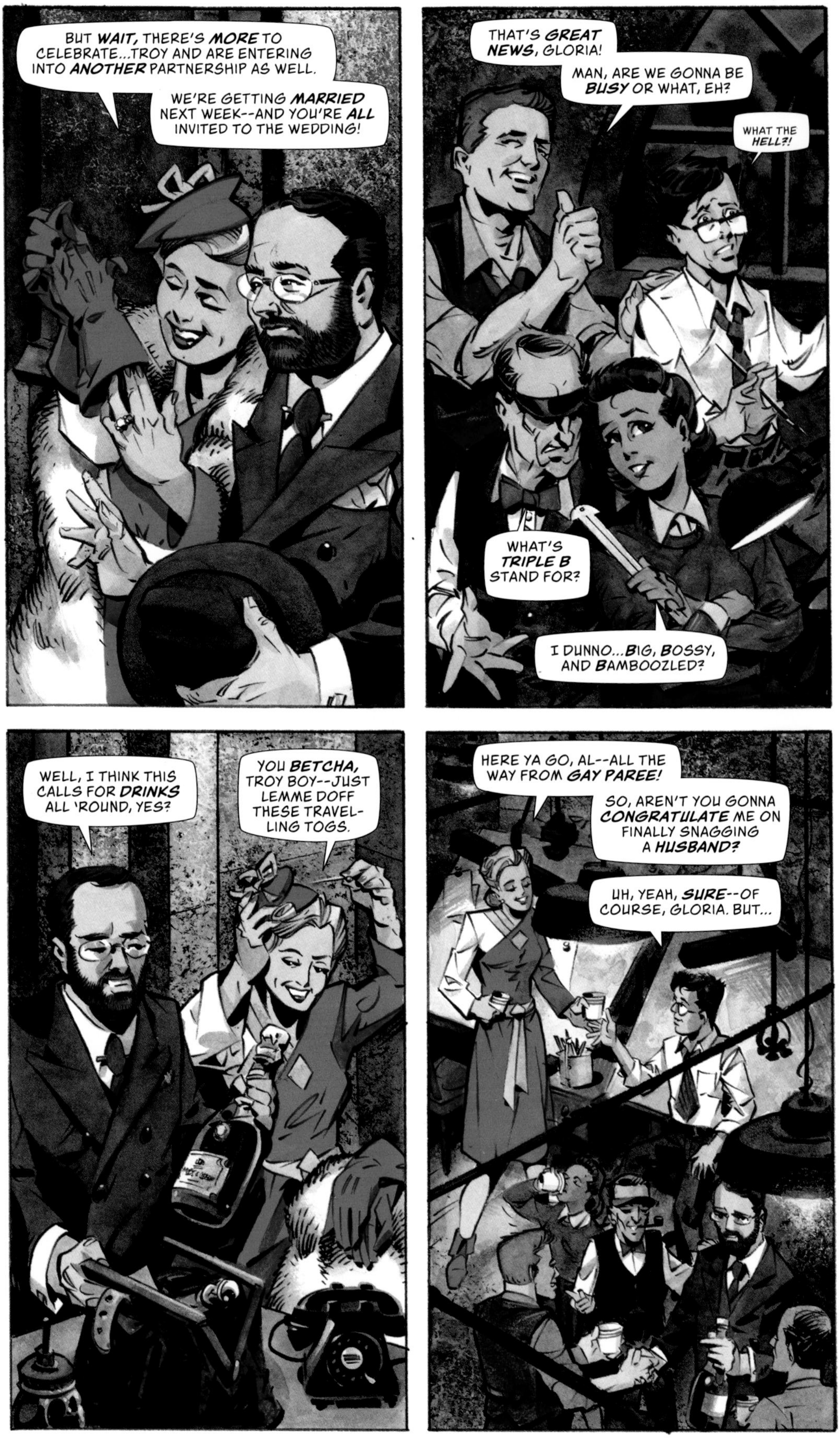
BUT WAIT, THERE'S MORE TO CELEBRATE...TROY AND ARE ENTERING INTO ANOTHER PARTNERSHIP AS WELL.
WE'RE GETTING MARRIED NEXT WEEK--AND YOU'RE ALL INVITED TO THE WEDDING!
THAT'S GREAT NEWS, GLORIA!
MAN, ARE WE GONNA BE BUSY OR WHAT, EH?
WHAT THE HELL?!
WHAT'S TRIPLE B STAND FOR?
I DUNNO...BIG, BOSSY, AND BAMBOOZLED?
WELL, I THINK THIS CALLS FOR DRINKS ALL 'ROUND, YES?
YOU BETCHA, TROY BOY--JUST LEMME DOFF THESE TRAVEL-LING TOGS.
HERE YA GO, AL--ALL THE WAY FROM GAY PAREE!
SO, AREN'T YOU GONNA CONGRATULATE ME ON FINALLY SNAGGING A HUSBAND?
UH, YEAH, SURE--OF COURSE, GLORIA. BUT...

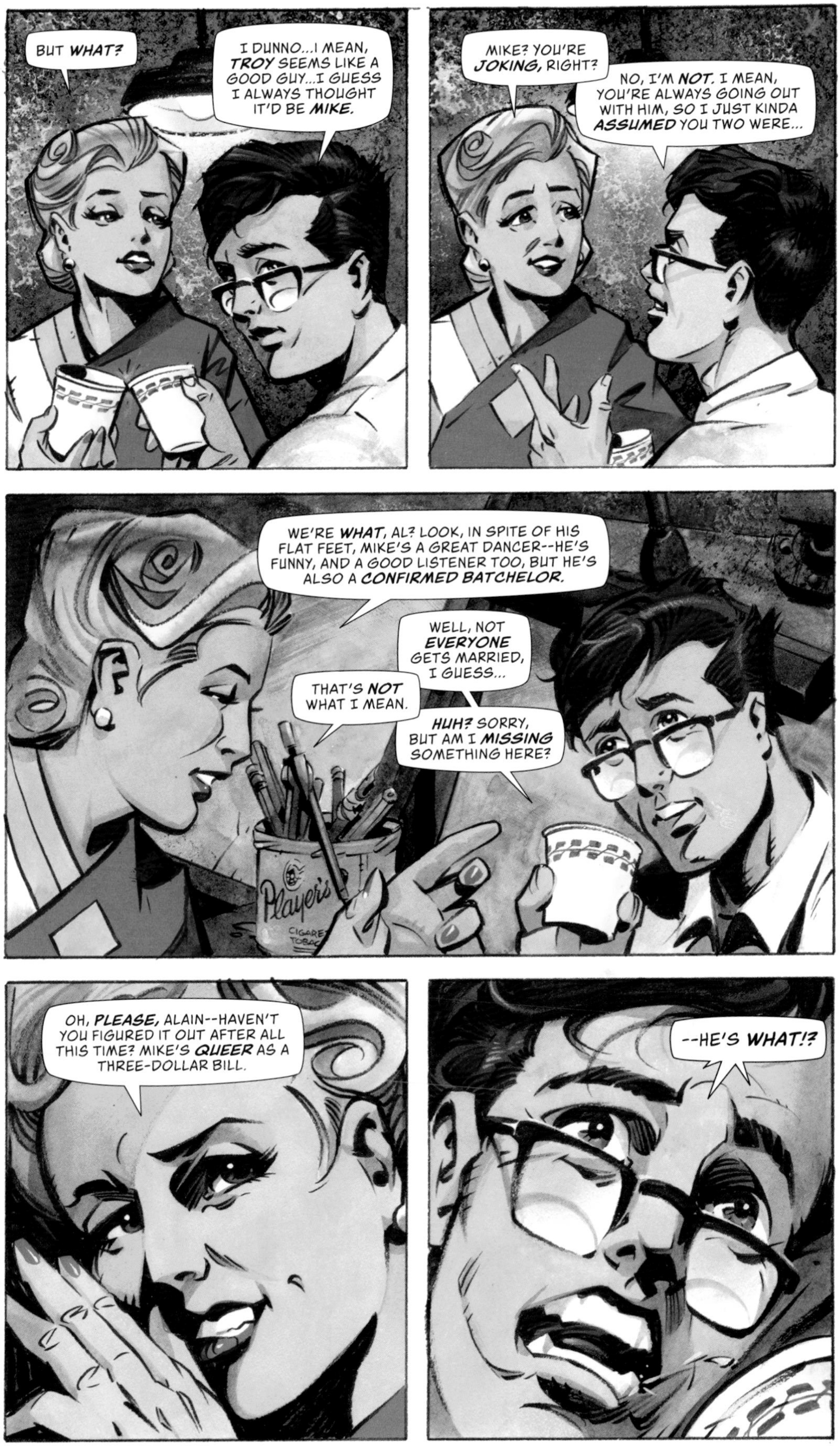
BUT WHAT?
I DUNNO...I MEAN, TROY SEEMS LIKE A GOOD GUY...I GUESS I ALWAYS THOUGHT IT'D BE MIKE.
MIKE? YOU'RE JOKING, RIGHT?
NO, I'M NOT. I MEAN, YOU'RE ALWAYS GOING OUT WITH HIM, SO I JUST KINDA ASSUMED YOU TWO WERE...
WE'RE WHAT, AL? LOOK, IN SPITE OF HIS FLAT FEET, MIKE'S A GREAT DANCER--HE'S FUNNY, AND A GOOD LISTENER TOO, BUT HE'S ALSO A CONFIRMED BATCHELOR.
WELL, NOT EVERYONE GETS MARRIED, I GUESS...
THAT'S NOT WHAT I MEAN.
HUH? SORRY, BUT AM I MISSING SOMETHING HERE?
Player's
OH, PLEASE, ALAIN--HAVEN'T YOU FIGURED IT OUT AFTER ALL THIS TIME? MIKE'S QUEER AS A THREE-DOLLAR BILL.
--HE'S WHAT!?

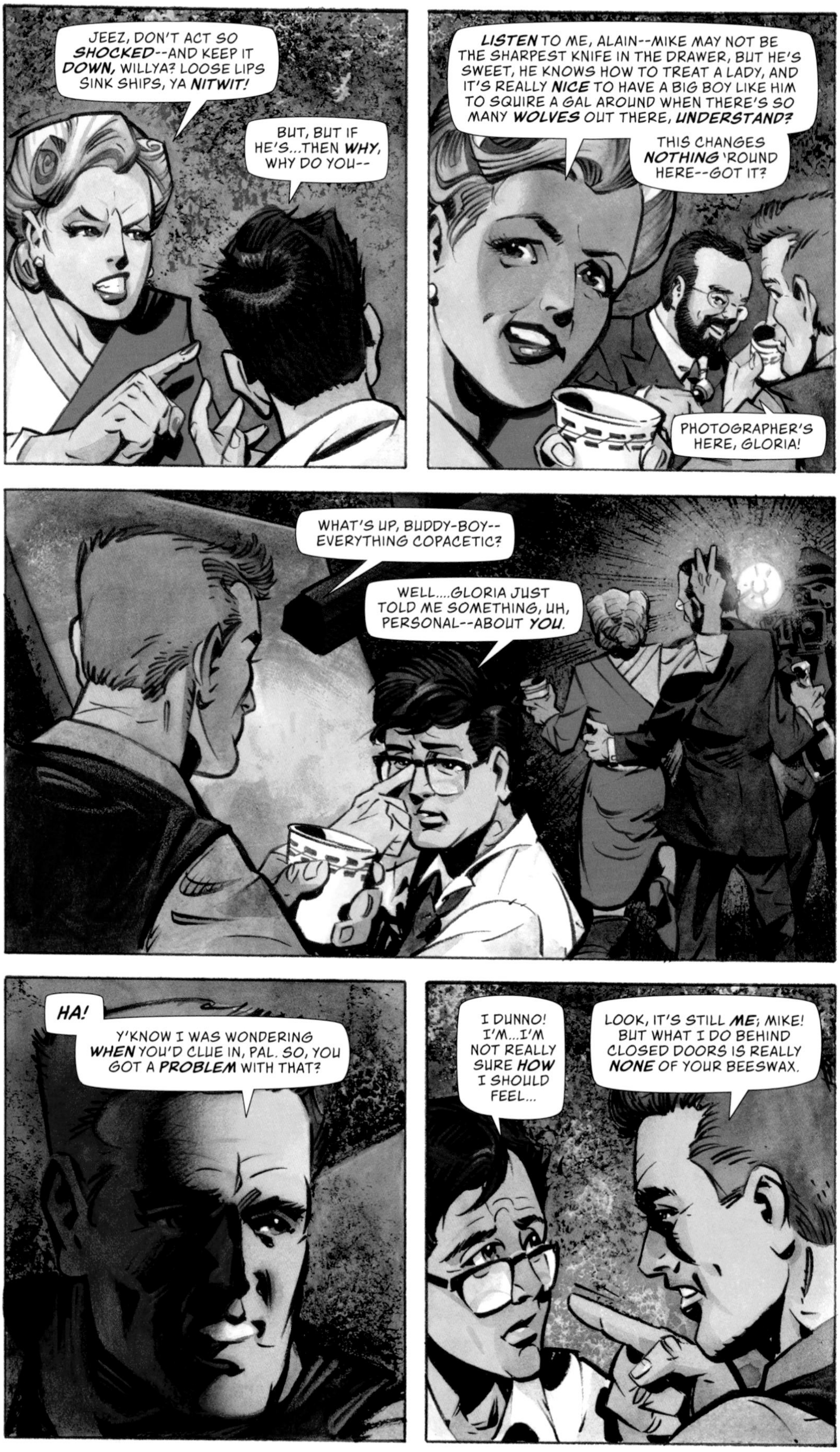
JEEZ, DON'T ACT SO SHOCKED--AND KEEP IT DOWN, WILLYA? LOOSE LIPS SINK SHIPS, YA NITWIT!
BUT, BUT IF HE'S...THEN WHY, WHY DO YOU--
LISTEN TO ME, ALAIN--MIKE MAY NOT BE THE SHARPEST KNIFE IN THE DRAWER, BUT HE'S SWEET, HE KNOWS HOW TO TREAT A LADY, AND IT'S REALLY NICE TO HAVE A BIG BOY LIKE HIM TO SQUIRE A GAL AROUND WHEN THERE'S SO MANY WOLVES OUT THERE, UNDERSTAND?
THIS CHANGES NOTHING 'ROUND HERE--GOT IT?
PHOTOGRAPHER'S HERE, GLORIA!
WHAT'S UP, BUDDY-BOY--EVERYTHING COPACETIC?
WELL....GLORIA JUST TOLD ME SOMETHING, UH, PERSONAL--ABOUT YOU.
HA!
Y'KNOW I WAS WONDERING WHEN YOU'D CLUE IN, PAL. SO, YOU GOT A PROBLEM WITH THAT?
I DUNNO! I'M...I'M NOT REALLY SURE HOW I SHOULD FEEL...
LOOK, IT'S STILL ME; MIKE! BUT WHAT I DO BEHIND CLOSED DOORS IS REALLY NONE OF YOUR BEESWAX.

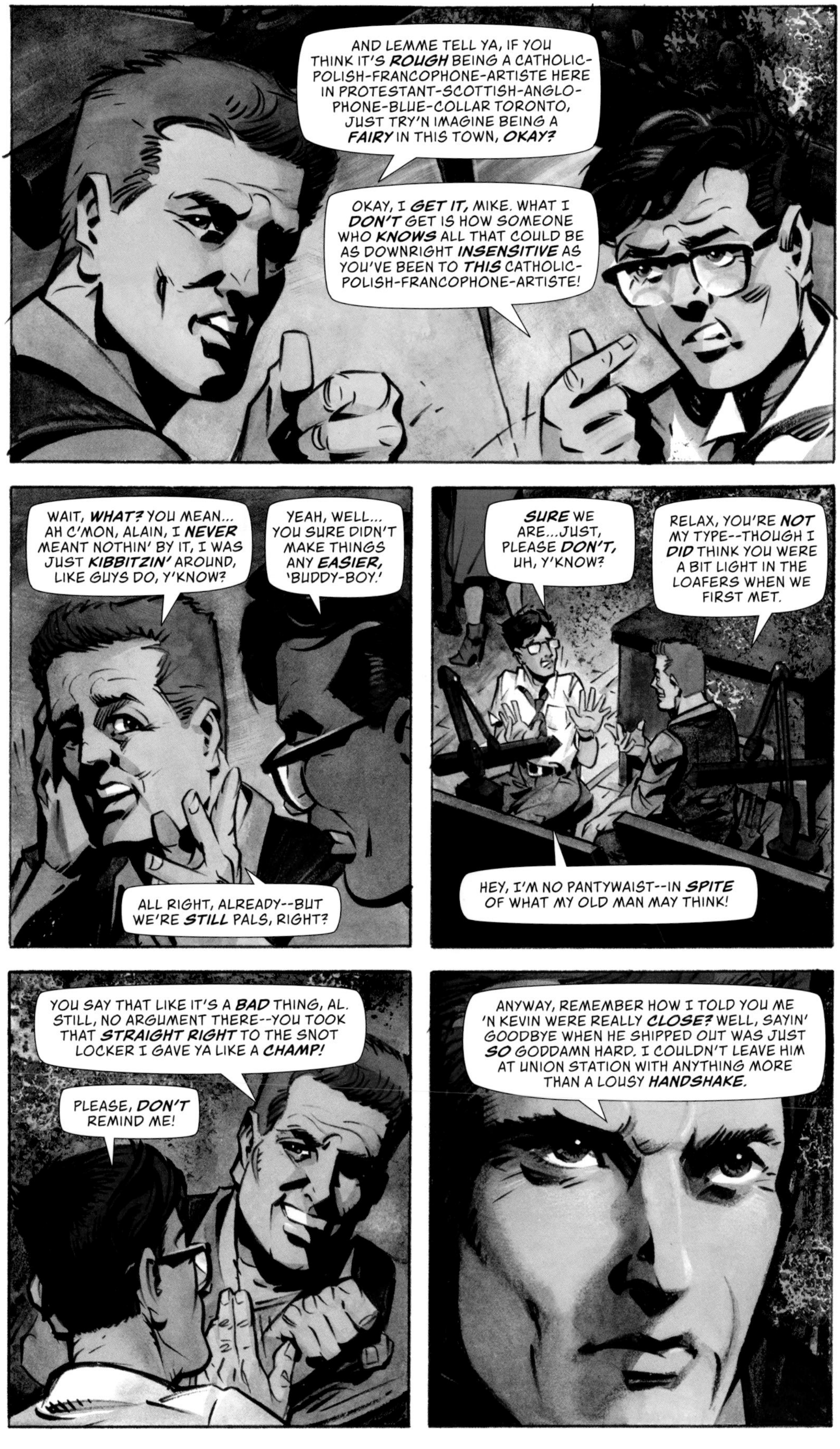
AND LEMME TELL YA, IF YOU THINK IT'S ROUGH BEING A CATHOLIC-POLISH-FRANCOPHONE-ARTISTE HERE IN PROTESTANT-SCOTTISH-ANGLO-PHONE-BLUE-COLLAR TORONTO, JUST TRY'N IMAGINE BEING A FAIRY IN THIS TOWN, OKAY?
OKAY, I GET IT, MIKE. WHAT I DON'T GET IS HOW SOMEONE WHO KNOWS ALL THAT COULD BE AS DOWNRIGHT INSENSITIVE AS YOU'VE BEEN TO THIS CATHOLIC-POLISH-FRANCOPHONE-ARTISTE!
WAIT, WHAT? YOU MEAN... AH C'MON, ALAIN, I NEVER MEANT NOTHIN' BY IT, I WAS JUST KIBBITZIN' AROUND, LIKE GUYS DO, Y'KNOW?
YEAH, WELL... YOU SURE DIDN'T MAKE THINGS ANY EASIER, 'BUDDY-BOY.'
ALL RIGHT, ALREADY--BUT WE'RE STILL PALS, RIGHT?
SURE WE ARE...JUST, PLEASE DON'T, UH, Y'KNOW?
RELAX, YOU'RE NOT MY TYPE--THOUGH I DID THINK YOU WERE A BIT LIGHT IN THE LOAFERS WHEN WE FIRST MET.
HEY, I'M NO PANTYWAIST--IN SPITE OF WHAT MY OLD MAN MAY THINK!
YOU SAY THAT LIKE IT'S A BAD THING, AL. STILL, NO ARGUMENT THERE--YOU TOOK THAT STRAIGHT RIGHT TO THE SNOT LOCKER I GAVE YA LIKE A CHAMP!
PLEASE, DON'T REMIND ME!
ANYWAY, REMEMBER HOW I TOLD YOU ME 'N KEVIN WERE REALLY CLOSE? WELL, SAYIN' GOODBYE WHEN HE SHIPPED OUT WAS JUST SO GODDAMN HARD. I COULDN'T LEAVE HIM AT UNION STATION WITH ANYTHING MORE THAN A LOUSY HANDSHAKE.

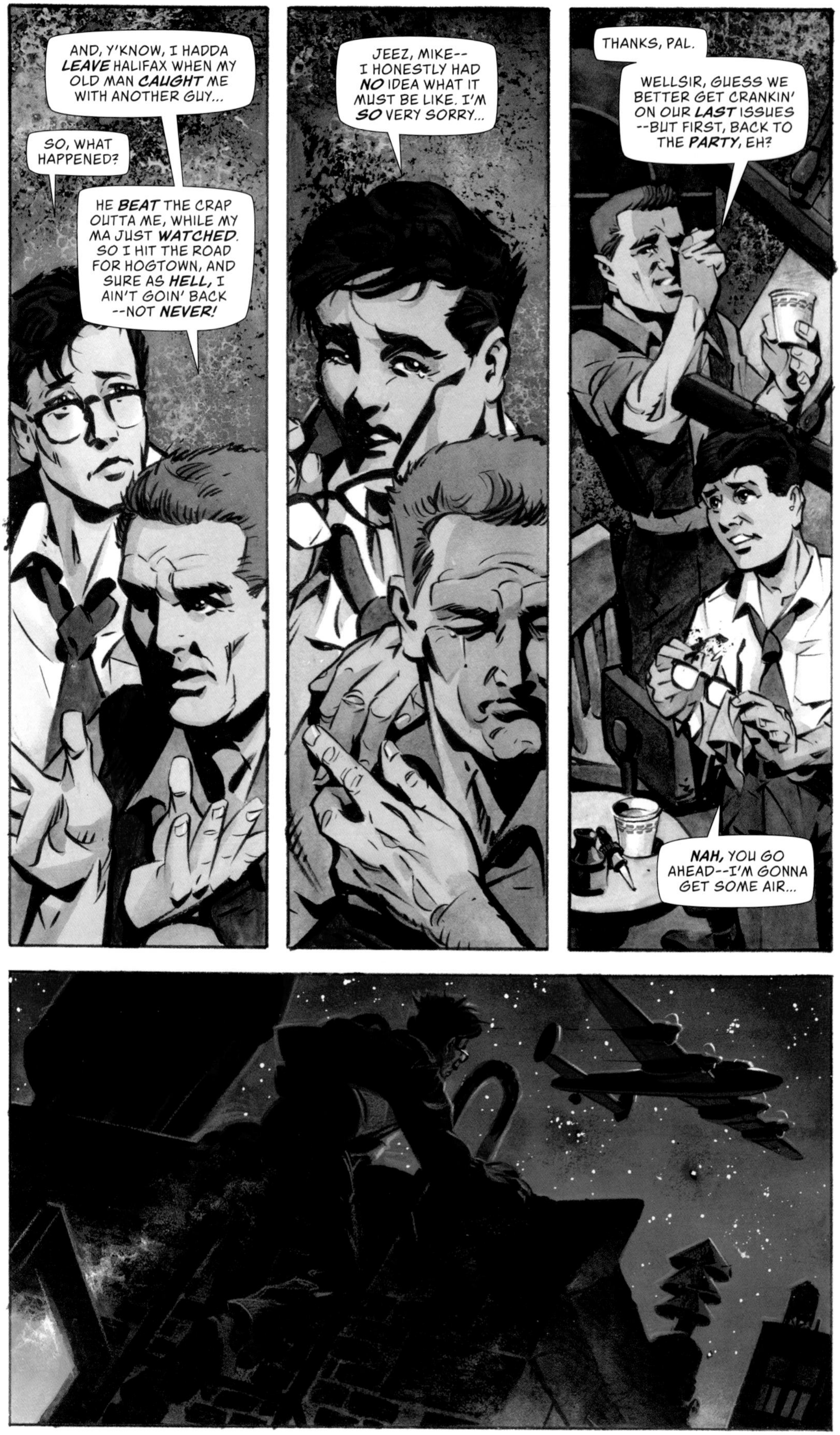
AND, Y'KNOW, I HADDA LEAVE HALIFAX WHEN MY OLD MAN CAUGHT ME WITH ANOTHER GUY...
SO, WHAT HAPPENED?
HE BEAT THE CRAP OUTTA ME, WHILE MY MA JUST WATCHED. SO I HIT THE ROAD FOR HOGTOWN, AND SURE AS HELL, I AIN'T GOIN' BACK --NOT NEVER!
JEEZ, MIKE-- I HONESTLY HAD NO IDEA WHAT IT MUST BE LIKE. I'M SO VERY SORRY...
THANKS, PAL.
WELLSIR, GUESS WE BETTER GET CRANKIN' ON OUR LAST ISSUES --BUT FIRST, BACK TO THE PARTY, EH?
NAH, YOU GO AHEAD--I'M GONNA GET SOME AIR...

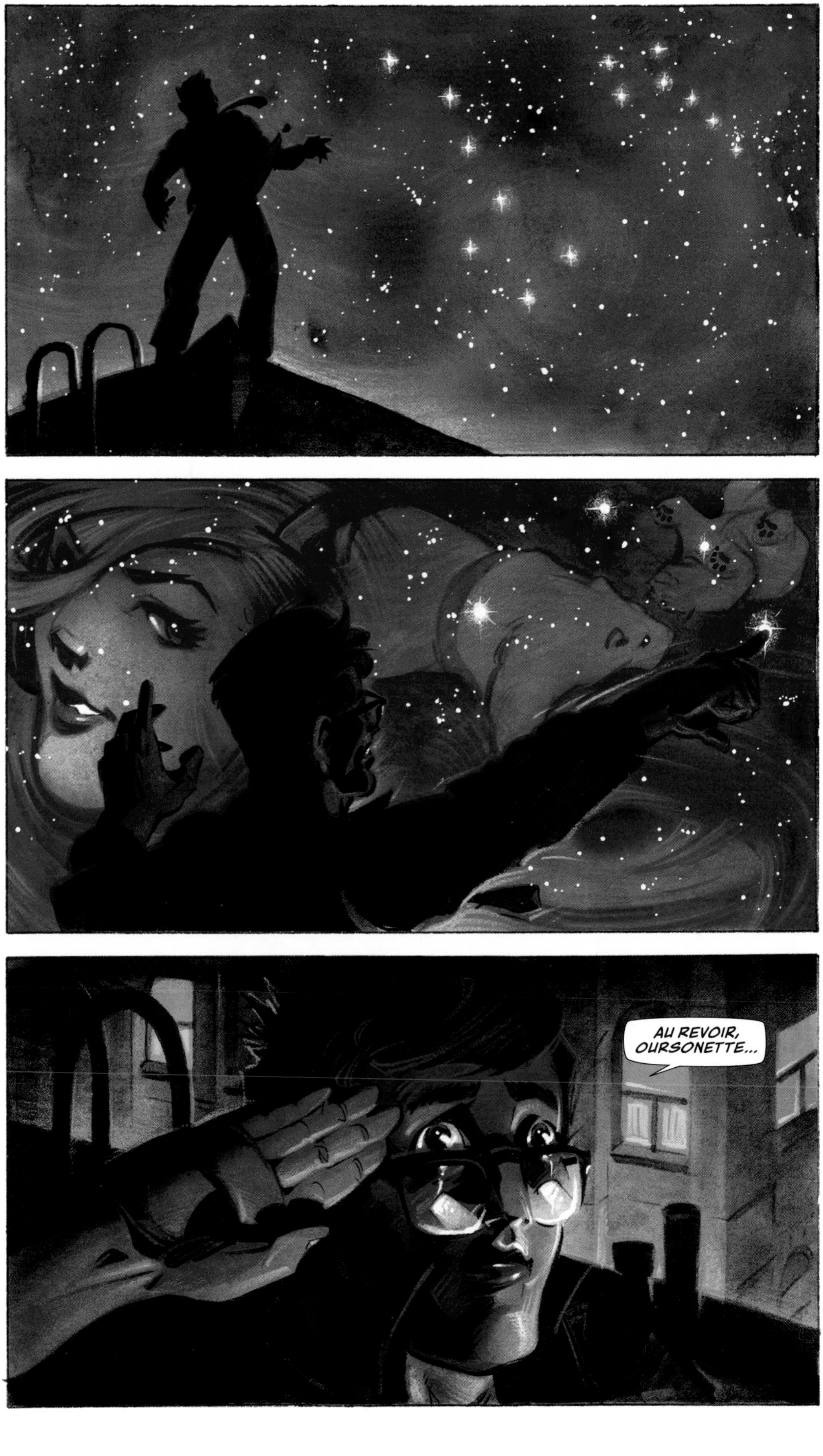
AU REVOIR, OURSONETTE...

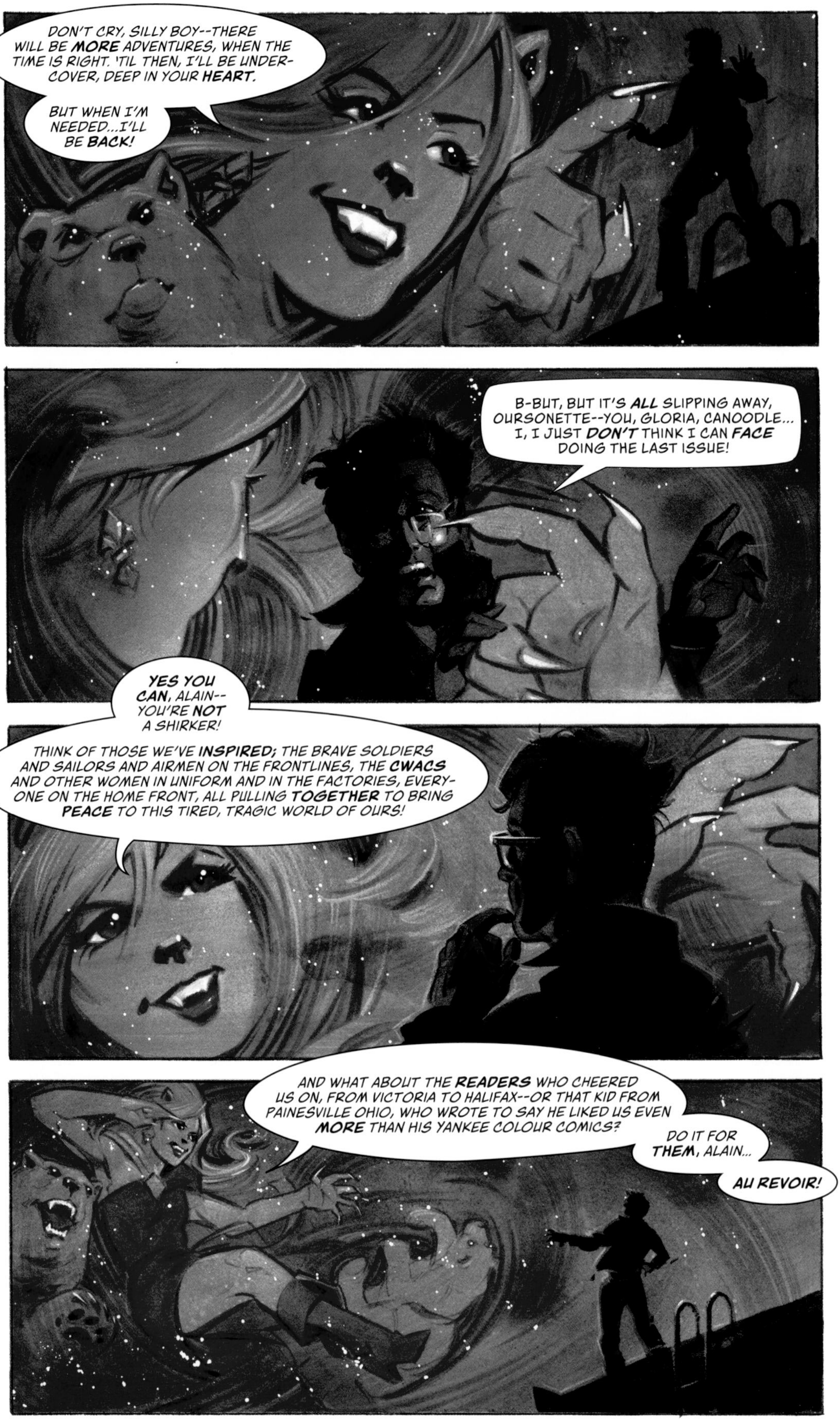
DON'T CRY, SILLY BOY--THERE WILL BE MORE ADVENTURES, WHEN THE TIME IS RIGHT. 'TIL THEN, I'LL BE UNDER-COVER, DEEP IN YOUR HEART.
BUT WHEN I'M NEEDED...I'LL BE BACK!
B-BUT, BUT IT'S ALL SLIPPING AWAY, OURSONETTE--YOU, GLORIA, CANOODLE... I, I JUST DON'T THINK I CAN FACE DOING THE LAST ISSUE!
YES YOU CAN, ALAIN--YOU'RE NOT A SHIRKER!
THINK OF THOSE WE'VE INSPIRED; THE BRAVE SOLDIERS AND SAILORS AND AIRMEN ON THE FRONTLINES, THE CWACS AND OTHER WOMEN IN UNIFORM AND IN THE FACTORIES, EVERY-ONE ON THE HOME FRONT, ALL PULLING TOGETHER TO BRING PEACE TO THIS TIRED, TRAGIC WORLD OF OURS!
AND WHAT ABOUT THE READERS WHO CHEERED US ON, FROM VICTORIA TO HALIFAX--OR THAT KID FROM PAINESVILLE OHIO, WHO WROTE TO SAY HE LIKED US EVEN MORE THAN HIS YANKEE COLOUR COMICS?
DO IT FOR THEM, ALAIN...
AU REVOIR!

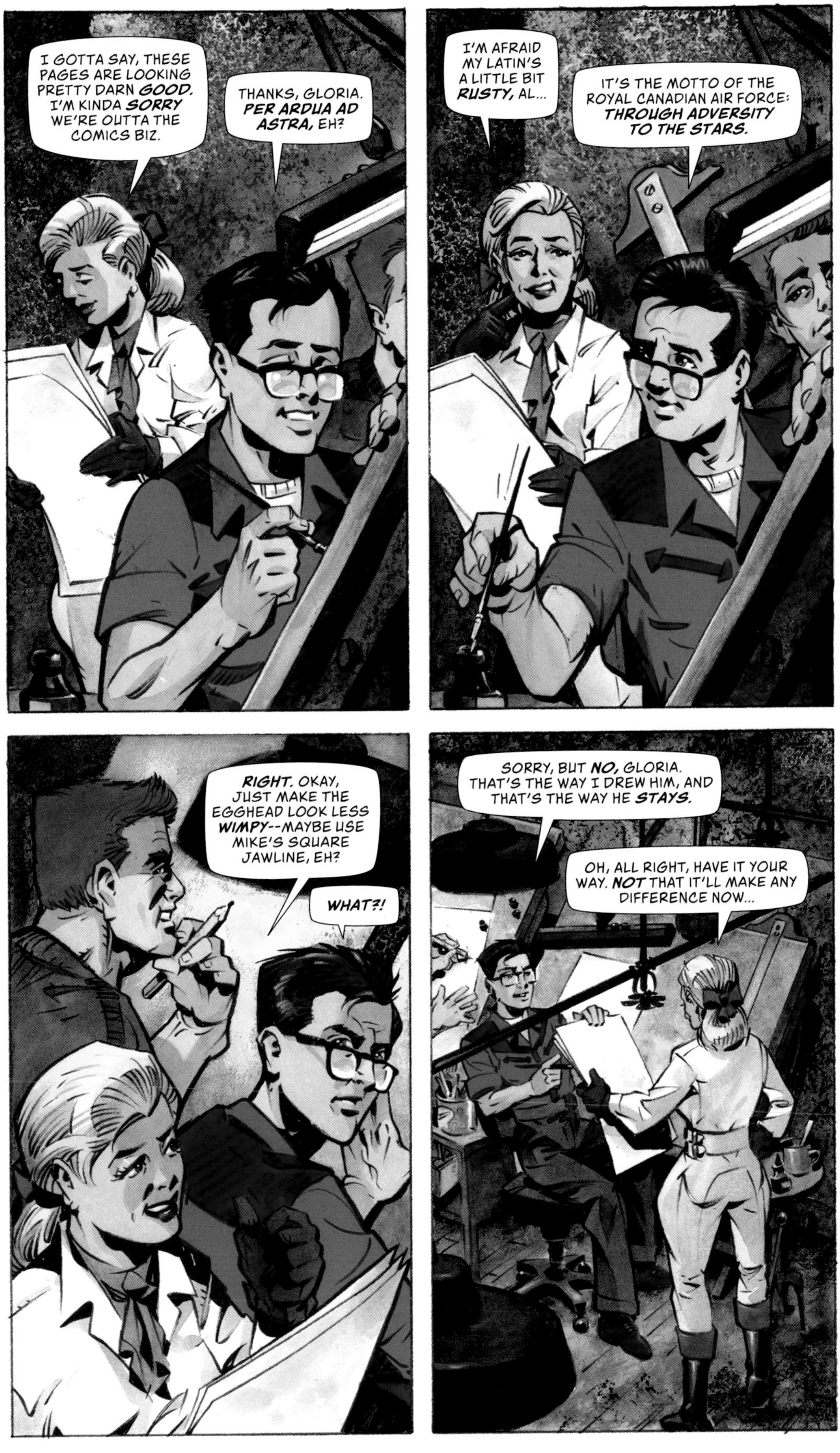
I GOTTA SAY, THESE PAGES ARE LOOKING PRETTY DARN GOOD. I'M KINDA SORRY WE'RE OUTTA THE COMICS BIZ.
THANKS, GLORIA. PER ARDUA AD ASTRA, EH?
I'M AFRAID MY LATIN'S A LITTLE BIT RUSTY, AL...
IT'S THE MOTTO OF THE ROYAL CANADIAN AIR FORCE: THROUGH ADVERSITY TO THE STARS.
RIGHT. OKAY, JUST MAKE THE EGGHEAD LOOK LESS WIMPY--MAYBE USE MIKE'S SQUARE JAWLINE, EH?
WHAT?!
SORRY, BUT NO, GLORIA. THAT'S THE WAY I DREW HIM, AND THAT'S THE WAY HE STAYS.
OH, ALL RIGHT, HAVE IT YOUR WAY. NOT THAT IT'LL MAKE ANY DIFFERENCE NOW...

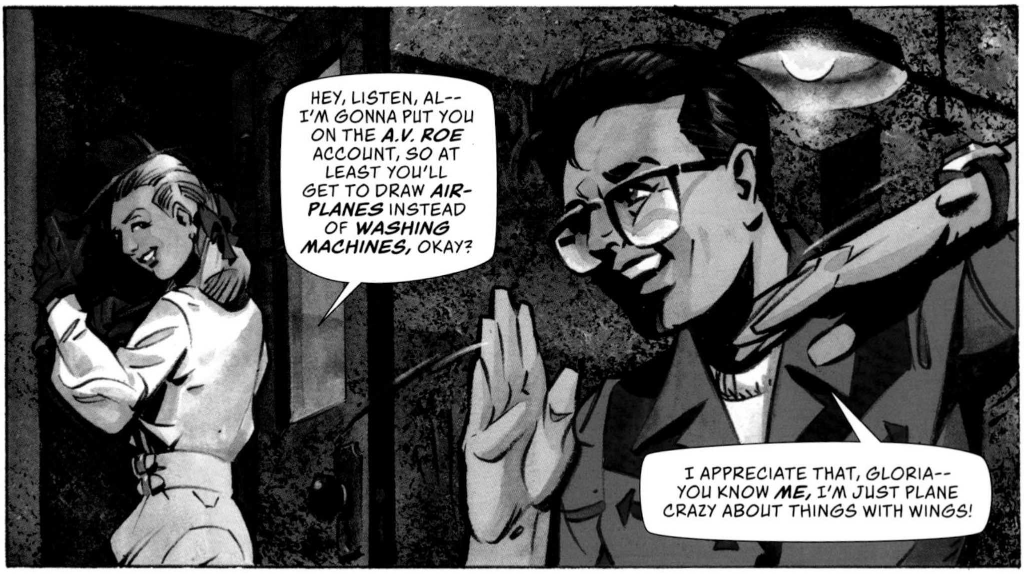
HEY, LISTEN, AL-- I'M GONNA PUT YOU ON THE **A.V. ROE** ACCOUNT, SO AT LEAST YOU'LL GET TO DRAW **AIR-PLANES** INSTEAD OF **WASHING MACHINES,** OKAY?
I APPRECIATE THAT, GLORIA-- YOU KNOW **ME,** I'M JUST PLANE CRAZY ABOUT THINGS WITH WINGS!

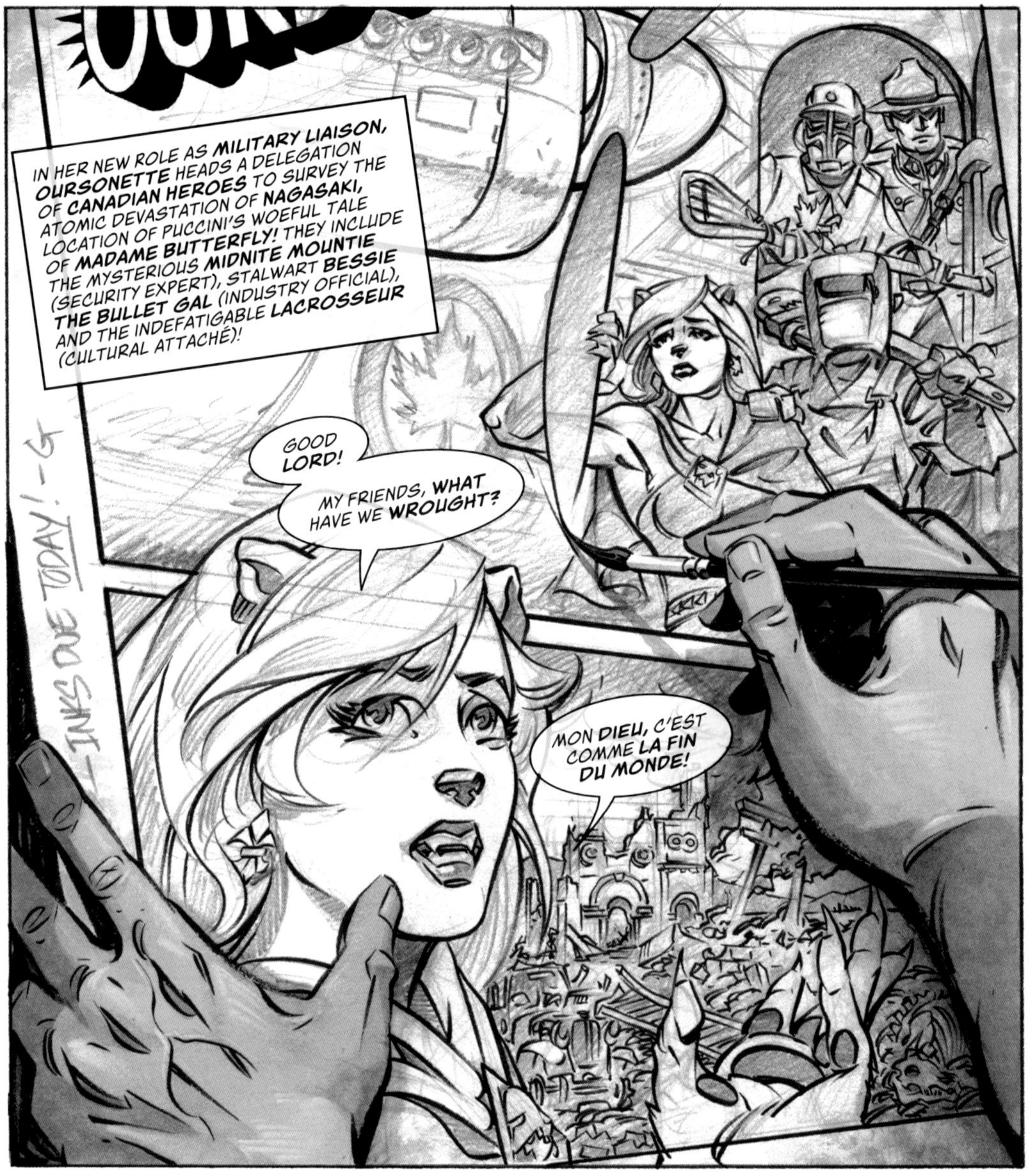
IN HER NEW ROLE AS **MILITARY LIAISON, OURSONETTE** HEADS A DELEGATION OF **CANADIAN HEROES** TO SURVEY THE ATOMIC DEVASTATION OF **NAGASAKI,** LOCATION OF PUCCINI'S WOEFUL TALE OF **MADAME BUTTERFLY!** THEY INCLUDE THE MYSTERIOUS **MIDNITE MOUNTIE** (SECURITY EXPERT), STALWART **BESSIE THE BULLET GAL** (INDUSTRY OFFICIAL), AND THE INDEFATIGABLE **LACROSSEUR** (CULTURAL ATTACHÉ)!
GOOD **LORD!**
MY FRIENDS, **WHAT** HAVE WE **WROUGHT?**
MON **DIEU,** C'EST COMME **LA FIN DU MONDE!**
INKS DUE TODAY! -G

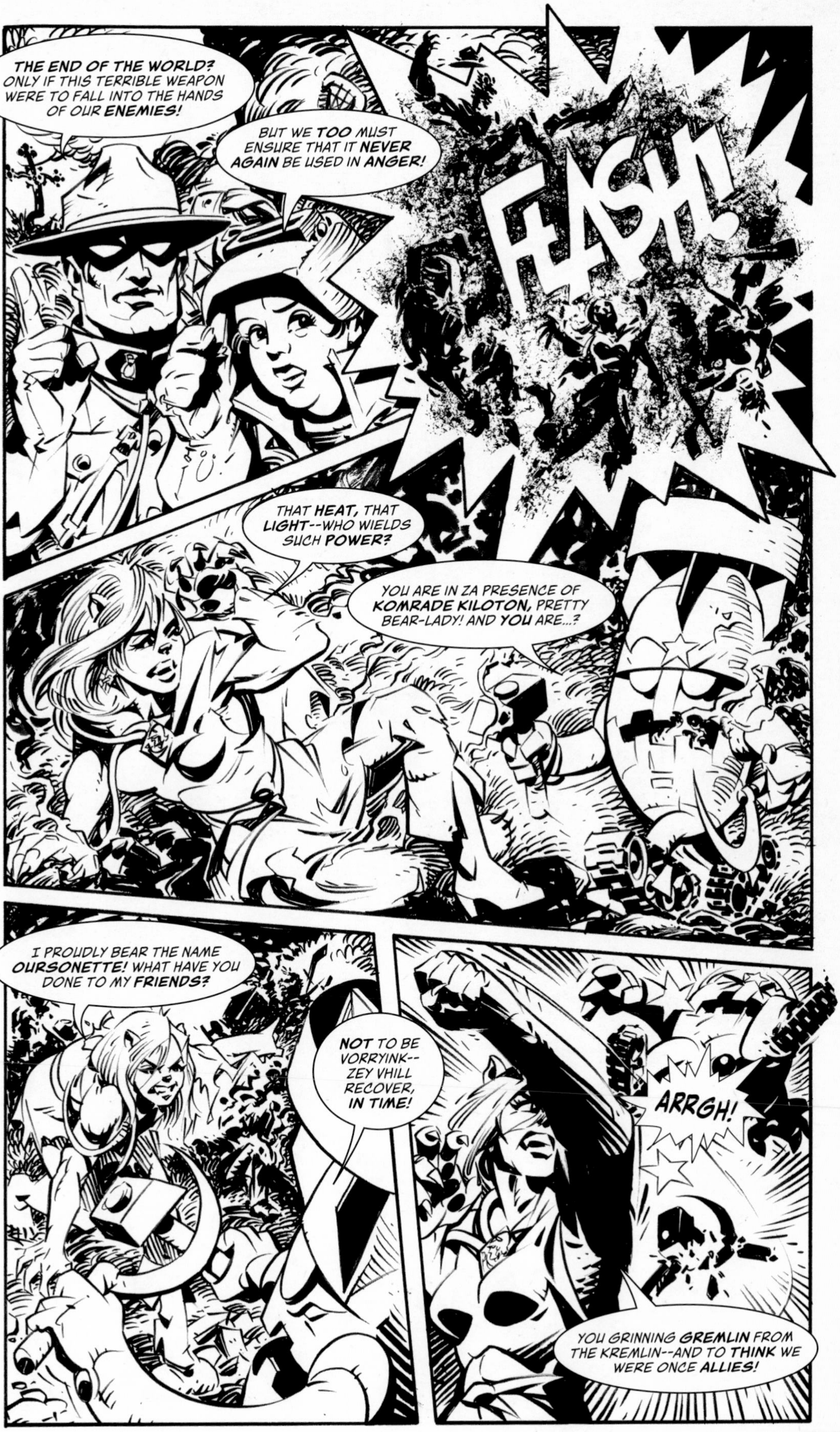
THE END OF THE WORLD? ONLY IF THIS TERRIBLE WEAPON WERE TO FALL INTO THE HANDS OF OUR ENEMIES!
BUT WE TOO MUST ENSURE THAT IT NEVER AGAIN BE USED IN ANGER!
FLASH!
THAT HEAT, THAT LIGHT--WHO WIELDS SUCH POWER?
YOU ARE IN ZA PRESENCE OF KOMRADE KILOTON, PRETTY BEAR-LADY! AND YOU ARE...?
I PROUDLY BEAR THE NAME OURSONETTE! WHAT HAVE YOU DONE TO MY FRIENDS?
NOT TO BE VORRYINK--ZEY VHILL RECOVER, IN TIME!
ARRGH!
YOU GRINNING GREMLIN FROM THE KREMLIN--AND TO THINK WE WERE ONCE ALLIES!

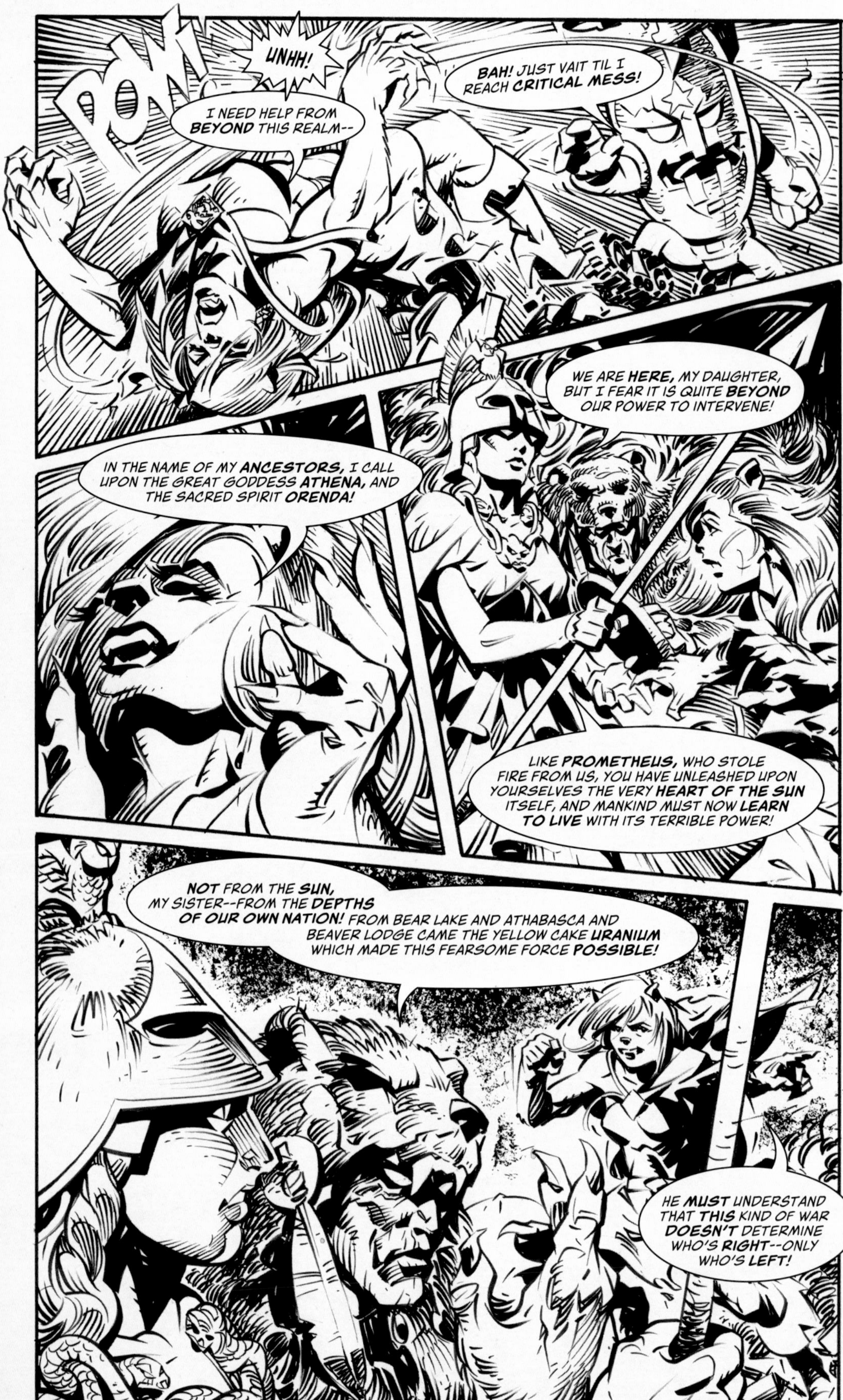
POW!
UNHH!
I NEED HELP FROM BEYOND THIS REALM--
BAH! JUST VAIT TIL I REACH CRITICAL MESS!
WE ARE HERE, MY DAUGHTER, BUT I FEAR IT IS QUITE BEYOND OUR POWER TO INTERVENE!
IN THE NAME OF MY ANCESTORS, I CALL UPON THE GREAT GODDESS ATHENA, AND THE SACRED SPIRIT ORENDA!
LIKE PROMETHEUS, WHO STOLE FIRE FROM US, YOU HAVE UNLEASHED UPON YOURSELVES THE VERY HEART OF THE SUN ITSELF, AND MANKIND MUST NOW LEARN TO LIVE WITH ITS TERRIBLE POWER!
NOT FROM THE SUN, MY SISTER--FROM THE DEPTHS OF OUR OWN NATION! FROM BEAR LAKE AND ATHABASCA AND BEAVER LODGE CAME THE YELLOW CAKE URANIUM WHICH MADE THIS FEARSOME FORCE POSSIBLE!
HE MUST UNDERSTAND THAT THIS KIND OF WAR DOESN'T DETERMINE WHO'S RIGHT--ONLY WHO'S LEFT!

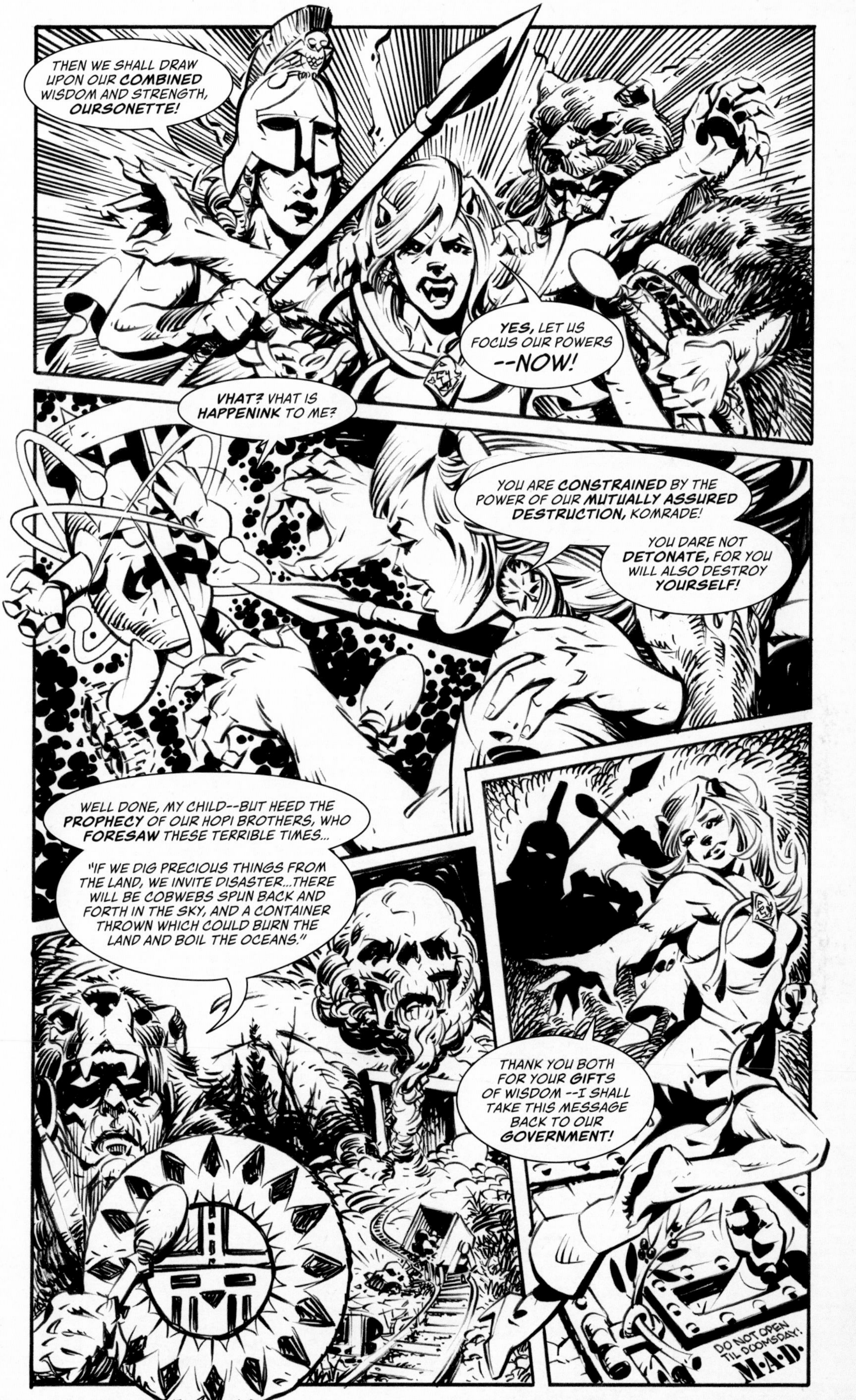
THEN WE SHALL DRAW UPON OUR COMBINED WISDOM AND STRENGTH, OURSONETTE!
YES, LET US FOCUS OUR POWERS --NOW!
VHAT? VHAT IS HAPPENINK TO ME?
YOU ARE CONSTRAINED BY THE POWER OF OUR MUTUALLY ASSURED DESTRUCTION, KOMRADE!
YOU DARE NOT DETONATE, FOR YOU WILL ALSO DESTROY YOURSELF!
WELL DONE, MY CHILD--BUT HEED THE PROPHECY OF OUR HOPI BROTHERS, WHO FORESAW THESE TERRIBLE TIMES...
"IF WE DIG PRECIOUS THINGS FROM THE LAND, WE INVITE DISASTER...THERE WILL BE COBWEBS SPUN BACK AND FORTH IN THE SKY, AND A CONTAINER THROWN WHICH COULD BURN THE LAND AND BOIL THE OCEANS."
THANK YOU BOTH FOR YOUR GIFTS OF WISDOM --I SHALL TAKE THIS MESSAGE BACK TO OUR GOVERNMENT!
DO NOT OPEN TIL DOOMSDAY!
M·A·D·

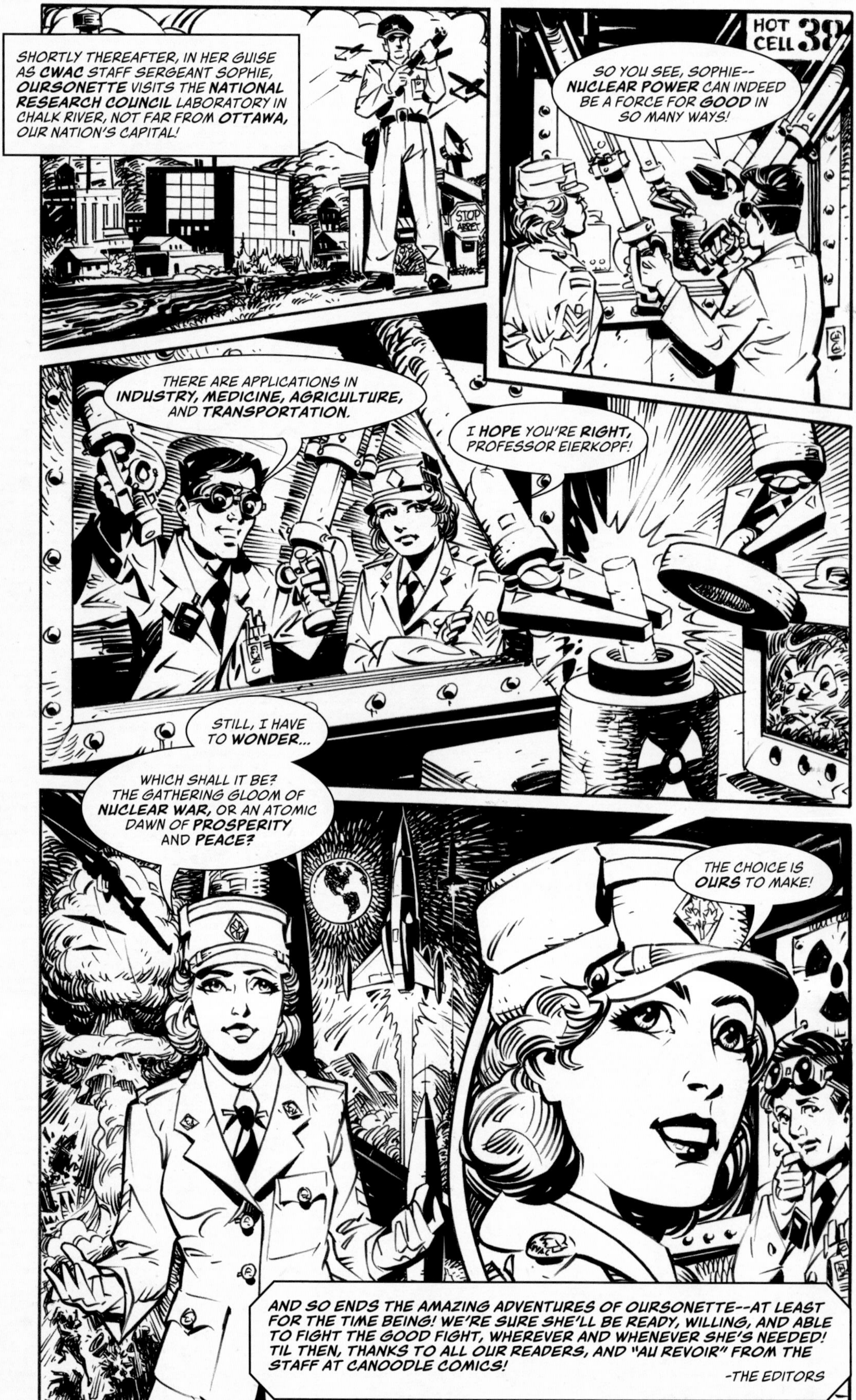
SHORTLY THEREAFTER, IN HER GUISE AS CWAC STAFF SERGEANT SOPHIE, OURSONETTE VISITS THE NATIONAL RESEARCH COUNCIL LABORATORY IN CHALK RIVER, NOT FAR FROM OTTAWA, OUR NATION'S CAPITAL!
STOP
HOT CELL 38
SO YOU SEE, SOPHIE-- NUCLEAR POWER CAN INDEED BE A FORCE FOR GOOD IN SO MANY WAYS!
THERE ARE APPLICATIONS IN INDUSTRY, MEDICINE, AGRICULTURE, AND TRANSPORTATION.
I HOPE YOU'RE RIGHT, PROFESSOR EIERKOPF!
STILL, I HAVE TO WONDER...
WHICH SHALL IT BE? THE GATHERING GLOOM OF NUCLEAR WAR, OR AN ATOMIC DAWN OF PROSPERITY AND PEACE?
THE CHOICE IS OURS TO MAKE!
AND SO ENDS THE AMAZING ADVENTURES OF OURSONETTE--AT LEAST FOR THE TIME BEING! WE'RE SURE SHE'LL BE READY, WILLING, AND ABLE TO FIGHT THE GOOD FIGHT, WHEREVER AND WHENEVER SHE'S NEEDED! TIL THEN, THANKS TO ALL OUR READERS, AND "AU REVOIR" FROM THE STAFF AT CANOODLE COMICS!
-THE EDITORS

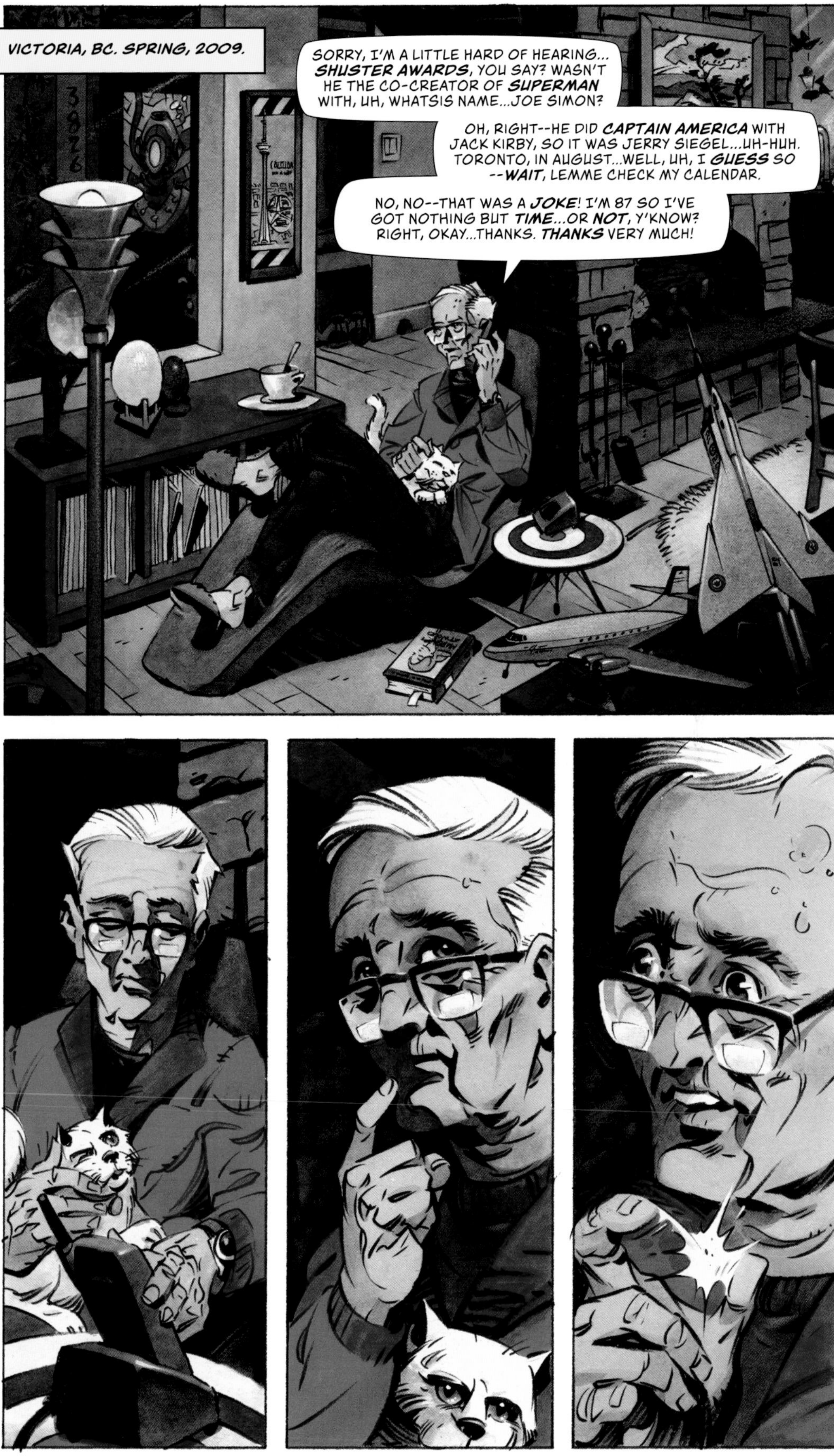
VICTORIA, BC. SPRING, 2009.
SORRY, I'M A LITTLE HARD OF HEARING... SHUSTER AWARDS, YOU SAY? WASN'T HE THE CO-CREATOR OF SUPERMAN WITH, UH, WHATSIS NAME...JOE SIMON?
OH, RIGHT--HE DID CAPTAIN AMERICA WITH JACK KIRBY, SO IT WAS JERRY SIEGEL...UH-HUH. TORONTO, IN AUGUST...WELL, UH, I GUESS SO --WAIT, LEMME CHECK MY CALENDAR.
NO, NO--THAT WAS A JOKE! I'M 87 SO I'VE GOT NOTHING BUT TIME...OR NOT, Y'KNOW? RIGHT, OKAY...THANKS. THANKS VERY MUCH!

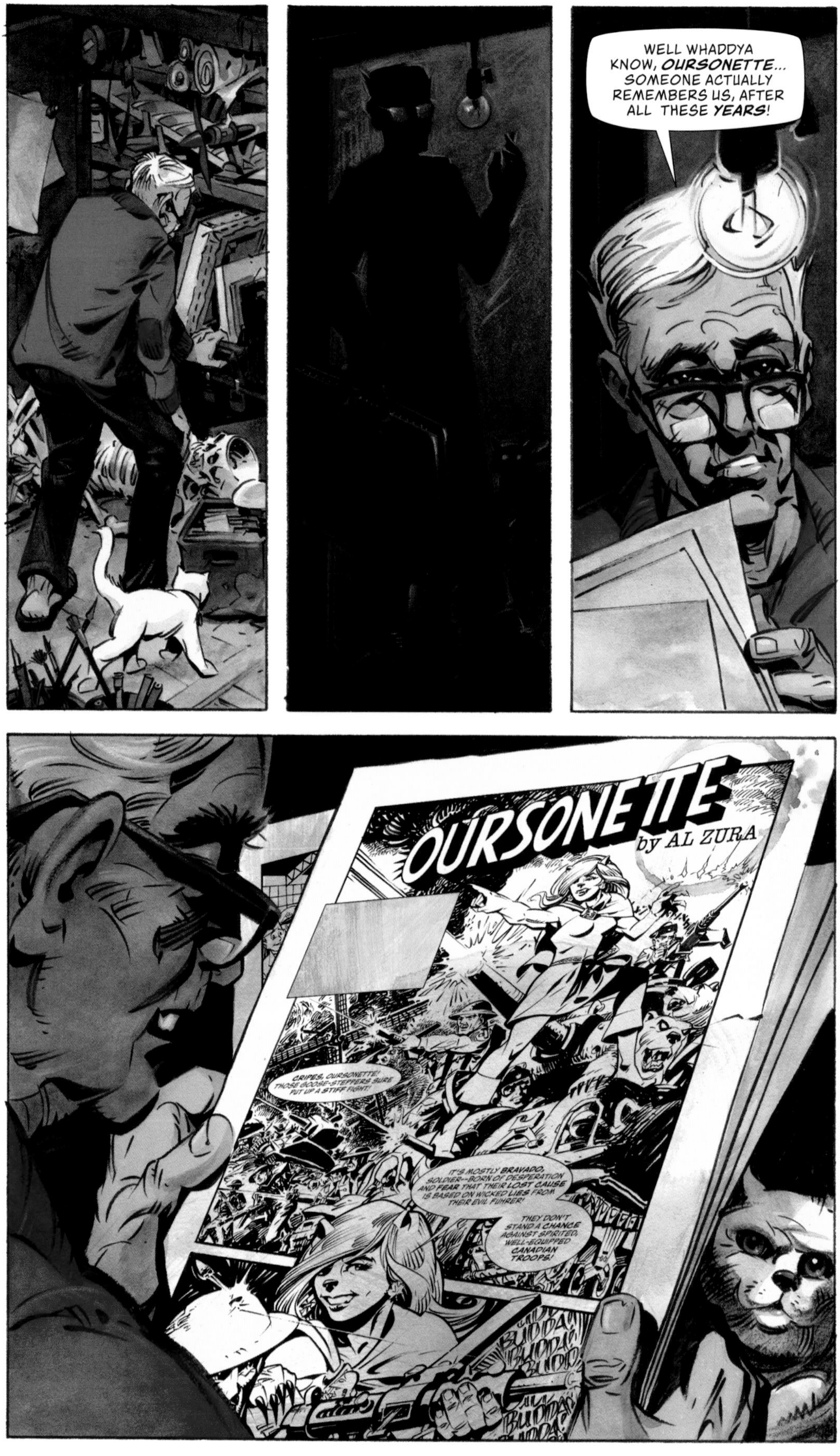
WELL WHADDYA KNOW, OURSONETTE... SOMEONE ACTUALLY REMEMBERS US, AFTER ALL THESE YEARS!
OURSONETTE
by AL ZURA
CRIPES, OURSONETTE! THOSE GOOSE-STEPPERS SURE PUT UP A STIFF FIGHT!
IT'S MOSTLY BRAVADO, SOLDIER--BORN OF DESPERATION AND FEAR THAT THEIR LOST CAUSE IS BASED ON WICKED LIES FROM THEIR EVIL FUHRER!
THEY DON'T STAND A CHANCE AGAINST SPIRITED, WELL-EQUIPPED CANADIAN TROOPS!

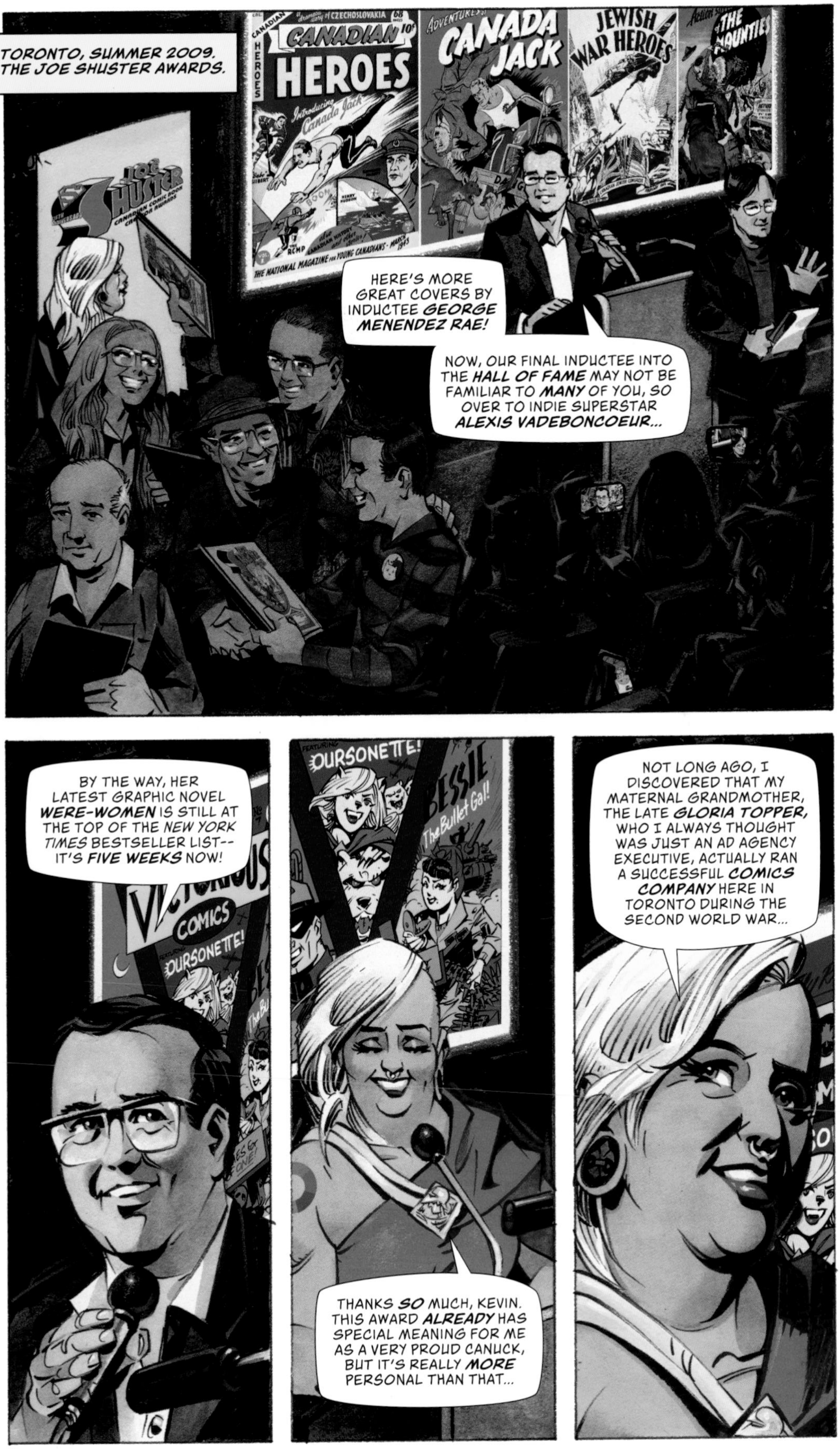

TORONTO, SUMMER 2009. THE JOE SHUSTER AWARDS.
HERE'S MORE GREAT COVERS BY INDUCTEE GEORGE MENENDEZ RAE!
NOW, OUR FINAL INDUCTEE INTO THE HALL OF FAME MAY NOT BE FAMILIAR TO MANY OF YOU, SO OVER TO INDIE SUPERSTAR ALEXIS VADEBONCOEUR...
BY THE WAY, HER LATEST GRAPHIC NOVEL WERE-WOMEN IS STILL AT THE TOP OF THE NEW YORK TIMES BESTSELLER LIST-- IT'S FIVE WEEKS NOW!
THANKS SO MUCH, KEVIN. THIS AWARD ALREADY HAS SPECIAL MEANING FOR ME AS A VERY PROUD CANUCK, BUT IT'S REALLY MORE PERSONAL THAN THAT...
NOT LONG AGO, I DISCOVERED THAT MY MATERNAL GRANDMOTHER, THE LATE GLORIA TOPPER, WHO I ALWAYS THOUGHT WAS JUST AN AD AGENCY EXECUTIVE, ACTUALLY RAN A SUCCESSFUL COMICS COMPANY HERE IN TORONTO DURING THE SECOND WORLD WAR...

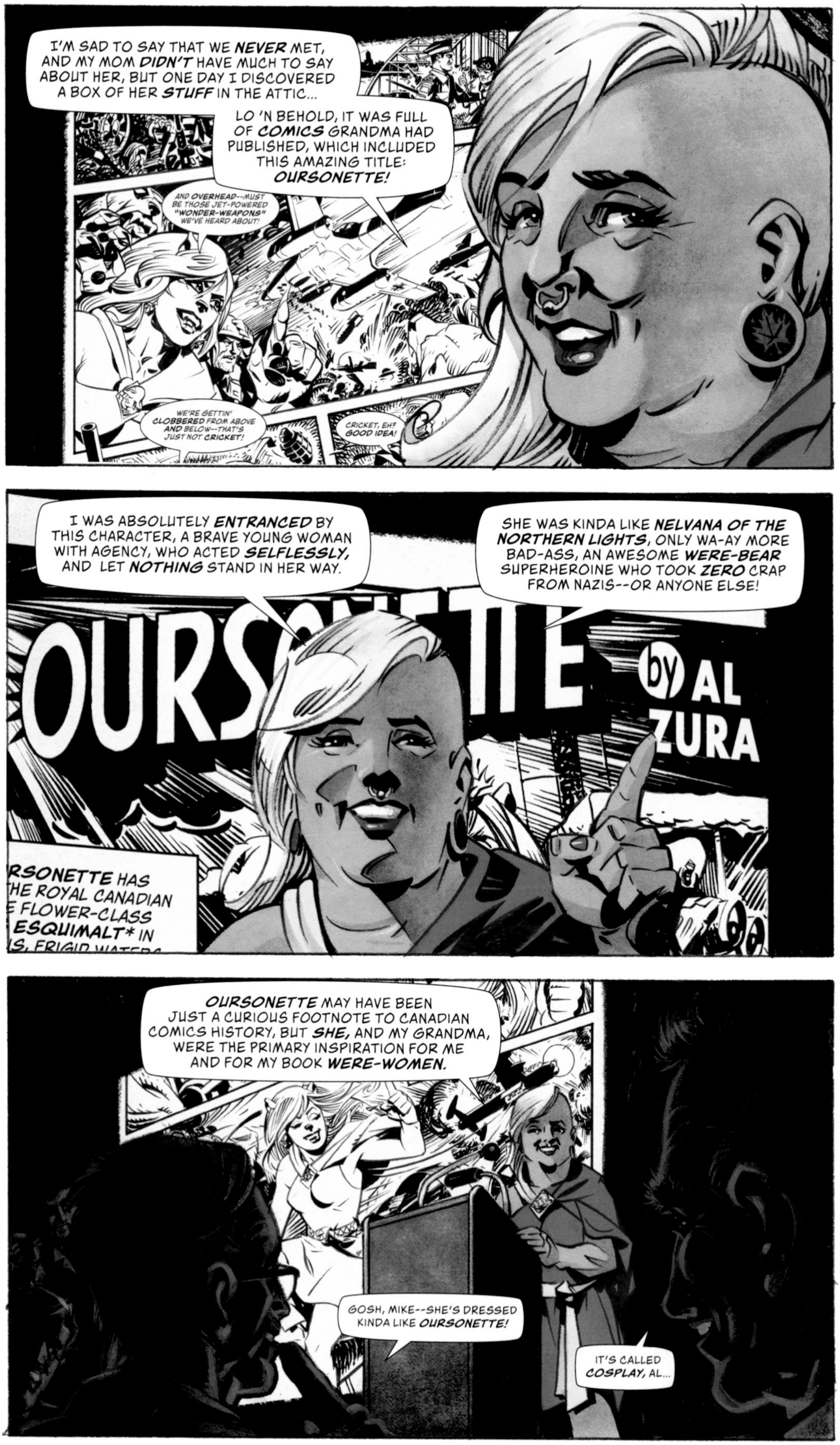
I'M SAD TO SAY THAT WE NEVER MET, AND MY MOM DIDN'T HAVE MUCH TO SAY ABOUT HER, BUT ONE DAY I DISCOVERED A BOX OF HER STUFF IN THE ATTIC...
LO 'N BEHOLD, IT WAS FULL OF COMICS GRANDMA HAD PUBLISHED, WHICH INCLUDED THIS AMAZING TITLE: OURSONETTE!
AND OVERHEAD--MUST BE THOSE JET-POWERED "WONDER-WEAPONS" WE'VE HEARD ABOUT!
WE'RE GETTIN' CLOBBERED FROM ABOVE AND BELOW--THAT'S JUST NOT CRICKET!
CRICKET, EH? GOOD IDEA!
I WAS ABSOLUTELY ENTRANCED BY THIS CHARACTER, A BRAVE YOUNG WOMAN WITH AGENCY, WHO ACTED SELFLESSLY, AND LET NOTHING STAND IN HER WAY.
SHE WAS KINDA LIKE NELVANA OF THE NORTHERN LIGHTS, ONLY WA-AY MORE BAD-ASS, AN AWESOME WERE-BEAR SUPERHEROINE WHO TOOK ZERO CRAP FROM NAZIS--OR ANYONE ELSE!
by AL ZURA
OURSONETTE MAY HAVE BEEN JUST A CURIOUS FOOTNOTE TO CANADIAN COMICS HISTORY, BUT SHE, AND MY GRANDMA, WERE THE PRIMARY INSPIRATION FOR ME AND FOR MY BOOK WERE-WOMEN.
GOSH, MIKE--SHE'S DRESSED KINDA LIKE OURSONETTE!
IT'S CALLED COSPLAY, AL...

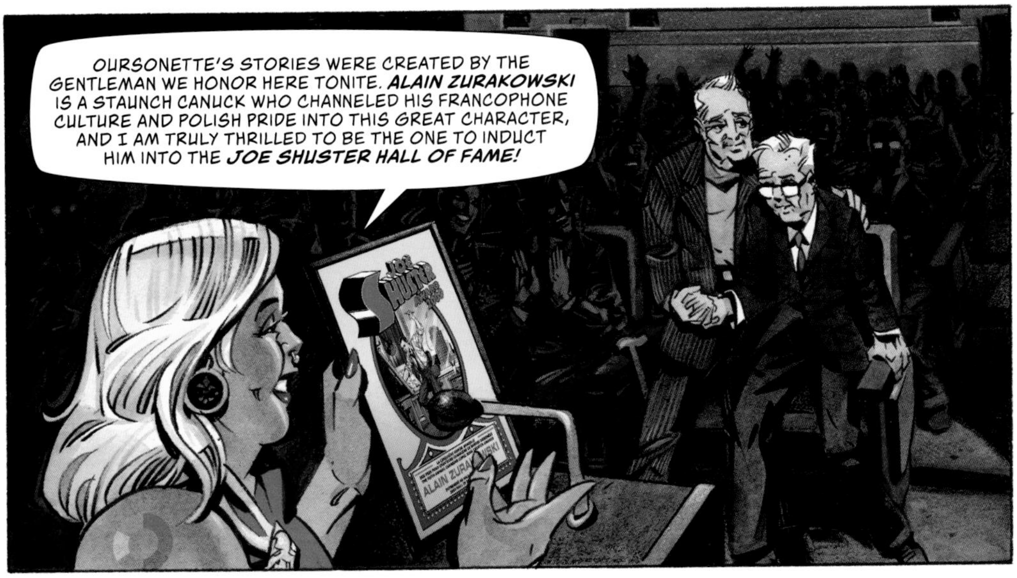
OURSONETTE'S STORIES WERE CREATED BY THE GENTLEMAN WE HONOR HERE TONITE. ALAIN ZURAKOWSKI IS A STAUNCH CANUCK WHO CHANNELED HIS FRANCOPHONE CULTURE AND POLISH PRIDE INTO THIS GREAT CHARACTER, AND I AM TRULY THRILLED TO BE THE ONE TO INDUCT HIM INTO THE JOE SHUSTER HALL OF FAME!

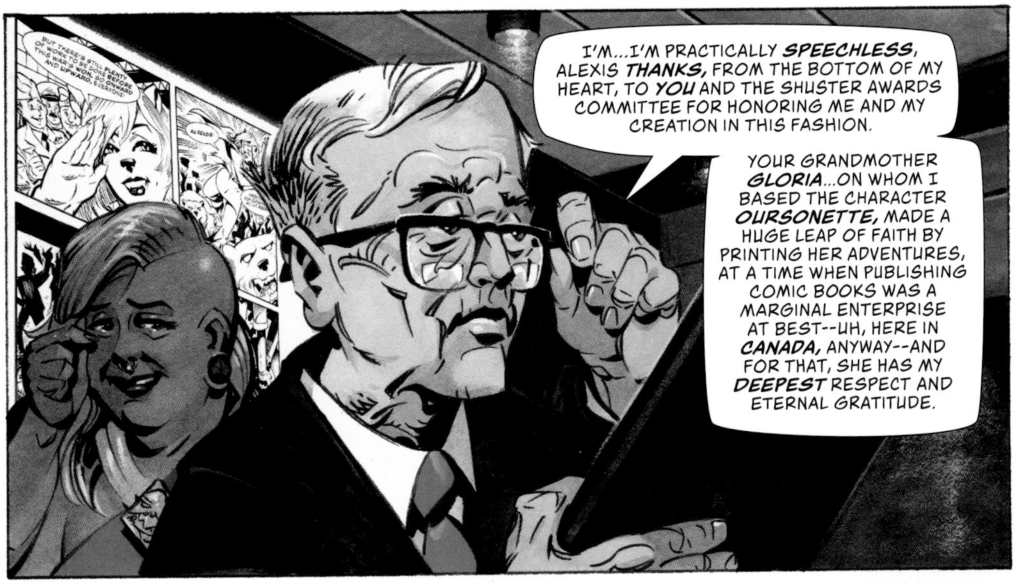
I'M...I'M PRACTICALLY SPEECHLESS, ALEXIS. THANKS, FROM THE BOTTOM OF MY HEART, TO YOU AND THE SHUSTER AWARDS COMMITTEE FOR HONORING ME AND MY CREATION IN THIS FASHION.
YOUR GRANDMOTHER GLORIA...ON WHOM I BASED THE CHARACTER OURSONETTE, MADE A HUGE LEAP OF FAITH BY PRINTING HER ADVENTURES, AT A TIME WHEN PUBLISHING COMIC BOOKS WAS A MARGINAL ENTERPRISE AT BEST--UH, HERE IN CANADA, ANYWAY--AND FOR THAT, SHE HAS MY DEEPEST RESPECT AND ETERNAL GRATITUDE.

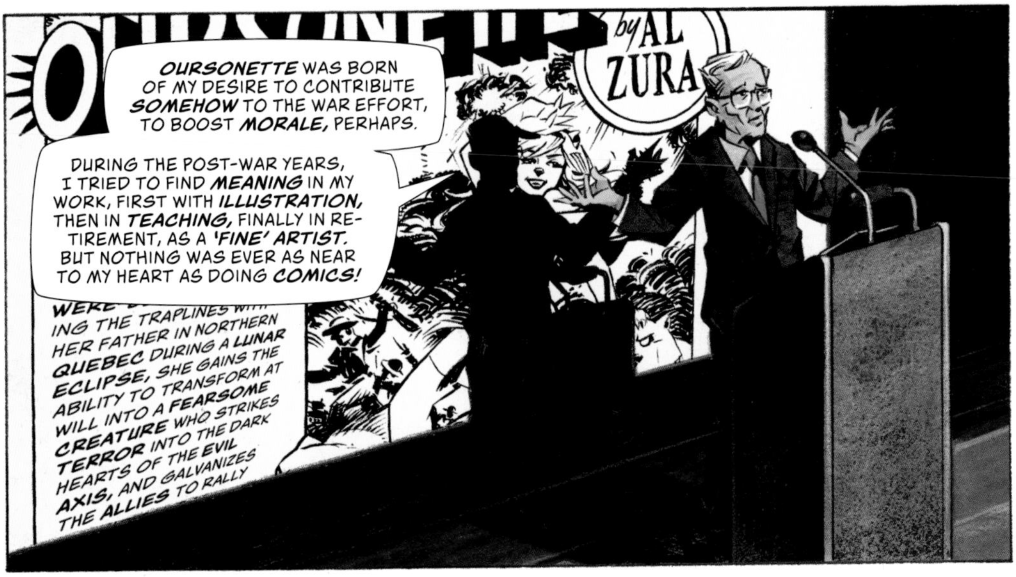
by AL ZURA
OURSONETTE WAS BORN OF MY DESIRE TO CONTRIBUTE SOMEHOW TO THE WAR EFFORT, TO BOOST MORALE, PERHAPS.
DURING THE POST-WAR YEARS, I TRIED TO FIND MEANING IN MY WORK, FIRST WITH ILLUSTRATION, THEN IN TEACHING, FINALLY IN RE-TIREMENT, AS A 'FINE' ARTIST. BUT NOTHING WAS EVER AS NEAR TO MY HEART AS DOING COMICS!
ING THE TRAPLINES WITH HER FATHER IN NORTHERN QUEBEC DURING A LUNAR ECLIPSE, SHE GAINS THE ABILITY TO TRANSFORM AT WILL INTO A FEARSOME CREATURE WHO STRIKES TERROR INTO THE DARK HEARTS OF THE EVIL AXIS, AND GALVANIZES THE ALLIES TO RALLY

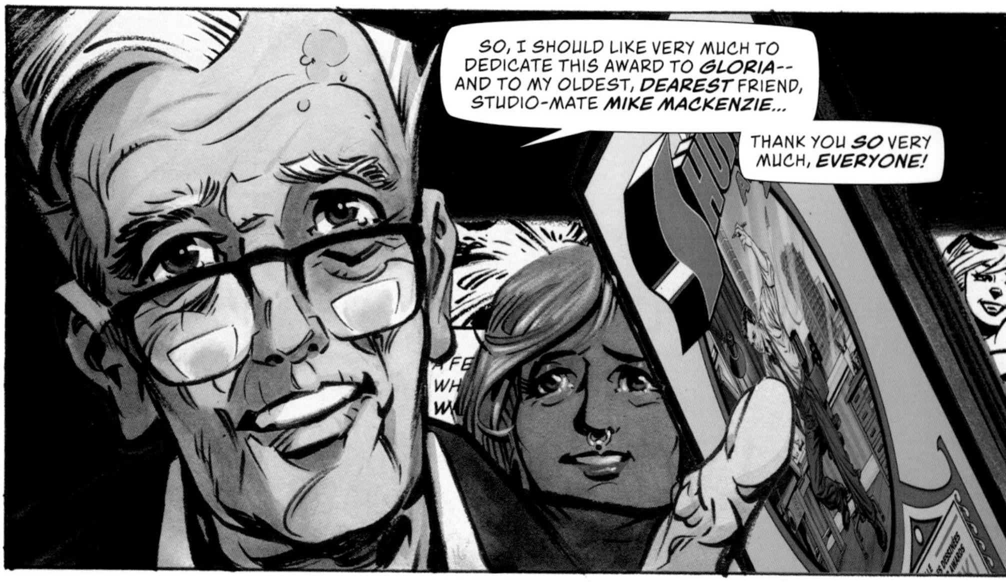
SO, I SHOULD LIKE VERY MUCH TO DEDICATE THIS AWARD TO GLORIA-- AND TO MY OLDEST, DEAREST FRIEND, STUDIO-MATE MIKE MACKENZIE...
THANK YOU SO VERY MUCH, EVERYONE!

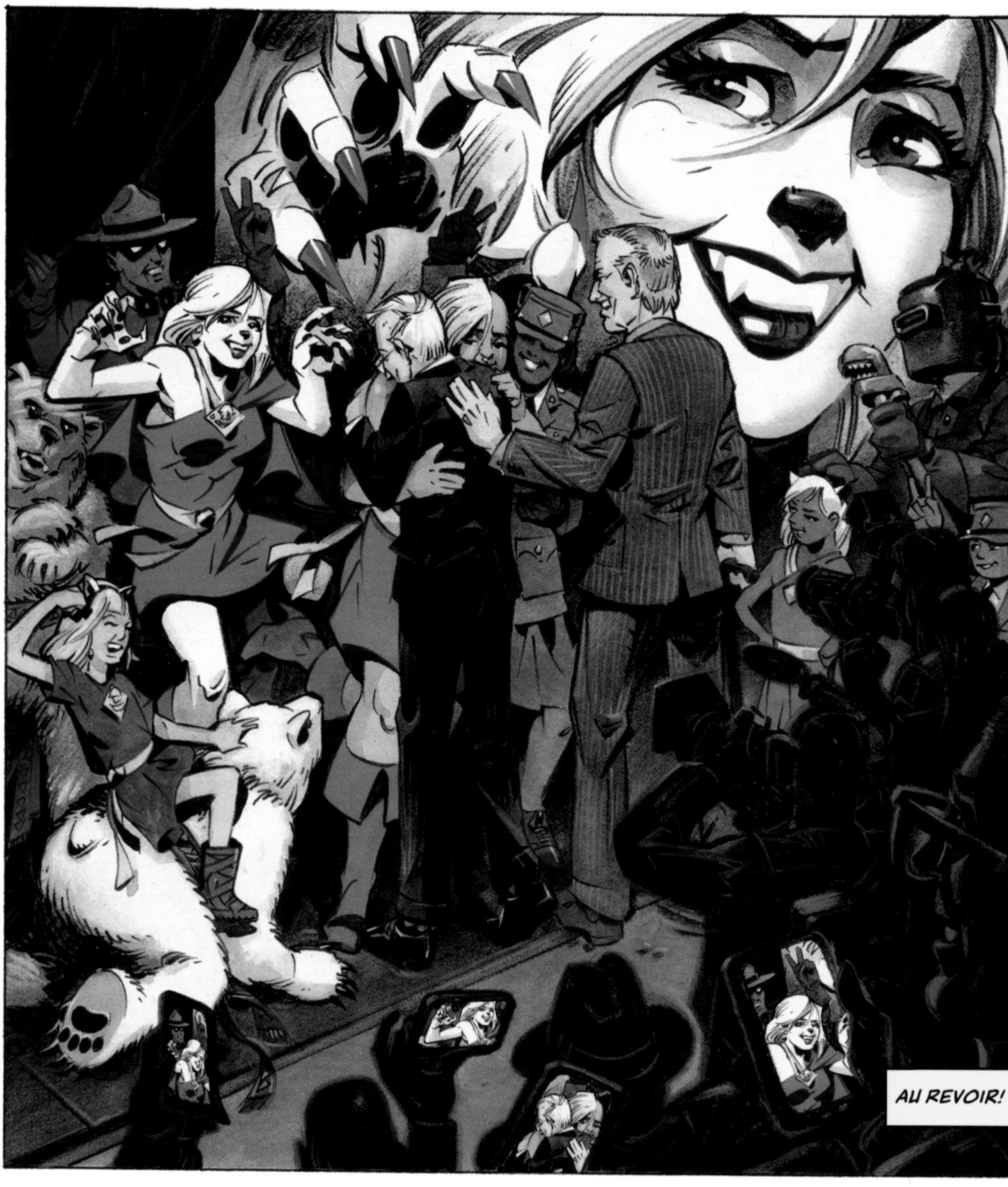
AU REVOIR!

AFTERWORD

Farewell, *chère* Oursonette! You owe a lot to my old but no longer living pal, Alan Walker, king of the nerds, who put together *The Great Canadian Comic Books* about the "Canadian whites" long ago, and who had a huge collection of Dubble Bubble gum cards.

In addition, I would like to thank all the same people Ken thanks, and add my agent Karolina Sutton, the comics historian, curator, and publisher Hope Nicholson—who initially brought me back to thinking about this world through her republication of *Brok Windsor*, and who was crucial to the creation of the *Angel Catbird* series—and Mark Medley of the *Globe and Mail*, who invited me to write a story about an important day in Canadian history. I chose VE Day; I was there, though in the Soo, not Toronto.

And finally I would like to thank Ken Steacy himself, who built my small story out with a full cast 'n backstory, whose passion for getting period details right is daunting, 'n whose enthusiasm is unflagging. Nobody says 'n like Ken!

MARGARET ATWOOD

Margaret Atwood began drawing comics in 1946 at age six, wanted to be The Dragon Lady when she grew up but was bad at smoking, ran a strip called Kanadian Kultchur Komix *in the 1970s, and has continued drawing comics to this very day, though for some unknown reason she failed to become a professional. Instead she wandered off into the hinterland of print. She is best known for her novels, which include* Cat's Eye, The Handmaid's Tale, Alias Grace, The Blind Assassin, *and the MaddAddam series. She sometimes draws flying catbirds.*

And so we bid a fond farewell to Oursonette, though I hope she will make good on her promise to return some day in some form, in the not-too-distant future. Meanwhile, making comics can be a solitary endeavour, but it's also dependent on help from a creative community, so I'd like to express my appreciation to the following folks who made her adventures possible…

To Margaret, first and foremost, I offer my boundless admiration for her skill as a storyteller, and profuse thanx for entrusting her were-bear to my care as her tale evolved. Her wit, wisdom, and world-building made playing in Oursonette's sandbox an absolute joy!

To *Globe and Mail* editor Mark Medley and art director Bryan Gee, and illustration historian Dr. Jaleen Grove, thanx so much for assigning yours truly the illo that accompanied *Oursonette*, Margaret's lovely, bittersweet story, which ran on July 1st, 2017, Canada's 150th birthday.

To sterling editor Daniel Chabon, whose stewardship of this challenging project has been greatly appreciated throughout. Thanx also to assistant editor Brett Israel, designer Jason Rall, and the rest of the gang at Dark Horse Comics, purveyors of the very best in comics and graphic novels.

To historian Ivan Kocmarek, and herstorian Trina Robbins, whose love for Canuck comics is deep and abiding, thanx again for taking us forward into the past.

To Karen Gillmore, Lia Gliddens, Janine Johnston, and Georgia Ma, many thanx for their skillful and timely art assists.

To Meredith MacLean at the Canadian War Museum in Ottawa, Arlene Gehmacher at the Royal Ontario Museum in Toronto, and Nancy Dauphinee at the Ashton Armoury Museum in Victoria, my gratitude for their help with getting the period zeitgeist just right.

To my wonderful wife Joan, whose support and equanimity kept me focussed during *War Bears'* long gestation, my eternal gratitude and deep love.

KEN STEACY

Ken Steacy decided at age eleven to become a professional comic book author/illustrator, a dream he realized in 1974. Since then, he has worked in the industry as writer, artist, art director, editor, and publisher, and in addition to creating his own intellectual property he has chronicled the exploits of Astro Boy, Iron Man, Harry Potter, 'n the Star Wars gang. Ken has also collaborated with other writers, including Douglas Coupland, Harlan Ellison, 'n Trina Robbins. The recipient of an Eisner and an Inkpot award, in 2009 Ken was inducted into the Joe Shuster Canadian Comic Book Hall of Fame, a lifetime achievement award for contributions to the industry. He currently teaches Comics & Graphic Novels at Camosun College in Victoria, BC, a visual storytelling program he co-created with his wife, author/illustrator Joan Steacy.

ADDENDUM

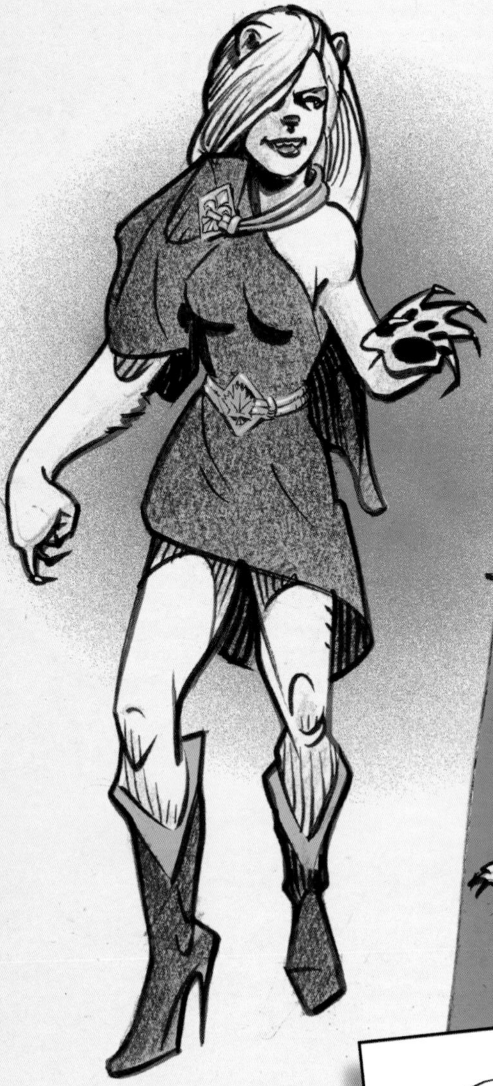

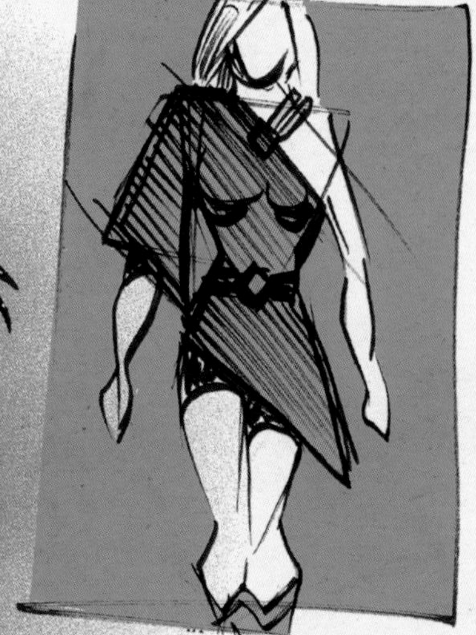

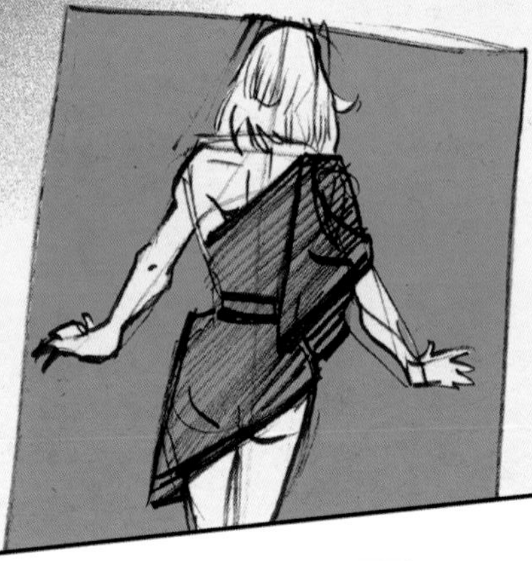

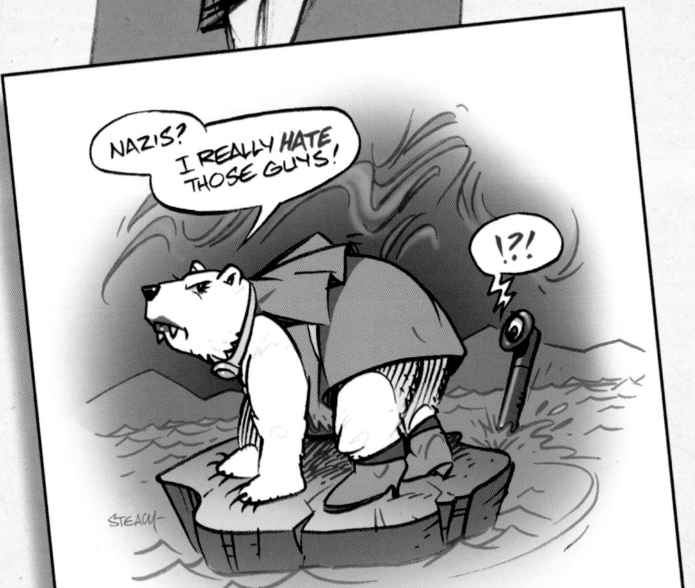
NAZIS?
I REALLY HATE THOSE GUYS!
!?!
STEACY

What follows is OURSONETTE, Margaret's original story which was written for the Globe & Mail, *Canada's national newspaper. It ran on Canada Day, July 1st, 2017, as part of our country's 150th birthday celebrations. I created the illustration opposite, and two spot illos for the digital version of the story on the* Globe's *website.*

After that are the covers to the original three-issue miniseries, alongside the monochrome versions.

This page features Oursonette's transitional character design, and a cartoon of her transforming into an actual polar bear, which I dubbed "Ourson-not!"

Enjoy! —KEN

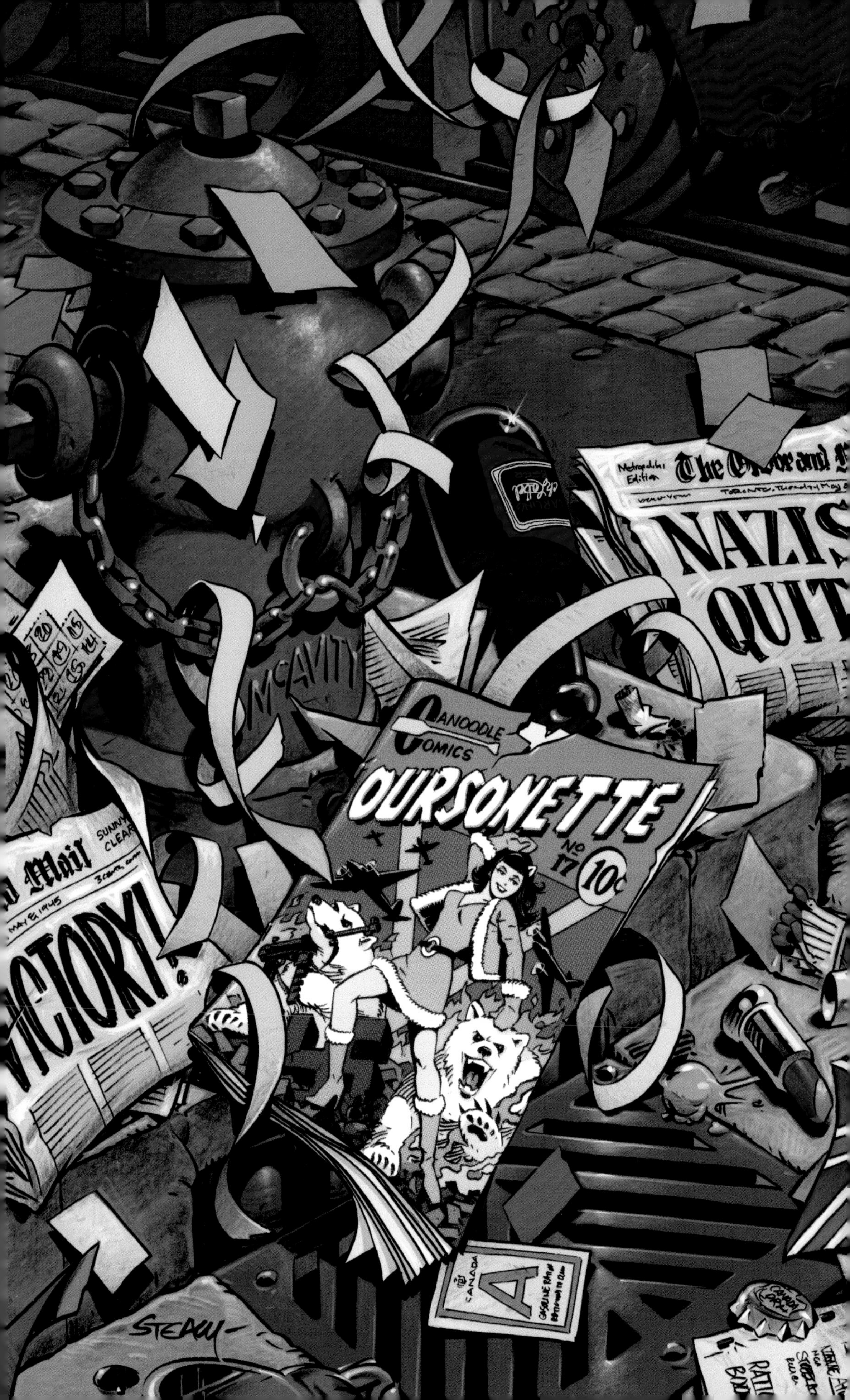

CANOODLE COMICS
OURSONETTE
No 17
10¢
NAZIS
QUIT
Mail
SUNNY
CLEAR
McAVITY
CANADA
STEACY

OURSONETTE
by Margaret Atwood

Paper was fluttering down from the sky. Typed pages, blanks, tickertape, hole puncher confetti, streamers—it was like a blizzard! Where did it come from? Who had been saving it all up over the past five years?

And to think of the trouble we had getting enough paper for *Oursonette*, Al thought bitterly. We had to grovel, we had to deal, we had to steal, we practically sold our souls. And for what?

Sourpuss, he told himself. It's the end of the war. You should be happy. Everyone else is.

At least he'd got the day off: around eleven, Canadian Pacific had called it quits. As soon as he stepped out the door he'd found himself shouldering his way through a surging mass of grinning, singing humanity. Women and men were still pouring onto Yonge Street from office buildings and side streets: dozens, hundreds, multiplying by the second. The noise was deafening: drums, bugles, bagpipes, tin horns, rattling New Year's Eve noisemakers, anything that could be whacked or blown. Hit tunes blared from Victory Loan loudspeakers. Somewhere in the distance—was that a hymn? "Abide With Me:" doleful enough for him. He wasn't in the mood for Glenn Miller.

The sky was blue, the sun was shining. That did nothing to cheer him up. Overhead, a couple of RCAF Mosquitoes were showing off, wing-dipping and buzzing the Lancaster bomber that was dumping more paper into the air. Flags everywhere: the Canadian Red Ensign, the Union Jack, the Stars and Stripes, the Hammer and Sickle, the Chinese flag; the French one, the Polish one, others he was vague about. Faces on posters: the King and Queen, serene; Churchill scowling; FDR grinning widely, even though he was dead; Uncle Joe with his tiger smile. Some Chinese guy. A group of dancers, hand in hand; couples locked in embrace. A barbershop quartet in uniform, mangling "The White Cliffs of Dover". He might have been among them if his feet weren't so flat and his lungs had been better, though recently they'd been accepting men scrawnier than him.

Well, he'd done his bit anyway: *Oursonette* was good for morale, especially in the beginning when things had been going so badly. Oursonette brought a smile amid the gloom. She stiffened the resolve. Several letter-writers had told him that.

"Look out where you're going," said a voice. He was jostled roughly aside, but then he was grabbed and kissed. His face came away wet: tears, not his. Some girl weeping with joy. He rubbed his mouth: who knew who else she'd been kissing?

Now there was an uproarious old geezer with a bottle, no tie or hat, his fly undone, offering him a drink. He turned it down, because it could be home brew, and "blind drunk" meant something.

A streetcar moved past him at the speed of a slug, a bunch of teenagers clinging to the front, waving at him, stretching out their hands. "Hop on!" they yelled. He'd never done such a thing at their age, and it was too late now. He was twenty-one, old enough to know better.

"Hey Four-eyes, how about a smooch?" A CWAC, in uniform, hair mussed, lipstick like raspberries mashed around her mouth. She ought to know better, too, though the women who joined the CWAC were definitely loose, or so it was said.

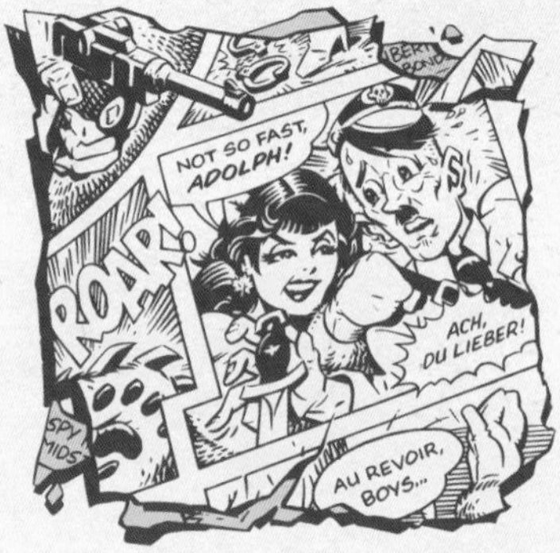
NOT SO FAST, ADOLPH!
ROAR!
ACH, DU LIEBER!
AU REVOIR, BOYS...

Not all of them though: Oursonette was CWAC, and she was a heroine. No man could get near her because she had to save her powers for fighting Nazi spies. She'd been so pure, so brave. What would become of her now? Would she be scrapped for parts, like a ruined tank? It was so unfair.

He picked his way along King Street West, going against the flow. His feet hurt, as they frequently did. Finally he reached the Pickering Hotel. It was the hangout for the inky boys; you could usually find some of them in there, stoking themselves up before hitting the drawing board again. If you were fulltime the pace could be blistering.

The place was half-empty—everyone was out celebrating, he supposed—but Gloria and Mike were at their regular table. They used the place as their impromptu office. Gloria was drinking a cup of the burnt toast crumbs and charred grain that the Pickering liked to term coffee. Mike was finishing off a beer and a hamburger, mustard smearing his chin. Al never touched those hamburgers, not since Mike told him that the meat was ground-up pig snouts. Then he said it was a joke, but Al wasn't so sure about that. Mike didn't care much what he put into his mouth.

"Hi, boy genius, how's tricks?" Mike said. Al wished he would chew and swallow before talking.

"Join us, Al," said Gloria.

"Why are you eating that?" Al slid into the booth. He'd have to order something—the Pickering frowned on free sitting. He'd opt for the orange Jell-O, even though Mike said it was made out of horse's hooves.

"Because he's hungry," said Gloria in her husky voice. She blew out smoke from under her wavy blonde Veronica Lake sideflop, extruding her lips into a red O. "He's always hungry. He's a growing boy." She smiled at Mike as if he was a two-year-old and had done a cute thing just by eating, which was how she always smiled at him.

That annoyed Al—what was so special about Mike except that he knew how to draw? Other than that he was quite stupid: Gloria was the brains behind Canoodle Features. She picked the artists, she okayed the ideas, she supervised the printing, the distribution, the ads. She kept the books. She'd inherited the business, which had printed signs, posters, and streetcar ads before the war, so she'd already known the basics.

"I'm getting back in shape," said Mike. "As a carnivore. Now that the war's over we're going to see a lot of meat. An explosion of meat! It'll be like someone dropped this enormous meat bomb!"

"I can hardly wait," said Gloria. "No more meat tokens! Roast lamb, that's my favourite."

"We're sunk," Al said.

"What?" Mike said. "What d'you mean, sunk? We just won the dad-ratted war!" He'd been told by Gloria not to swear around her, not real swearing, so most of the time he didn't.

"Who do you mean by 'we'?" said Gloria to Al. She

was no dumb bunny, except in the matter of Mike.

"Mike means the allies. I mean us," said Al. "All of us. You and Mike. Canoodle Features. The rest of them, too: Bell and Wow, Johnny Canuck, Nelvana, the works. And Oursonette."

"But Oursonette's doing great!" said Mike. "The fan club—it doubled since the last issue! And the numbers are great too! Right, Gloria?"

"Twenty thousand copies," said Gloria. "Maybe twenty-five, I'll know in a week. Not as good as Bell's numbers, but we're climbing." She paused, gave Al a level look. "Or we were climbing, until now."

The last episode of *Oursonette* had indeed been a triumph: she'd parachuted behind enemy lines in her nifty fur-trimmed outfit with the short skirt that showed a lot of leg—"Show more leg," Gloria had said—and her fur-topped boots. Then, after an interlude when she'd been captured, tied up, and almost brutally tortured, she'd called on her two bear allies, broken free of her bonds with their aid, changed into her white bear form, and subdued a whole nest full of enemy agents.

She wasn't allowed to actually kill them—that would have been too unfeminine, said Gloria—but she'd tied them up in bundles, using telegraph wire, and she and her two bear allies had carted them through the lines, dodging machine-gun bullets and artillery fire—dubba dubba dubba, ack-ack-ack! After another narrow escape, she'd met up with the Brits and Canucks under the command of Field Marshall Montgomery, drawn by Al from a newspaper photo. She'd then switched back into her human form.

"Got a little present for you, boys," she'd said. She was charmingly offhand about her own heroic exploits.

"Oursonette! How can we thank you?" they'd said, as they usually did.

"No need," Oursonette had said. "We're winning! That's thanks enough. Au revoir!" Oursonette often said "Au revoir!" Her name was more or less French, which was good because Al was partial to the Van Doos, especially since Ortona. "Au revoir" was the only French thing Oursonette ever said, but you got the idea.

There was a closeup of her heart-shaped face, her roguish, long-lashed wink. Then she'd changed back into her bear form and headed into the woods with her two bear allies.

When he'd first pitched Oursonette to Gloria, she'd been unsure. "A bear?" she'd said. "I dunno, Al. Could it maybe be a tiger? Or a lynx?"

"What's wrong with a bear?"

"It's not...face it, Al, a bear's not sexy. Bears are more cuddly, like teddy bears. Or else they're ferocious."

Al had been hurt. "You don't get it," he'd said. "The bear's a tribute to Uncle Joe. Russia—the U.S.S.R—they're helping us win the war, right?"

"So?"

"It's a symbol. Like, a mascot. The Russian Bear. Except I made it white, so it's more, I dunno. More pure."

"You're very sweet, Al," Gloria had said. "You need a girl friend." She's paused, blown out more smoke, stared up at the ceiling, as she did when pondering. "Okay, give it a whirl. If it works I'll take you off Bessie the Bullet Gal. But do it fast, we need to keep pushing if we want to gain on Bell."

But that had been a long time ago: three years at least. Now, in the Pickering dining lounge, Gloria was frowning while she lit another cigarette. She offered him the pack even though she knew he was quitting on account of his lungs. "I'm thinking like you," she said. "A year ago I thought I'd be offering you a full-time slot. Get you out of the mail room at C.P. But now..."

"What're you both talking about?" said Mike. "Want some pie? I'm having some. Lemon chiffon!"

"It's not real lemons," said Al.

"War's over, honey," Gloria said. "That embargo on American comics is gonna come off. I give it six months, a year maximum. All-colour Americans—they'll be back. Captain Marvel, Batman, Wonder Woman, the whole shooting match. Mickey Mouse, you name it. Then this place will be flooded. Black and whites like ours will be finished. Oh, Al, and that Russian bear—I don't see that being so popular, coming up. How're they going to divide things? The Yanks, the Russies. It's not gonna be so lovey-dovey soon, trust me."

Mike said, "Cripes. I need another beer."

"It's okay, sweetie, we've got a fallback," Gloria said to him. "We'll slide back into the posters and ads. The factories are gonna be making all kinds of new things. Vaccuum cleaners, toasters, cars—trust me, they're gonna be big! You heard of televisions? In a few years, just watch! Then they'll need to sell it, all of it, and that means ads. You'll have lots to draw!"

Fine for Mike, but what about me? Al thought. He didn't want to draw cars. They lacked purpose. He'd been just a kid when the war started, so it was all he could really remember. The waste paper collections, the balls of tinfoil they'd been urged to save, the ration books, the radio broadcasts from the front, the newsreels, the airplane cards; the smells, the sounds, the textures: would it all simply vanish, as if those efforts counted for nothing? He had a vision of people—millions of people, intent on a single goal, marching forward together, but suddenly faltering, coming to a standstill, then wandering away in different directions as if they had amnesia. What would everyone do? He couldn't imagine.

And his Oursonette. She wasn't a real woman, a real bear-woman, true, but he would miss her a lot. They'd been through so much together. The U-boat attack, the tank battle, the advance through Holland when she'd brought food to the starving, the time when she'd rescued those French resistance fighters; the Maquis, up in the mountains. The people she'd guided through the Alps, into the safety of Switzerland. That had been a suitable job for a bear. He'd learned so much geography from her, he'd been with her every step of the way. Together they'd renounced their so-called normal life to dedicate themselves to the cause.

Au revoir, he whispered to her silently; but she was already fading. Lost, lost. He felt like crying. Would he find someone else to draw? Maybe not. Maybe his life was already over.

"Buck up, Al," Mike said to him. "You're young and reckless! You've got a whole new future ahead of you! Have a beer!"

"Can you draw washing machines?" Gloria said. "Boxes of soap flakes? Cute housewives in aprons hanging out the sheets, pitching woo to their laundry? Sexy little kiss mouths?"

"Yeah, I guess so," Al said listlessly.

"Good," said Gloria. "'Cause trust me: it's gonna be big!"

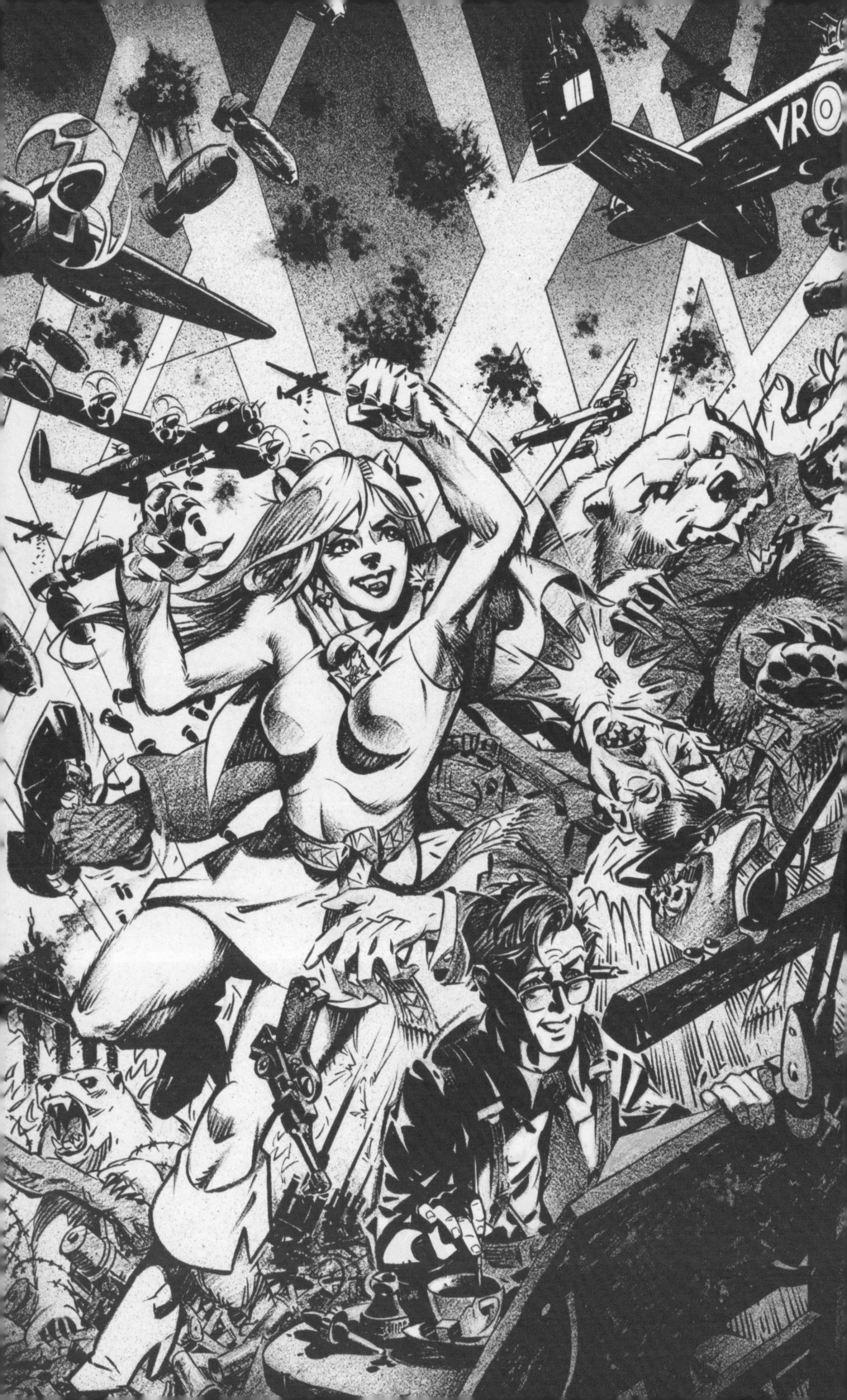
VR

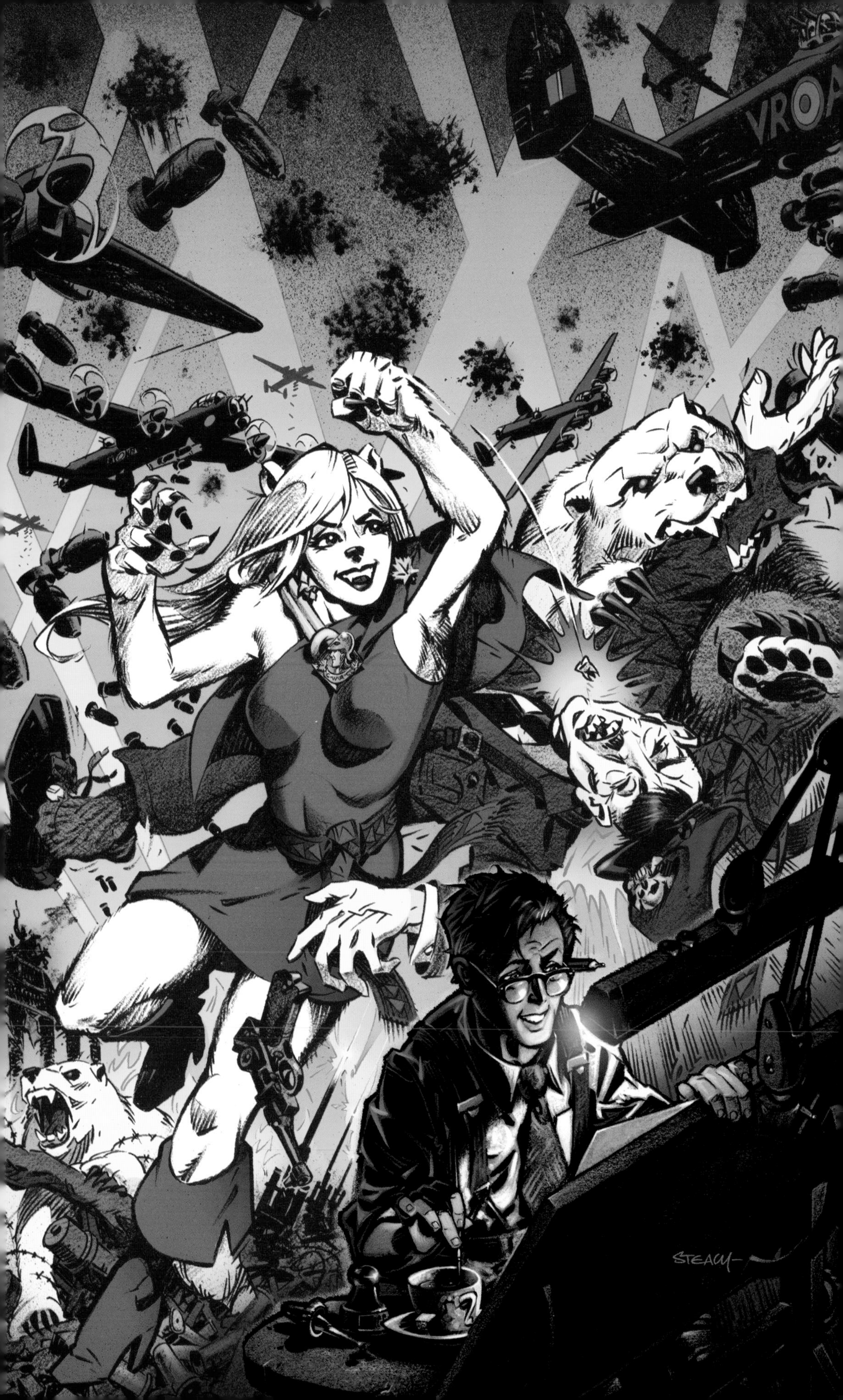
VROA
STEACY

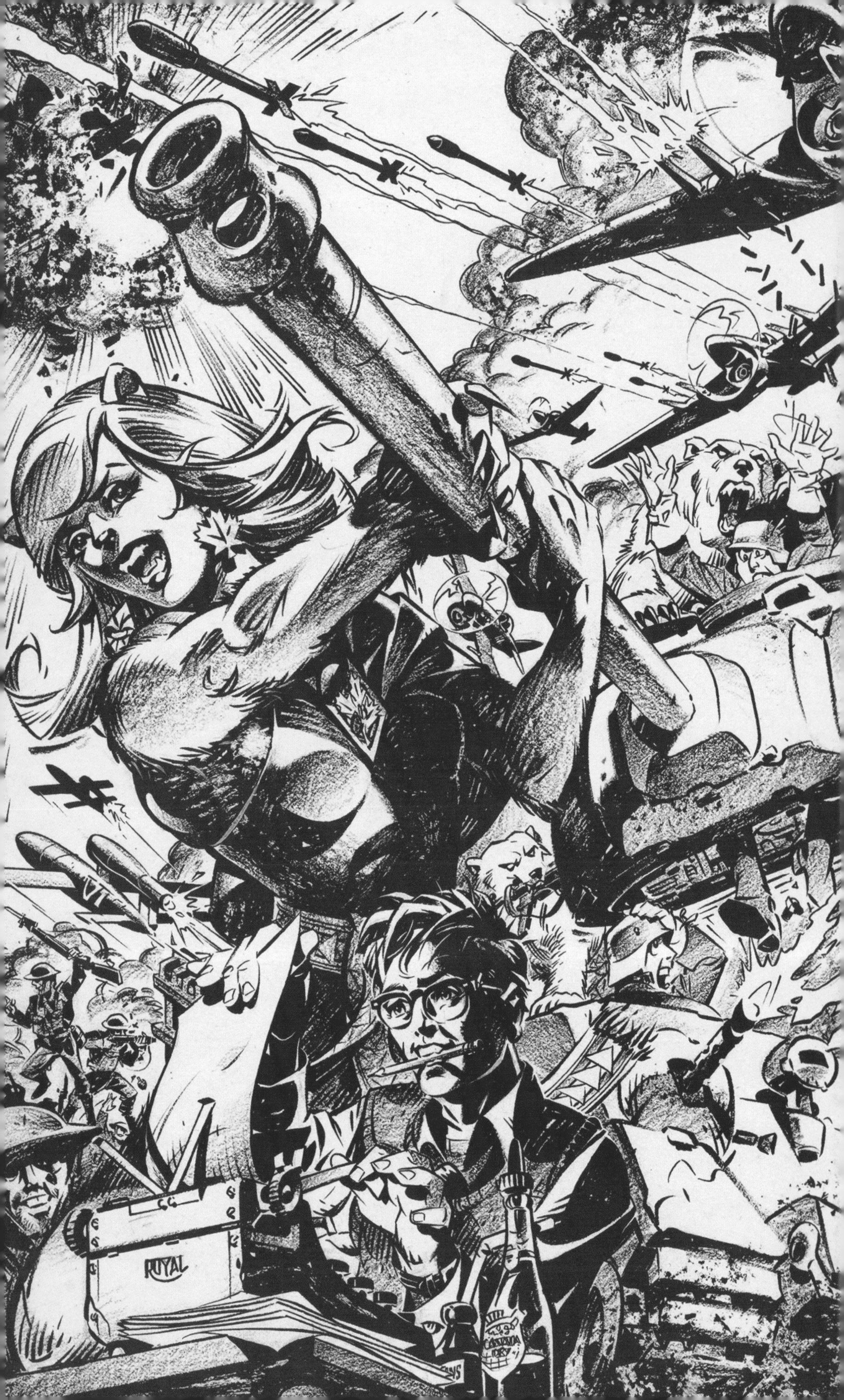
ROYAL
CANADA DRY

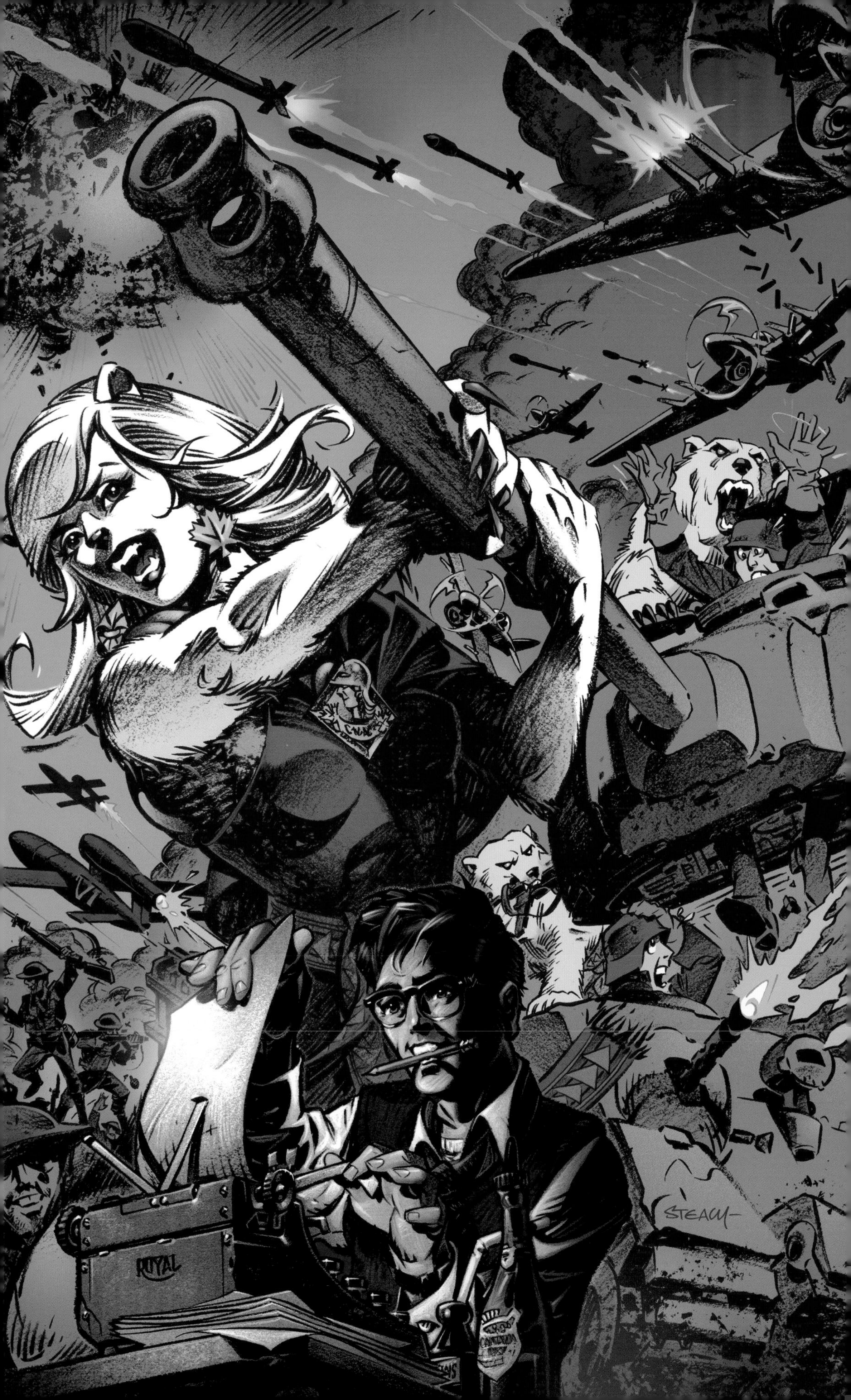
STEACY
ROYAL

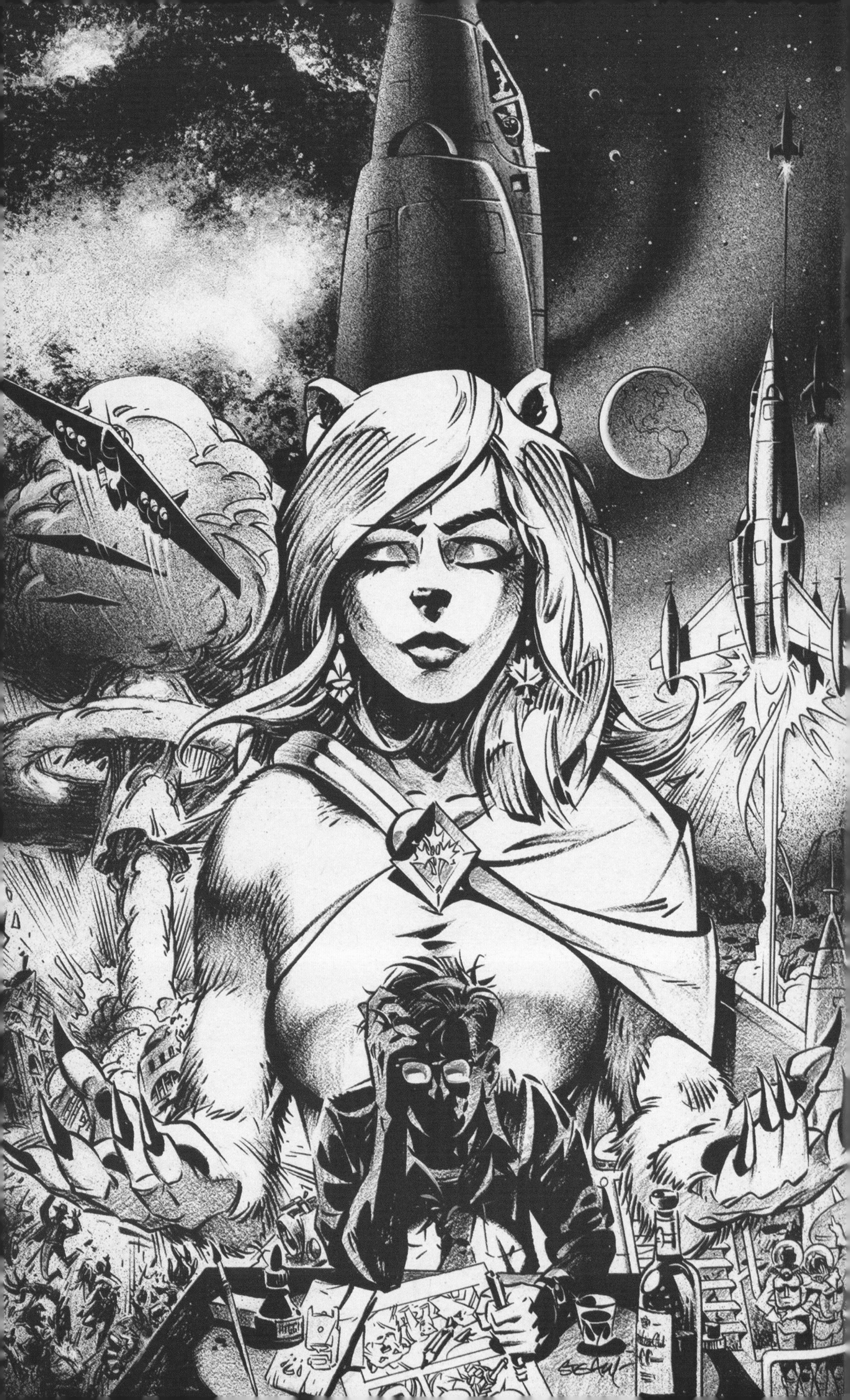

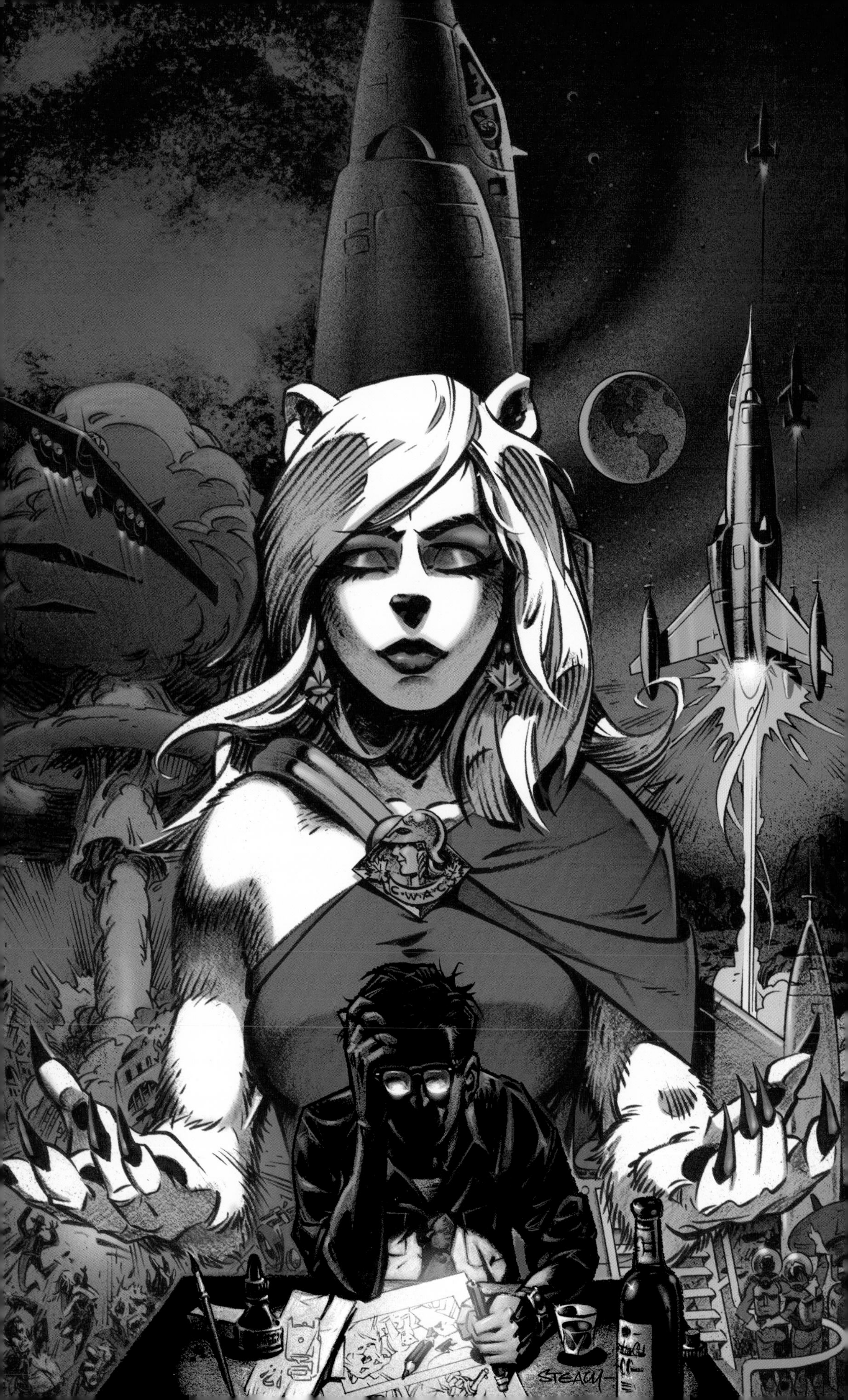
C·W·A·C
STEACY

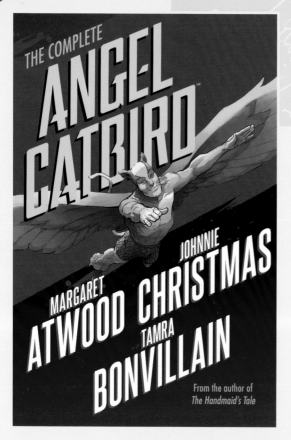

SUPER:POWERED BY CREATORS!

BLACK HAMMER
Jeff Lemire and Dean Ormston
VOLUME 1: SECRET ORIGINS
ISBN 978-1-61655-786-7 | $14.99

VOLUME 2: THE EVENT
ISBN 978-1-50670-198-1 | $19.99

DREAM THIEF
Jai Nitz and Greg Smallwood
VOLUME 1
ISBN 978-1-61655-283-1 | $17.99

VOLUME 2: ESCAPE
ISBN 978-1-61655-513-9 | $17.99

THE BLACK BEETLE
Francesco Francavilla
NO WAY OUT
ISBN 978-1-61655-202-2 | $19.99

KARA BOCEK
ISBN 978-1-50670-537-8 | $12.99

THE ANSWER!
Mike Norton and Dennis Hopeless
ISBN 978-1-61655-197-1 | $12.99

BLOODHOUND
Dan Jolley, Leonard Kirk, and Robin Riggs
VOLUME 1: BRASS KNUCKLE PSYCHOLOGY
ISBN 978-1-61655-125-4 | $19.99

VOLUME 2: CROWBAR MEDICINE
ISBN 978-1-61655-352-4 | $19.99

**MICHAEL AVON OEMING'S
THE VICTORIES**
Michael Avon Oeming
VOLUME 1: TOUCHED
ISBN 978-1-61655-100-1 | $9.99

VOLUME 2: TRANSHUMAN
ISBN 978-1-61655-214-5 | $17.99

VOLUME 3: POSTHUMAN
ISBN 978-1-61655-445-3 | $17.99

VOLUME 4: METAHUMAN
ISBN 978-1-61655-517-7 | $17.99

HELLBOY: SEED OF DESTRUCTION
(third edition)
Mike Mignola
ISBN 978-1-59307-094-6 | $17.99

ORIGINAL VISIONS—
THRILLING TALES!

"These superheroes ain't no boy scouts in spandex. They're a high-octane blend of the damaged, quixotic heroes of pulp and detective fiction and the do-gooders in capes from the Golden and Silver Ages." —Duane Swierczynski

ALENA
Kim W. Andersson
Since arriving at a snobbish boarding school, Alena's been harassed every day by the lacrosse team. But Alena's best friend Josephine is not going to accept that anymore. If Alena does not fight back, then she will take matters into her own hands. There's just one problem . . . Josephine has been dead for a year.

$17.99 | ISBN 978-1-50670-215-5

ASTRID: CULT OF THE VOLCANIC MOON
Kim W. Andersson
Formerly the Galactic Coalition's top recruit, the now-disgraced Astrid is offered a special mission from her old commander. She'll prove herself worthy of another chance at becoming a Galactic Peacekeeper . . . if she can survive.

$19.99 | ISBN 978-1-61655-690-7

BANDETTE
Paul Tobin, Colleen Coover
A costumed teen burglar by the *nome d'arte* of Bandette and her group of street urchins find equal fun in both skirting and aiding the law, in this enchanting, Eisner-nominated series!

$14.99 each
Volume 1: Presto!
ISBN 978-1-61655-279-4
Volume 2: Stealers, Keepers!
ISBN 978-1-61655-668-6
Volume 3: The House of the Green Mask
ISBN 978-1-50670-219-3

BOUNTY
Kurtis Wiebe, Mindy Lee
The Gadflies were the most wanted criminals in the galaxy. Now, with a bounty to match their reputation, the Gadflies are forced to abandon banditry for a career as bounty hunters . . . 'cause if you can't beat 'em, join 'em—then rob 'em blind!

$14.99 | ISBN 978-1-50670-044-1

HEART IN A BOX
Kelly Thompson, Meredith McClaren
In a moment of post-heartbreak weakness, Emma wishes her heart away and a mysterious stranger obliges. But emptiness is even worse than grief, and Emma sets out to collect the pieces of her heart and face the cost of recapturing it.

$14.99 | ISBN 978-1-61655-694-5

HENCHGIRL
Kristen Gudsnuk
Mary Posa hates her job. She works long hours for little pay, no insurance, and worst of all, no respect. Her coworkers are jerks, and her boss doesn't appreciate her. He's also a supervillain. Cursed with a conscience, Mary would give anything to be something other than a henchgirl.

$17.99 | ISBN 978-1-50670-144-8

THE ONCE AND FUTURE QUEEN
Adam P. Knave, D.J. Kirkbride, Nick Brokenshire, Frank Cvetkovic
It's out with the old myths and in with the new as a nineteen-year-old chess prodigy pulls Excalibur from the stone and becomes queen. Now, magic, romance, Fae, Merlin, and more await her!

$14.99 | ISBN 978-1-50670-250-6

MISFITS OF AVALON
Kel McDonald
Four misfit teens are reluctant recruits to save the mystical isle of Avalon. Magically empowered and directed by a talking dog, they must stop the rise of King Arthur. As they struggle to become a team, they're faced with the discovery that they may not be the good guys.

$14.99 each
Volume 1: The Queen of Air and Delinquency
ISBN 978-1-61655-538-2
Volume 2: The Ill-Made Guardian
ISBN 978-1-61655-748-5
Volume 3: The Future in the Wind
ISBN 978-1-61655-749-2

THE SECRET LOVES OF GEEK GIRLS
Hope Nicholson, Margaret Atwood, Mariko Tamaki, and more
The Secret Loves of Geek Girls is a nonfiction anthology mixing prose, comics, and illustrated stories on the lives and loves of an amazing cast of female creators..

$14.99 | ISBN 978-1-50670-099-1

THE SECRET LOVES OF GEEKS
Gerard Way, Dana Simpson, Hope Larson, and more
The follow-up to the smash hit *The Secret Loves of Geek Girls*, this brand new anthology features comic and prose stories from cartoonists and professional geeks about their most intimate, heartbreaking, and inspiring tales of love, sex, and dating. This volume includes creators of diverse genders, orientations, and cultural backgrounds.

$14.99 each | ISBN 978-1-50670-473-9

ZODIAC STARFORCE: BY THE POWER OF ASTRA
Kevin Panetta, Paulina Ganucheau
A group of teenage girls with magical powers have sworn to protect our planet against dark creatures. Known as the Zodiac Starforce, these high-school girls aren't just combating math tests—they're also battling monsters!

$12.99 | ISBN 978-1-61655-913-7

SPELL ON WHEELS
Kate Leth, Megan Levens, Marissa Louise
A road trip story. A magical revenge fantasy. A sisters-over-misters tale of three witches out to get back what was taken from them.

$14.99 | ISBN 978-1-50670-183-7

THE ADVENTURES OF SUPERHERO GIRL
Faith Erin Hicks
What if you can leap tall buildings and defeat alien monsters with your bare hands, but you buy your capes at secondhand stores and have a weakness for kittens? Faith Erin Hicks brings humor to the trials and tribulations of a young, female superhero, battling monsters both supernatural and mundane in an all-too-ordinary world.

$16.99 each | ISBN 978-1-61655-084-4
Expanded Edition | ISBN 978-1-50670-336-7

DARKHORSE.COM
AVAILABLE AT YOUR LOCAL COMICS SHOP OR BOOKSTORE | TO FIND A COMICS SHOP IN YOUR AREA, VISIT COMICSHOPLOCATOR.COM
For more information or to order direct: •On the web: DarkHorse.com •Email: mailorder@darkhorse.com •Phone: 1-800-862-0052 Mon.–Fri. 9 AM to 5 PM Pacific Time.

Alena™, Astrid © Kim W. Andersson, by agreement with Grand Agency. Bandette™ © Paul Tobin and Colleen Coover. Bounty™ © Kurtis Wiebe and Mindy Lee. Heart in a Box™ © 1979 Semi-Finalist, Inc., and Meredith McClaren. Henchgirl™ © Kristen Gudsnuk. Misfits of Avalon™ © Kel McDonald. The Secret Loves of Geek Girls™ © respective creators. The Adventures of Superhero Girl™ © Faith Erin Hicks. Zodiac Starforce™ © Kevin Panetta and Paulina Ganucheau. Spell on Wheels™ © Kate Leth and Megan Levens. Dark Horse Books® and the Dark Horse logo are registered trademarks of Dark Horse Comics, Inc. All rights reserved. (BL 6041)

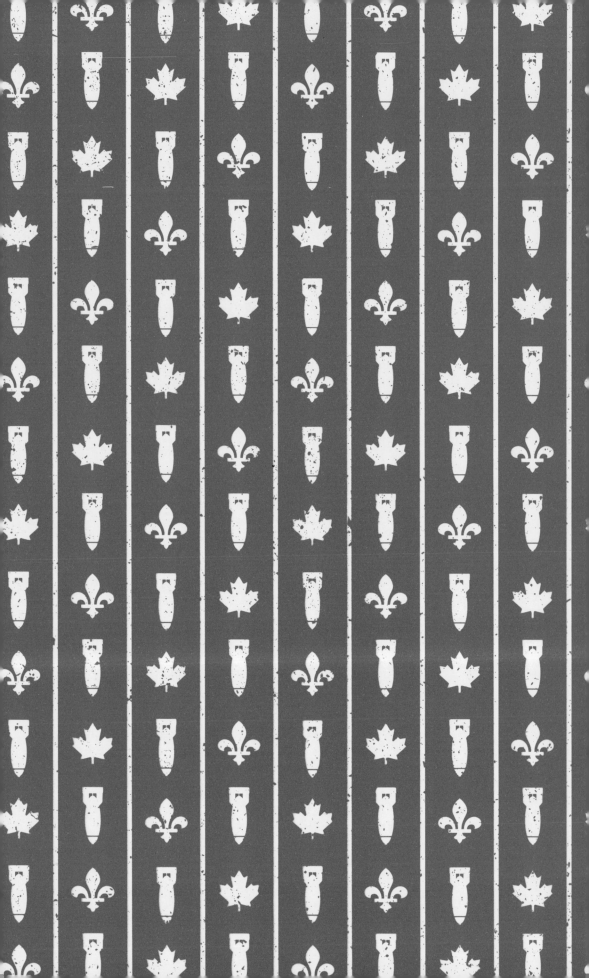